IMAGE AS INSIGHT

MARGARET R. MILES

Image as Insight

*Visual Understanding in Western Christianity
and Secular Culture*

BEACON PRESS ◆ BOSTON

The quotations in chapter four from *Meditations
on the Life of Christ* are from Ira Ragusa, Trans.,
*Meditations on the Life of Christ: An Illustrated
Manuscript of the Fourteenth Century*. Completed
from the Latin and edited by Ira Ragusa and
Rosalie B. Green. Copyright © 1961 by Princeton
University Press. Text pp. 166, 170, 171, 172, 173,
174, 177, 191 reprinted with permission of Princeton
University Press.

Beacon Press books are published under the auspices
of the Unitarian Universalist Association of
Congregations in North America,
25 Beacon Street, Boston, Massachusetts 02108

Library of Congress Cataloging in Publication Data

Miles, Margaret Ruth.
  Image as insight.

  Bibliography: p.
  Includes index.
  1. Christian art and symbolism. 2. Art —
Language. 3. Visual communication. 4. Visual
perception. I. Title.
BV150.M47 1985   246   85–47528
ISBN 0-8070-1006-5 (cloth)
ISBN 0-8070-1007-3 (paper)

For Owen

Contents

CONTENTS

Illustrations

Preface

Authorship is moral responsibility. An author who understands her printed work as inevitably and irreducibly containing a political statement can assist the reader by specifying the relation of her book to what she identifies as a crucial task of this historic moment. Let us then, author and reader, begin by being clear about the task of discourse to which this book is addressed and to which it offers a contribution.

I understand the most significant and pressing task of contemporary discourse to be respectful and appreciative attention to those persons, contemporary and historical, who have not been recognized as participating in and contributing to the articulation of a governing cultural view of the human person in the world. Who defines what is thought of simply as "reality"? Who specifies the position of each individual in relation to what is considered most real and most valuable?

Wittgenstein's axiom "The master of the language is the master of us all" articulates the assumption that "it is the world of words that creates the world of things." [1] This gives an absolute advantage to language users, those whose primary tool for relating to the world is trained linguistic skill. It renders inaudible and invisible those whose primary mode of understanding and relating to the world is not verbal. Not only does this view of reality as verbally constituted unjustly exclude all people some of the time, and some people all of the time, but it also forces discourse to entertain and respond only to itself — to discourse — rather than to perceptive, affective, and intellectual experience.

Although the task I have identified is a contemporary one — the opening of reality-defining discourse to others besides language users — I begin with historical cultures that have not shared our exaggerated esteem for language and its exclusive prerogative for describing and defining reality. Historically in western christian societies, images provided representations of the nature of reality and the range of human possibilities that intimately informed the emotional, spiritual, and intellectual lives of individuals. From study of several of these cultures, we can begin to conceive alternatives to the "world of words" that will help us respect both historical and contemporary persons who are not represented by the skilled language users who claim to speak for them.[2] As Freud said, "We are obliged to use the coinage of the country we are exploring."

Although the politically and socially subordinate and the culturally under-privileged do not speak through historical verbal texts authored by privileged, educated, and usually powerful men, I do not despair of access to the ideas and feelings of "ordinary" historical people. One way to discover the cultural messages from which they constructed self-images and values is to use publicly available visual images as historical evidence. We must teach ourselves to look — literally look — long and attentively at the visual images at which historical people looked. The images with which they lived were few in number, concentrated in content, and supported and extended by the presence of an interpreting community. This book seeks to illustrate the potential fruitfulness of trained attention to visual evidence.

In my own discipline, historical theology, both the theologians of the past and those who presently study them have often claimed to speak not from a limited and culturally conditioned perspective but from a "God's eye view," universally. In our time this "universal" discourse is beginning to be questioned, evaluated, and often dismissed in whole or in part by persons who speak from different geographical, physical, social, and cultural experience. From within the discourse defined by christian theological and historical concerns, strong objections are being brought by feminists, by gay and lesbian people, and by people of the second and third worlds against claims to universality of perspectively biased theological statements. The problem they identify will not be solved by hastily making sure that our language is inclusive or simply acknowledging diversity and then continuing with what we have always done. We must find the methods and the materials that reveal the story of contemporary and historical persons who have not been recognized as participants in historical and theological work because they were not skilled language users.

For five years I have taught a course in the history of christian thought at the Harvard Divinity School, and I have become increasingly aware of the inadequacy of a history of western Christianity that begins and remains with verbal texts. My struggle to find a method for coordinating visual and verbal material has taught me a great deal about the culturally and educationally conditioned resistances, practical difficulties, and experimental awkwardnesses that accompany the attempt to draw historical information from visual images. These resistances, in myself and my students, have led me to search for a more comprehensive hermeneutic. In the course of this search, I went to Rome, surely the place to begin looking at historical christian imagery. I went with an interest not dissimilar to that of an illiterate medieval worshipper in images that order, sustain, and comfort a human being in the midst of the overwhelming and potentially disorienting beauty and pain of a human life.

This book emerges from, and will return to, many conversations. During my M.A. program in humanities at San Francisco State University, I had a fine teacher who knew how to train the weak and lazy eye, who insisted on the viewing of a slide long beyond its entertainment value and on the coordination of eye and intellect in discussion of the image. I am still learning from and teaching my students the visual method of Matthew Evans. In my doctoral work at the Graduate Theological Union and the University of California, Berkeley, another superb historian and teacher, Peter L. R. Brown, who himself works as fluently with visual as with verbal evidence, set an example of the fully competent teacher that has become the model for my own teaching and writing. Most recently, it was in conversation with my colleagues Clarissa Atkinson, Constance Buchanan, Marilyn Massey, and Sharon Welch that I have come to understand the content and agenda of my work as a matter of moral responsibility, a political statement. This book is also a part of conversations with student-colleagues, many of whose faces, insights, and questions occur to me as I write. The book is also part of a conversation with a reader — you — whom I imagine questioning, prompting, arguing, encouraging me. Finally, the book is an anticipation of future conversations that will help me to remember what I have forgotten to say, to carry an idea a step further, or to make me want to retract some of my suggestions for further polishing.

In this book, I explore only one aspect of a task that, if it is to be effective, must engage the insights, energies, and committed labor of a great diversity of people of many perspectives and talents. The goal is not simply the consciousness-raising of a few individuals, but the most pervasive readjustment of human society ever conceived: equalization of the dignity of all human beings.

I am grateful to the Harvard Divinity School for freedom from institutional and teaching duties during the academic year 1982–83. I am also indebted to the John Simon Guggenheim Foundation for the opportunity to study and write in Rome during my sabbatical leave. A National Endowment for the Humanities summer stipend supported a fruitful summer of preparation before I went to Rome. An appointment as scholar-in-residence at the Rockefeller Study and Conference Center, Bellagio, Italy, provided the peace and comfort conducive to the revision of the manuscript in May 1983. My heartfelt thanks to Professors Rudolf Arnheim, Natalie Zemon Davis, and Elisabeth Schüssler Fiorenza for reading the manuscript and making important suggestions and to Barbara M. Buchanan for suggesting the title. The book is more readable because of the help of two excellent editors, Wendy J. Strothman and Caroline L. Birdsall. Finally, I am grateful to David Gillerman, who collected the photographs in Italy, and to Evelyn Rosenthal for typing the manuscript.

3 September 1984
Cambridge, Massachusetts

IMAGE AS INSIGHT

◆ 1 ◆

Introduction

The Logos is more readily perceived by
the eye than by the ear.
Heraclitus

Religion, it has frequently been said, both articulates and responds to the life experience, the ideas, and the ultimate concerns of human beings and communities. A viable religious orientation must organize and lead in fruitful directions the loves and fears, the thoughts and emotions of human beings who think, feel, anticipate, and remember, who doubt, and who — whether we like it or not — necessarily live by faith. Religion is first and foremost a way of managing *this* world, the only world we know, which presses us continuously for response, for adjustments, and for decisions. Even the most explicitly other-worldly religious orientations are primarily responses to the exigencies of *this* life.[1] They address the questions What is the most fruitful and satisfying way to conduct a human life? and What set of assumptions, beliefs, and actions provides the most accurate formulation of the facts of experience?

One way religions address these questions is the formulation of concepts that organize a bewildering and potentially overwhelming conglomeration of awarenesses and experiences — "it's the richness of the mixture," one of Saul Bellow's heroes groans. Language itself arises from the need to identify and name features of thought and experience; in turn, language so thoroughly informs and limits thought and experience that it is almost impossible for anyone to conceive what is not communally recognized and named. Concepts,

◆ 1

built with and communicable by language, can be arranged in comprehensive systems that provide comfort and the assurance that one is oriented. By the use of such concepts, religions seek to order the mind to what is intrinsically and universally valuable so that none of the richness of the texture of human life will be lost. Without swamping the psyche, they seek to be inclusive — to describe everything that contributes to the beauty and goodness of human life.

Religion has also repeatedly been described as a way of seeing. "Seeing," in academic parlance, has been used so frequently as a metaphor for understanding that its primary literal sense has been neglected. Religion is a way of seeing not merely in the figurative sense. Religious "seeing" implies perceiving a quality of the sensible world, a numinosity, a "certain slant of light," in which other human beings, the natural world, and objects appear in their full beauty, transformed. The transient, intensely experienced occasions on which we experience "eyesight as insight" [2] have frequently been described as a clue to the nature and structure of reality and the first step toward realization of the ultimate fulfillment of human being as symbolized by the idea of the vision of God. Jonathan Edwards gives a particularly vivid account of the mingling of intensity of feeling, religious sensitivity, and strong visual experience in his *Personal Narrative*:

After this my sense of divine things gradually increased, and became more and more lively, and had more of that inward sweetness. The appearance of every thing was altered; there seemed to be, as it were, a calm, sweet cast, or appearance of divine glory, in almost every thing. God's excellency, his wisdom, his purity and love, seemed to appear in every thing; in the sun, moon, and stars; in the water, and all nature; which used greatly to fix my mind. I often used to sit and view the moon . . . and in the day, spent much time in viewing the clouds and sky, to behold the sweet glory of God in these things; in the mean time singing forth with a low voice my contemplations of the Creator and Redeemer. [3]

That such experiences are normative — rather than freakish and illusory — is a traditional religious claim. Moreover, visual experiences of the transformation of the world provide concentration and energy for the gradual conversion into daily life of what was originally strong but unassimilated experience. [4]

Objects of the natural world are capable of evoking religious awareness, and these objects provide the strongest and most enduring images of the religious life. For Augustine, the spontaneous and dynamic movement of the spirit found its visual parallel in fire: "Inardescimus et imus," he wrote: "We are inflamed and we go." [5] Fire, water, light, space, color — these powerful visible properties of the natural world underlie the power of every religious image. [6] Figurative "seeing" is dependent on literal seeing, and the religious life must be conceived and articulated by the use of metaphors based on natural objects if its concepts are not to remain lifeless.

Objects can train the eye, can reveal "the world in a grain of sand." How does eyesight become insight? How is the eye to be trained to look not through and beyond things to their ideal prototypes but more deeply into them, so that the fully experienced beauty of natural objects becomes religious exprience? If the experience of beauty is allowed to expand of itself, if it is not stopped short by conceptual restrictions, it yields a somatic as well as an intellectual religious sense.[7] Both the problem of training the eye and the problem of integrating fleeting experiences of "eyesight as insight" bring us to a consideration of the role of artistic images in human communities.

Susanne Langer's essay "The Cultural Importance of Art," after discussing the primacy of discursive language for conceptual expression, continues:

There is, however, an important part of reality that is quite inaccessible to the formative influence of language: that is the realm of so-called "inner experience," the life of feeling and emotion. The reason why language is so powerless here is not, as many people suppose, that feeling and emotion are irrational; on the contrary they seem irrational because language does not help to make them conceivable and most people cannot conceive anything without the logical scaffolding of words.[8]

Ordinary discursive language does not give adequate expression to "the intricate dynamic pattern" of feeling, in that the words we use to describe feeling give only the most general and unnuanced impressions of what we feel. "The primary function of art is to objectify feeling so that we can contemplate and understand it," Langer continues. "Art objectifies the sentience and desire, the self-consciousness and world-consciousness, emotions and moods, that are generally regarded as irrational because words cannot give us clear ideas of them."[9]

Every culture does in fact educate its members, by commission or omission, to particular styles of feeling, toward the development of a rich range of affections and emotions or toward a limited and limiting vocabulary of feeling. The arts one lives with educate or stultify the life of feeling. The verbal arts — poetry, narrative, ritual, and liturgy — as well as the visual arts give shape to the emotional lives of individuals and cultures. They articulate and extend, or fail to do so, momentary experiences of eyesight as feeling-toned insight.[10]

An incident through which I became aware of how easily the seeing of an artistic object can inform the seeing of natural objects illustrates this point. Several years ago I attended an exhibit of the American sculptor Duane Hanson. Knowing nothing about his work, I entered the exhibit and saw a group of people standing around a young man who was leaning on a wall. Wondering what was the matter with him, I looked more closely and saw that "he" was a trompe l'oeil sculpture. The exhibit was composed of a variety of such sculptures — a fat woman sunning herself on a deck chair, a couple of house painters about to begin work, a junkie sprawled on the floor, oblivious to his surroundings. As I walked around or stood and stared at these figures, I slowly lost my fascination with the materials and technique by which they were made so lifelike and realized that they were, simultaneously, completely characteristic of the people one looks at every day and beautiful.

The lifelike realism of the sculptures, which I at first considered an artistic gimmick, quickly became a training of vision. And this incident was neither an accident nor a freak occurrence, but an instance of the visual arts achieving one of their primary tasks. As one of the first impressionist painters, in prophetic response to the nearly universal critical rejection of the new style, said, "You will soon see nature as we do."

The function of art is to identify and articulate a range of subjective patterns of feeling and to give objective form to feeling. But its function is not exhausted when the community recognizes and affirms certain complex configurations of the life of feeling. Religion needs art to orient individuals and communities, not only conceptually but also affectively, to the reality that creates and nourishes, in solitude and in community, human life. Religion, as we have seen, is a complex of concepts about the self, the world, and God; it is also an altered perception of the meaning and value of the sensible world, a different way of seeing. Both are cognitive functions; both involve an organization of experience, but they are different in content and they train different capacities in human beings. Rudolf Arnheim has said, "Perceiving achieves, at the sensory level, what in the realm of reasoning is known as understanding." [11] Both are skilled operations; for the untrained eye, eyesight is not insight, just as, for the unprepared mind, religious concepts make no sense. Because religion irreducibly involves both concepts and altered perceptions, the training of both eye and mind is fundamental to the quickening of religious sensibility.

Let us set aside talk about religion in general and consider western Christianity in particular. Were historic christian communities aware of responsibility for educating members perceptively and affectively as well as conceptually? Do we not immediately think of Christianity as the religion of the Word, the Logos? Could not the history of western Christianity be read as the progressive articulation of doctrinal concepts, as reflected in the History of Christian Doctrine course that has been the traditional approach to the study of western Christianity? Have we not read or been told time and again that early christian leaders struggled ceaselessly to stamp out the remnants of pagan idolatry that repeatedly threatened the religion of the Word "from below" — from the uneducated masses who were unable to worship "spiritually," that is, verbally? [12]

This book attempts to demonstrate that closer study of western Christianity reveals a continuous integration of visual imagery in christian worship and piety. From the first sites of christian worship that we can still examine, frescoes, and, by the fourth century, mosaics and three-dimensional free-standing sculpture accompany and provide the setting for worship throughout the Roman world. We cannot assume that this religious imagery played the minimal role of illustration or decoration. In the absence of unambiguous textual testimony concerning the significance of imagery in the first three centuries of christian worship, the historian may follow one of two options. Either she may interpret the handful of relevant but ambiguous texts or she may infer, on the evidence of the ubiquity of visual images in the sites of christian worship, that this imagery was thoughtfully and purposely created by the christian community.

By the fourth century there is abundant evidence of the importance of vision in worship. Magnificent church buildings appeared throughout the Roman world with costly and exquisite contents — candelabra, vessels, hangings, precious draperies, lamps, floor and wall mosaics, and frescoes. No contemporary interpreter of what must have been a race to build christian basilicas gives any indication that the overpowering magnificence of the interiors of these churches was criticized on any grounds in the fourth century. It is striking that images were accepted by Christians whose association of images with pagan worship might well have led them to exclude the visual arts. Moreover, the acceptance of images in fourth-century christian worship argues for continuity in the use of images from the period before the Peace of the Church rather than for a dramatic contrast between the imageless simplicity of early christian worship and the abrupt "corruption" of the church in its political legitimation.[13]

By the fourth century, then, images were accepted, albeit not uncritically, as appropriate in the setting of christian worship. A careful contextual analysis of third- and fourth-century texts[14] indicates awareness of a potential problem with the strong visual component in worship and piety, the danger that a worshipper could become attached to the image rather than to its prototype. Yet none of the texts that caution against illegitimate attachment to images urges the rejection of all images. Rather, these texts indicate an awareness that a powerful tool is always double-edged, capable equally of providing valuable help and of promoting addiction to the tool itself. Would it not have been easier simply to reject a devotional tool so susceptible to abuse? That this was not the conclusion of the fourth-century churches indicates a recognition that the great value of images outweighed their danger. The picture we can reconstruct from fourth-century verbal and visual sources is of the critical use of images as an important aspect of christian tradition.[15]

The practice and attitude toward visual images of fourth-century Christians were characteristic of christian communities throughout the medieval centuries. A voluminous theological literature concerning the use and value of

◆ 5

images emerged not only in the course of the century and a half of iconoclastic debate in the east but also in the west.[16]

Both historical theologians and art historians have been interested in the meaning of religious images. To locate the meaning of images, historical theologians have worked with treatises in which the professional theologians of the past articulated their ideas. But textual historical evidence limits our findings to the ideas of a few linguistically trained men. Art historians have also demonstrated the relation of religious ideas to the formation of styles in painting, sculpture, and architecture. For example, Erwin Panofsky's delightful book *Gothic Architecture and Scholasticism* discusses the structural and methodological connections between new methods of scholarship and new architectural forms in the twelfth century. Panofsky discusses a "cause and effect relationship" [17] between the scholastics' method of "systematic division" and the articulation of the visual arts and architecture "through an exact and systematic division of space." [18] The architect's arrangement of space, stone, and stained glass was based, in other words, on principles derived from the privileged discourse of his time.[19]

Neither the sources of the historical theologian nor those of the art historian, however, are likely to yield information about the significance of a cathedral for the people who worshipped there. These sources do not, for one thing, distinguish between the message *given* and the message *received*.[20] Can we possibly assume such an exact translation of intentions and ideas into building materials that the message received by medieval people necessarily would have been identical with the message given? Although some overlap must have occurred, it is safe to assume that the message given by the architect and the message received by an illiterate medieval worshipper could have been significantly different.

Discussions of the relations between theological or methodological ideas and artistic forms, then, may not help us recover the message received. The scriptural, classical, or even political referent of a fresco, a stained-glass window, or a cathedral may or may not have been part of the interpretive equipment of an illiterate worshipper. The worshipper sought and found a different kind of information from that pursued by modern scholars and art historians, knowledge conducive to living a fruitful life both in the present and after death. The perception and interpretation of an image or a building was governed not by the intention of its creator but by the vital interest of the viewer.

Let us grant, for the moment, our medieval viewer's general interest in life-orienting and -enhancing images. How are we to identify the more particular interests of different individuals or groups within a community? Since our medieval worshipper usually did not record her perceptions and impressions nor define for us how the images in her place of worship affected her ideas and emotions, we are left with the images themselves as evidence.

We must reconstruct on the evidence of the images themselves the spectrum of messages that were likely to be received by the worshippers who lived with them in vitally interested contemplation on a daily basis throughout their lives. Our job is thus complex and somewhat frightening, protected from guesswork only by an educated eye trained by long and patient looking. Moreover, we must be content with working hypotheses, suggestions, and the description of a range of probable interpretations rather than "proof" for a single meaning identical for all persons who had access to the image.

A further problem arises: The claim that historians must be prepared and equipped to involve ourselves with visual as well as verbal texts cannot be supported by a projection of the significance of modern experience of visual art. Medieval men and women's experience of religious images is far closer to modern experience of media images than to a modern person's visit to a museum.[21] Both contemporary media images and historical religious images were experienced daily. Moreover, three major differences between the visual experience of modern people and that of historical people must be taken into account when we try imaginatively to reconstruct the role of religious images in the life and worship of historical people.

First, modern understanding of physical vision in its popular version differs significantly from the understanding of medieval people. In the theory of vision described by Augustine,[22] the most influential christian author of the medieval and reformation periods, a fire within the body — the same fire that animates and warms the body — is collected with unique intensity behind the eyes; for an object to be seen by a viewer, this fire must be projected in the form of a ray that is focused on the object, thereby establishing a two-way street along which the attention and energy of the viewer passes to touch its object. A representation of the object, in turn, returns to the eye and is bonded to the soul and retained in the memory.[23]

This strong visual experience was formulated negatively as the fear of contamination by a dangerous or "unsightly" visual object or positively as belief in the miraculous power of an icon, when assiduously gazed upon, to heal one's disease. Popular beliefs and practices support the conclusion that medieval people considered visual experience particularly powerful for one's good or ill. The persistence of belief in the "evil eye" from classical times to the sixteenth century and beyond is a good example. The evil eye was thought of as a maleficent visual ray of lethal strength. A person who had the evil eye reportedly could touch and poison the soul or body of an enemy. The only protections against the evil eye were making the sign of the cross, keeping one's body thoroughly covered against the baleful touch, and, especially, never meeting the eye of such a person; to do so would be to connect the two visual rays and allow the evil ray direct access to one's soul.

This heightened, even exaggerated, respect for the power, for good or evil, of visual experience is very far from modern understandings of what occurs in vision. Modern theories of vision concentrate on the mechanics of vision without attention to the psychological, moral, or spiritual effects of visual experience; or sociological studies attempt, thus far largely unsuccessfully, to document the effect of media violence or more subtly transmitted values on young people; or psychological studies attempt to identify the unconscious imagery that organizes individual and communal psyches. None of these approaches highlights the power of physical vision to affect the psyche.

Despite the constant bombardment of images for commercial and entertainment purposes, images that compete to catch the eye and thus are highly effective in catching the wallet, modern people prefer to think of themselves as disengaged voyeurs. This is a form of self-deception that makes it difficult for us to sympathize with what we think of as the "superstition", of medieval people who were very conscious of themselves as powerfully and intimately affected by visual images.[24]

Second, we must notice in our examination of significant differences between modern visual experience and that of medieval people that historical Christians experienced religious images in the context of public worship and devotional piety. The individual viewer confronted the image as a member of an interpreting community, and the image itself was also part of the architectural and liturgical presentation of an ordered cosmos of being, reality, and value.[25] The position in the church building of the various depictions of Christ, the Virgin, saints, and scriptural events indicated their relative importance in the religious life of the community. Christ in Majesty, *Christus triumphans,* depicted in the half-dome of the apse *and* in the tympanum of the main portal of a Romanesque church informed the worshipper as she entered that the same Christ who presides over the cosmos is the "door" by which worshippers enter the liturgical gatherings of the faithful.[26] In a series of traditionally placed images, the worshipper received information concerning the meaning and relative importance of the various figures and events.

In addition, religious images were interpreted verbally and reinforced by the liturgy of the churches in which they appeared. In the sacraments conducted in this setting, priests reenacted the same cosmically significant activity, the same paradigmatic events that worshippers saw around them on walls, doors, and windows. The dramatic hieratic quality of the scriptural scenes of the stained-glass windows, spoken and sung in the lectionary of readings and hymns, was reflected in the unity of word, object, and gesture in the sacraments. The field from which to begin to understand the meaning of any particular religious image to worshippers, then, is the occasion of public worship of the christian community.

Another difference between a religious image in use in a worshipping community and the same image in a modern museum is that the worshipper's perception of an image is not an aesthetic appreciation. Rather, the image is valued because of its power to move, to focus the senses and the mind, and to offer a mnemonic aid that gathers the worshipper's strongest and most fundamental ideas, emotions, and memories in an enriched present. An image deplored by an art critic or a theologian may nevertheless contain the power to carry the worshipper to the psychic place in which worship occurs. The taste of cultivated people may have little to do with the images most valued by a worshipper. Certainly, a good deal of the most powerfully moving religious art is also "great art" by the standards of the art connoisseur. But taste, a concept unknown before the Renaissance, does not explain why a particular image or subject was highly esteemed in one historical time and place but not in another. The prevalence of a subject or a style at a particular time and place must lead us to explore its relevance to the religious needs of a worshipping community.

The third major difference between modern visual experiences and those of historical people has already been suggested — the tremendous increase in the quantity of images seen by a typical modern person. Pre-sixteenth-century women or men, depending on the social class to which they belonged, may have seen only the relatively few images in their local church throughout their lives. The visual, as well as the verbal, overload of modern people requires that all the senses, and especially vision, act much more as "data reduction agencies" than as windows.[27] It is likely that our capacity for vision is — or will shortly be — congenitally fatigued by the sheer volume of images with which most modern people cope.

These three fundamental differences of assumptions and experiences constitute a challenge not only for understanding the historical importance of religious images in the life of the christian community but also for historical hermeneutics in general. Every student of history understands about another age only the meanings and values he is prepared by his own sensitivities and values to recognize. Historical interpretation reflects the perspective of the historian, and historians, as modern people, are usually not prepared — either educationally or psychologically — to give to historical visual evidence the same interest and attention that they give to verbal texts. Yet it is inadequate, to say the least, to attempt to understand a historic community entirely from study of the writings of a few of its most uncharacteristic members.

Recognition that the full task of historical understanding involves the interpretation of both verbal and visual texts will have important results for the reconstruction of a usable history for many modern people who have not found their own situations and interests reflected in historical verbal texts. These texts, almost exclusively the product of culturally privileged, highly educated, male, and most frequently monastic authors, constitute the great bulk of the literary products of Christianity before the modern period. From these writings, we can learn a great deal about how their authors thought, something about how they felt, and sometimes a bit about how they lived. But we cannot expect to learn from them how the large majority of the people in their cultures thought, felt, and lived.

To further complicate matters, in the face of the most glaring differences of experience among people within a community, historical authors frequently spoke with the universalizing self-confidence of those who had not yet learned, by painful historical circumstances, to respect the sociology of knowledge, who had no awareness of the "indignity of speaking for others." [28] In our own time, however, neither philosophy nor theology nor historical interpretation can ignore the inevitable perspectival bias that permeates assumptions, methods, and the facts selected as significant.[29] Awareness of the necessarily relative nature of every human perspective has given us an interest in the perspectives of historical people whose perceptions and ideas are not represented in literary works which present the authors' ideas as universally valid.

Many social and cultural historians are now correcting the one-sidedness of the "history of great ideas and the men who had them" approach with important studies of technological, economic, and demographic conditions. These studies often give very different pictures of historical communities from the often profoundly unhistorical "tradition" we have received concerning them. But even this valuable evidence is not sufficient — necessary as it is — to enable historians to reconstruct a tentative account of the subjective lives of historical people. Understanding historical communities and individuals requires the important addition of visual evidence to the texts and other data that are the raw material of historical interpretation. Both verbal and visual texts[30] must be used to illuminate, to correct, and to supplement the impressions we get from each. Only then are we able to understand how the lives of human beings were organized psychologically, spiritually, and intellectually—how, that is, their lives were formed, informed, and supported by words and images.

This book deals with different source materials to explore the history of different people of the past and to begin to reconstruct the historical antecedents of different contemporary people from those that traditional historical work has served.

By far the largest group whose history can be approached by using visual images in addition to verbal texts is women. The use of visual images as historical evidence promises to provide a range and depth of material for women's history that is simply unavailable in verbal texts, the great majority of which were neither written by nor read by historical women. Popular texts, records, and letters are, of course, highly informative and valuable but are often not extant for a time and place we would like to explore, nor do they help us to reconstruct from the material used by historical women themselves the complexity of their affective lives. The work of feminist historians has, on the basis of available verbal data, identified historical misogyny; it has also revealed hitherto unknown or ignored women's writings or evidence of women's lives and activities in the writings and records of men.[31] The evidence these historians are uncovering reveals both a great deal of misogyny and the existence of interesting, creative, and sometimes powerful historical women[32] who were able to obtain education, leisure, and an unusual degree of autonomy.

Preliminary to a balanced account of verbal and visual evidence, we must examine the visual evidence for its own sake. If we were, for the moment, to put all of our historical literary texts back on the shelf, to shelve even our knowledge of them, and to reconstruct a history of Christianity on the evidence of visual texts alone, we would see immediately that from the earliest christian images there is a continuous depiction of women and the development of subjects and themes based on the experience of women. For a woman whose daily life centered around the worship of a christian community, these images may have been powerfully affirming in a way that twentieth-century women find difficult to imagine, flooded as we are with exploitive commercial images of women.[33] An understanding of the quantity and quality of self-esteem and the community's esteem for women must eventually be the result of careful interpretation of texts, records, and images in relation to one another.

When we attend to visual evidence, a different picture from that given by texts appears. For example, depictions of the various significant events in the life of the Virgin/Mother Mary presented to women a reflection or interpretation of their own experience. In addition, depictions of other women of scriptural, apocryphal, or historical significance were frequent not in isolated paintings or sculptures but in themes that, if we are to judge by the great number of these representations, held the imagination of Christians throughout the medieval period and well into the sixteenth century, even in Protestant areas. Saint Anne, the Virgin's mother, a married woman and an old woman, was a popular subject that reached its height in a cult of St. Anne at the end of the Middle Ages.[34] The sick woman, the woman with the issue of blood of the gospel accounts, was regularly the subject for images emphasizing great faith and divine healing. Paintings treating the martyrdom of women saints pictured women as capable of heroic strength of conviction. Another widely popular theme that we examine in more detail in Chapter 4 is that embodied by Mary Magdalene, a sinful woman but a woman uniquely loved by Christ and therefore an image of hope to everyone. The Old Testament story of Judith and Holofernes, a subject that grew in popularity from the fourteenth century on, presents a powerful, threatening, but nonetheless righteous woman. We may find, on further study, that women of the christian west in the fourteenth century were nourished, as Christians and as women, by a de-

◆ 11

veloped lexicon of images that presented and tacitly affirmed a wide spectrum of behavior, emotion, and experience.

But visual evidence in isolation from verbal evidence is seriously incomplete; the very prominence and popularity of medieval visual imagery of women may have contributed to a verbal backlash. The iconophobia that resulted in local iconoclastic activity periodically throughout the medieval period [35] and reached its height in the west in the Protestant reform of the sixteenth century may have been directly related to the misogyny that was frequently expressed in popular saints' lives and devotional material as well as in theological texts. Marian icons excited "both the greatest devotion from iconophiles, and the greatest hostility from iconophobes." [36] The iconoclasm associated with the Protestant reforms of the sixteenth century destroyed images of Mary with special venom, often despite the remonstrance of their leaders.[37]

The search for women's history illustrates the general rule that it is not any more sufficient to attend only to the visual images of late medieval piety than it is to use only verbal texts. Historical hermeneutics must develop a method that includes the use of both texts and images if the worlds of historical people are to be understood. Such a method needs to begin by determining, for a historical culture, the complex of texts and images available to persons within the culture.[38] From close study of these texts and images, we can describe how texts amd images illuminate one another. The relation of texts to images may then be seen as one of (1) complementarity or even redundancy, in which image and text offer similar and mutually reinforcing messages; (2) tension, in which text and image offer differing evidence that can be used to understand the community from which they come; or (3) contradiction, in which fundamental dissonance between texts and images signals either that texts and images represent different and unreconcilable groups within the community or that texts and images should be understood as mutually compensatory in the community they represent. At this point, we can describe the messages available from both texts and images and who within the community was likely to have received them.

This book offers a contribution to the responsible evaluation of images in relation to texts. I analyze what is needed and provide historical examples of the potential fruitfulness of a hermeneutic that includes visual and verbal texts. Since historical theological texts have received a disproportionate amount of skilled attention in relation to historical religious images, I focus my attention on images as the first step in the interpretive process I have outlined. Since the interest of historians has been largely on the people in historical communities who wrote and read texts, my interest is largely—but not entirely—on historical people who were primarily engaged with images.

The book, you will by now have realized, has a diversified agenda, the several aspects of which will be taken up in its various sections. The first section, Chapter 2, examines the hermeneutical principles, assumptions, and methods that have resulted in historians' concentration on verbal texts as historical evidence. It then proposes a hermeneutic of visual texts. The central section, Chapters 3–5, offers illustrations of visual images used as historical evidence. These historical examples were chosen somewhat arbitrarily on the basis of my own interest and preparation; it is my conviction that any historical situation will yield a similarly enriched picture if visual images are taken into account. The visual experience of worship in a fourth-century basilica is considered in Chapter 3. Chapter 4 treats the importance of images of women in the fourteenth century for the recovery of women's history. The practice and attitudes toward religious images of Protestants and Roman Catholics in the sixteenth century and their religious repercussions are discussed in Chapter 5.

The final section, Chapters 6 and 7, considers the contemporary use and abuse of images in North American culture. It explores the relevance of historical christian evaluations of images to the present cultural and religious situation. The significance for us of practices and attitudes of the past is their value to corroborate and support present experience, to offer alternatives to present values and practices, or to call into question, to contradict, or to judge the present ordering — so that nothing will be lost — of "the richness of the mixture."

◆ 2 ◆

Hermeneutics and
the History of Image Users

It is our needs that interpret the world.
FRIEDRICH NIETZSCHE

The recommendation that visual historical evidence be taken into account in our attempt to understand the ideas and images of people who were not linguistically trained — that is, specially privileged — has the ring of an obvious truth or methodological necessity about which no more need be said. But the fact that this "obvious" methodological suggestion has apparently been anything but obvious to most historians of ideas is our starting point for an exploration in this section of the hermeneutical assumptions that have made the use of visual historical evidence problematic for professional historians. Innocent as the proposal for the use of visual evidence sounds, it has important repercussions within the discipline of historical hermeneutics, affecting fundamental questions concerning the politics of historical inquiry.

History and the Historian

A century-long, complex discussion that began with the late nineteenth-century German philosopher Wilhelm Dilthey has led to a recognition of the inevitable perspectival bias, or human interest, that permeates historical knowledge. The honorific model of scientific work — even, as Dilthey proposed, scientific work of a different kind from that of the natural sciences — has been gradually relinquished as an accurate account of historical inquiry.

The Enlightenment goal of objective human knowledge, governed by adherence to the universal laws of reason, had been based on Descartes's confidence in the trustworthiness of the clear and distinct idea. For Descartes, the model of knowledge was mathematics. Thought must govern itself by rules of logic but it would then be rewarded with undoubtable knowledge. In reaction, the Romantic movement recognized an inevitable admixture of "the silken weavings of our afternoons," which leaves reason structurally flawed. While Enlightenment philosophers went into ecstasies over "Reason" as the universal human activity, participated in more or less fully by every human being, Romantic philosophers located the essence of universal humanity in affective activity. Descartes's "I think, therefore I am" became, to Rousseau, "I feel, therefore I am." Both claimed as universal an aspect of human being identified by an educated individual who claimed to speak for the whole human race.

The identification of the human activity of interpreting and responding to the world was first examined in relation to social situations and the part they play in the acquisition and formulation of knowledge by late nineteenth- and twentieth-century sociologists. In our time, social scientists, using a Marxist critique of Hegelian idealism, have begun to demonstrate how social class, economic conditions, and cultural environment form what is sought and recognized as knowledge, especially self-knowledge. Questions about what part or function of human being is considered essential, core, or distinctive may be answered very differently by persons of different races, social classes, genders, or educations.

Despite the recent acknowledgment by social scientists of the "sociology of knowledge," it is still, I believe, the analysis of human being as distinguished by a thinking and feeling activity or a subjective consciousness that implicitly or explicitly underlies contemporary historical work. If subjective consciousness is considered distinctive, normative, and universal, it is the history of *this* aspect of human being that is sought, formulated, and presented as "human" history.

The two kinds of historical work compiled and taught in academic institutions during the last century — the history of ideas and political history — analyze the most prominent components of subjective consciousness. "Man as thinker" and "man as actor" are treated in related approaches to historical study. These two human functions, and the men who exemplify them, are considered worthy of the committed labor of historians. It is assumed that when we have understood adequately the human saga of profound thought and heroic action, we will have understood what is significant, characteristic, and essential about humanity.

Historians' need for a self-constituting history — a history that reconstructs the development of thought that has culminated in our own habits of mind, principles of selectivity, and scholarly and personal problems — is the unrecognized motivation for work on the history of ideas and political history. The history of ideas is, first of all, a history of modern subjective consciousness, the historical antecedents of a human being who has been trained by his education to understand himself as constituted by a subjective activity that at once differentiates him from other human beings and constitutes his quintessential selfhood. The historian, when he reads historical texts, is predisposed by his "interest" to recognize in his sources the antecedents of his own self-constituting activity.

The history of ideas, however, claims the universality of the history it explores. It claims that since subjective consciousness is normative, it is also universal, so that all human beings participate — to a greater or lesser degree — in it. There is, then, no place in the history of ideas for historical or contemporary people who do not understand themselves as constituted primarily by subjective consciousness, that is, by interests that focus on man as thinker or man as actor.

But by what else might a "self" be constituted and organized for thought and action? It is hard to imagine a more presumptuous question or one that better demonstrates the lifelong privileged education to which I, along with most readers of this book, have been exposed, an education that has imperceptibly trained us to understand subjective consciousness as the normative human activity. Can we really suppose that if it were possible to ask a random sampling of historical and contemporary people what aspect of themselves they consider normative or universally human, they would answer — if our question did not immediately irritate them — that it is their subjectivity or consciousness? Would they not find belonging to a family or a social or national community, the struggle for physical necessities, or their position in the life cycle of the body, perhaps, to precede and determine their thought and activity?

It is important to emphasize that we are not discussing which aspect of human being alone constitutes the "real" human being. We would like to know what human function is understood, and by which members of a community, as organizing or orchestrating the other aspects of human being. I strongly suspect that the question would be answered differently by persons who have not been educated long and strenuously to think of themselves as thinkers and actors than by those who have. If the person we question understands individual subjective consciousness as ordering his life, he will answer by describing the worldview, the ideas, and the values he holds as distinguishing and informing his selfhood. But if a person sees her physical existence as central, she will answer by identifying her age, sex, work, children, or relationships based on birth and marriage as distinguishing her selfhood. This configuration of constituting interests is, incidentally, reminiscent of the method by which cultural anthropologists approach the study of previously unexplored cultures — cultures that cannot be presumed to have adopted a western intellectual bias about normative human being.

Just as the history of ideas focuses on "great ideas and the men who had them," political history inevitably produces a rendering of the deeds of an elite, the few leaders the results of whose ideas and decisions were suffered by scores of human beings who had no alternative but to suffer them. The method of the political historian is significant; he first accumulates all the evidence he can about the motives and structures of the particular events he studies and then comes to his conclusions by rethinking the decision-making process of the actor — the king, emperor, or prelate. We are no closer to the self-constituting ideas and images of the powerless and underprivileged with political history than we are with the history of ideas.

Language and the Historian

A further step brings us to another structural element of the model of human being as organized by an individual subjective consciousness — the crucial role of language. Modern linguistic philosophers make dramatic claims for the role of language in the constitution of a "self." Individuation is understood as a language event: "Being that can be understood is language," Gadamer wrote.[1] It is also a universal event: "What raises us out of nature is the only thing whose nature we can know: language," Habermas asserted. "Through its structure, autonomy and responsibility are posited for us. Our first sentence expresses unequivocally the intention of universal and unconstrained consensus." [2]

Congruent with Freud's statement that the ego has a verbal nucleus,[3] the constitution of subjective consciousness is a linguistic activity, the verbal use of imagination for the creation of "one's favorite character in fiction." Language simultaneously defines the individual — "raises us out of nature" — and plants us securely in the universally human.[4] It is, Habermas observed, impossible to speak without speaking universally; the formative act of the subjective consciousness is the first sentence one speaks. After this decisive break with nature, one's only prerogative is to become increasingly skilled at linguistic self-reflection or, failing this, to capitulate to what Mallarmé called "the common use of language," which he compares "to the exchange of a coin whose obverse and reverse no longer bear any but worn effigies, and which people pass from hand to hand in silence." [5]

The common use of language, however, the unexamined use of words deadened or at least fatigued by routine usage, has ontological implications, according to modern linguistic philosophers: To the extent that the subjective consciousness is gathered and organized by a fatigued language or a "base rhetoric," [6] the person will be removed from — and here the imagery is imported from the spatial/hierarchical language of classical ontology — the reality, the truth, and the beauty of his or her being. The subjective consciousness will be "in flight from itself." [7]

This analysis of the relation of language and subjective consciousness contains two important implications. First, if it is true that the relative strength of the ego — or subjective consciousness — is determined by a more or less adequate linguisticizing activity, a less adequate "verbal nucleus" may be remedially adjusted by analysis of the constituting language, and "the ego's flight from itself" may be reversed through language that has a therapeutic rather than a regressive effect.[8] The subjective rhetoric of guilt, depression, or addiction may be experimentally replaced with a new rhetoric of patient perseverance, self-forgiveness, and optimism. This rectification of language may be managed with the use of extremely simple phrases, even clichés,[9] or it may require the long, complex, and expensive process of the "talking cure," [10] the analysis of the relation of language and being originated, in its present form, by Freud.

Second, the assumptions and methods of the history of ideas have been profoundly affected by the analysis of language made explicit by contemporary linguistic philosophers. If it is true that the strength — and therefore the power — of the ego is determined by a more or less adequate use of language, then those persons in any culture who are skilled in language will be seen as more real than will less skilled persons. The historian will consider this skilled language user as representative of the culture because he is able to describe, and therefore to create, the reality experienced by his community. And so the historian concentrates on the words, the verbal texts, of language users when he attempts to reconstruct cultural perspectives, attitudes, and values.

Undeniably, the language users in a culture have a power that must be taken into account when one tries to understand the culture of which they are a part. Yet it cannot be assumed that their power and influence are total, or even representative, within their culture. The question of precisely who is affected by the speech or writing of language users, and of how those people are affected — that is, to what extent and in what specific area of life — is an important one to explore at the outset of any historical analysis based on the study of language users.

The relative distinction I have suggested between language users and non–language users comes from the semiologist Roland Barthes. Language users are the people, few in any culture, who actively change language by the skillful manipulation of words to present new perspectives, different values, or forceful insights. Non–language users, by far the majority in any culture, are those whose use of language is unselfconscious. These people take the mean-

◆ 19

ing, the intensity value, and the connotative value of words as self-evident, as contained in the words themselves, and therefore as existing in reality.[11]

Non–language users are frequently ignored by historians; they are often considered incapable of providing interesting or usable antecedents for modern subjective consciousness. They are seen as immersed in the physical contingencies of life and sustenance, transcending these pressing necessities only occasionally and then only in the interest of "superstition." Non–language users do not participate in the "fellowships of discourse" that define and create the culture. They are not members of the educational institutions and the elite intellectual groups that have appropriated intellectual discourse and have set the qualifications, the rules, and the gestures of discourse.[12] And yet the lives of non–language users were no less ordered by ideas and images than were those of language users. To dismiss their lives as uninteresting for historical understanding is the judgment of an educationally privileged elite that reflects an exclusive interest in the antecedents of modern subjective consciousness.

It has always been apparent, in the boredom of schoolchildren and college students who "hate history," that the academic history they are taught is not *their* history. It is not, in other words, a history of the past that discovers and formulates the antecedents of the self-constitution of the student, who is not yet thoroughly educated to think of herself as primarily a subjective consciousness. It is not her history in terms of the aspect of human being she considers normative. Neither is it likely to be her history in sociological terms. The most important differences of sex, perspectives of social class, experience, and values are ignored in the claim of the historical disciplines to produce "human" knowledge.

Do persons who do not define themselves primarily by either thought or independent activity "have" a history? Is there, for example, a history of the human body — of nourishment, sexuality, or power directed to the conditioning and control of the body? Could not such a history provide information of the first importance about the conditions in which both thought and activity take place?

The research of Michel Foucault began to provide a history of the body for certain limited historical periods and is most interesting both in its content and in its revelation of the different assumptions, methods, and evidence that a history of the body requires. Foucault's work on corporal and capital punishment, on medical attitudes toward illness, madness and their treatment, and on the societal control and deployment of sexuality has demonstrated that exclusive study of the antecedents of modern subjective consciousness is neither obvious nor necessary.

Let us leave for the moment the question of whether the emergence of individuality takes place, in real and important ways, in other than linguistic modes and further explore the claim that language is the vehicle of universality, access to "the transindividual reality of the subject." [13] Is language, as Gadamer claims, the concrete form of the connectedness of all human beings? [14] Is "intersubjectivity" community?

The most dramatic claims for the universality of language appear in those philosophers who assert or assume that intersubjectivity is identical with universality and that language forms the basis of human community. [15] The longing for a verbal form of intersubjectivity, [16] or a "common language," has obscured for many philosophers, historians, and hermeneuts the evident esotericism of a dialectic that can take place only between persons — whether contemporary or historical — who share the equivalent of "a common social background . . . and college education." [17]

Is language the exclusive basis of human community with its dependence for survival not only on heterosexual relationships but on heteropsychic relationships, that is, on some degree of respect for a variety of human beings? If the concrete bond of human community actually depends on a certain amount and kind of linguistic training by which a person acquires the habit of thinking of himself or herself as constituted by subjective consciousness, are not most members of the human race excluded by precisely the factor that was posited as universal? Why could not descriptions of the importance of language to human community be balanced by recognition that the common experience of embodiment, with all its vulnerability, beauty, and terror, offers no less a fundamental and concrete basis for human community? If a human body were understood as part of what is universal or normative about human being, differences as well as similarities of bodily experience would need to form part of the description of normative humanity.

If, however, language is regarded as the foundation of a common humanity, it is tempting to assume the universality of one's own perspective as an articulate representative of human being. The historian who operates with this assumption will likely neglect to make explicit, even to himself, an inevitable foreshortening of the historical evidence by his perspective and values, the perspective and values of a particular sex, social class, and education. The intellectual's traditional role of "representing or representative consciousness," of speaking "the truth for those who have yet to see it," of being the "conscience, consciousness, and eloquence" [18] of humanity results from the assumption of the universality of language. If language is universal, the language user can claim, without a qualm, to speak universally.

The predilection of language users for other language users can be illustrated by psychoanalysis, in this sense analogous to the historical disciplines. In psychoanalysis, as in the history of ideas, a "structuring of narratives" [19] occurs in which the concatenation of discrete occurrences that constitute the patient's life are composed into a history. Analyst and patient must share a "common social background of bourgeois origins and college education" if such verbal reconstruction is to be effective. Failing some degree of common preparation and perspective, a "linguistic distance" between patient and analyst will develop that will undermine the mutual "structuring of narratives." Just as the analyst is at sea with a patient whose linguistic training does not approximate his own, the historian is at sea with historical non–language users.

Language and Power

Wittgenstein's dictum "The master of the language is the master of us all" unambiguously identifies language with power. In doing so, it articulates the assumption shared by language users — historians among them — that the great books of history, containing the great ideas and perhaps originally presented as the great speeches, have influenced social and political institutions, values, changes, and continuities more than any other factor. It is not my intention to disparage the importance of language but to argue that claims for its power have been wishfully overdrawn by language users.

Michel Foucault has critiqued the exaggerated relation of power and rhetoric in his many discussions of the way power operates in culture. Critical of the axiom, common to idealism and to Marxism, that power operates by the use of ideology, Foucault emphasizes the primary operation of power on the human body: "Nothing is more material, physical, corporal, than the exercise of power." [20] The goal of power is not the management of consciousness so as to ensure agreeable, or at least docile, behavior, but the control of behavior — that is, labor and sexuality — into what constitutes the "normal." Moreover, Foucault criticizes the identification of power with repression: "Power would be a fragile thing if its only function were to repress . . . If, on the contrary, power is strong this is because . . . it produces effects at the level of desire — and also at the level of knowledge." [21]

Foucault writes that we must jettison our notions of knowledge as the personal acquisition of a few individuals who have freed themselves from the control of power and are therefore able to understand accurately and to think freely. Rather, "power produces knowledge . . . There is no power relation without the correlative constitution of a field of knowledge, nor any knowledge that does not presuppose and constitute at the same time power relations." [22]

Neither should we think of power as centralized or even localized within a culture, the possession of an individual, a group, or an institution. It is, rather,

a network of relations, constantly in tension, in activity . . . This power is exercised rather than possessed; it is not the privilege, acquired or preserved, of the dominant class, but the overall effect of its strategic positions . . . These relations go right down into the depths of society; . . . they define innumerable points of confrontation, focuses of instability, each of which has its own risks of conflict, of struggles, and of an at least temporary inversion of the power relations.[23]

This understanding of the operation of power within a culture not as a centralized institution or ideology but as a "network" containing myriad points at which power is exercised to coordinate the desires of individuals is an important starting point for the historical sections of this book. Both as a critique of the identification of rhetoric with power and as a model for the exploration of historic cultures, Foucault's description of power as primarily operative — and effective, while it is strong — in constellating and directing desire has important implications for historical method. This understanding of power dispenses with one of the most universally useful figures of historical study, the villain — the possessor of power to repress and compel. In the history of ideas, the villain is the thinker who first — or most fully and articulately — formulated an idea that, in our time, has come to appear oppressive.[24]

Contemporary historians' frequent description of the medieval Catholic church as a centralized oppressive power, for example, is modeled on the idea of power criticized by Foucault. It fails to account for the activity and creativity with which medieval communities worshipped and with which they supported — and were supported by — monasteries; it ignores the energy with which they built cathedrals. These are only the most external and visible indications that the Roman Catholic church was largely successful in constellating the desires and longings of medieval communities. Even this coordination of desire was not achieved by a planned manipulation but operated from a thousand coordinated points within and "right down to the depths of society." [25]

Only when the late-medieval church became weakened from within by a too frequently dishonorable clergy and from without by the formulation of critical and alternative groups such as the Waldensians, the Bogomils, and the Cathars did the Roman Catholic church install routine coercive measures in the office of the papal inquisition. The weakness of the institution prompted the emergence of the papal inquisition, which represented in its time a quantum leap in repressive technique over the almost entirely ineffective episcopal inquisition formally in effect since the beginning of the fourth century. The turn to an explicitly repressive agenda happened only when the collapse of effective power made feasible the ultimately self-defeating use of repressive force. "The notion of repression," Foucault writes, "is quite inadequate for capturing what is precisely the productive aspect of power." While power is strong, people accept it precisely because

it doesn't only weigh on us as a force that says no, but . . . it traverses and produces things, it induces pleasure, forms knowledge, produces discourse.

◆ 2 3

It needs to be considered as a productive network which runs through the whole social body, much more than as a negative insistence whose function is repression.[26]

The historian's identification of a villain is a way to avoid the painstaking work of examining the network by which constructive, "strong" power is brought to bear within a culture by "stimulation."[27] We need to locate neither the person nor the institution that is to blame for controlling and exerting power but the attractiveness of a constellation of power and its ability to produce cooperation within the culture.

This understanding is important for the reconstruction of the history of those usually called "powerless." The task is no longer to identify the powerless and the powerful within cultures as a sex, a class, or a social or ideological group of any kind. Nor is it the task of a historian to locate a persuasive rhetoric by which some members of a culture acquiesce in or support the repression of other individuals or groups. Rather, power is "a highly intricate mosaic."[28]

The training and skill of the historian, then, should be engaged in exploring the concrete occasions on which power is transacted, that is, the occasions on which it is effectively affirmed against resistance. Only by noting the small and apparently insignificant instances in which power is exercised[29] can we understand who "has" power, in which area of daily life, and to what extent. We need to look for the way in which the various kinds of power, wielded by different people within a community, are balanced by mutual resistance.

Although professional historians have not often been as articulate about their assumptions as have the philosophers whose statements I have used to outline various facets of the subjective consciousness, we can see by examining certain methodological features of traditional historical inquiry that an assumption that subject consciousness constitutes essential human being, pervasively informs the historians' method.

Interest and Historical Method

What are the characteristics of a historical study that begins with an interest[30] in identifying the antecedents of modern subjective consciousness? The first characteristic has already received our attention. Because subjective consciousness is verbally structured, its history will be a verbal history, a history of ideas. Its evidence will be the verbal texts of the past, written by the most skilled language users of their time. Any other kind of historical evidence will be regarded as enigmatic or obscure.

The second characteristic is more complex and requires more careful description. The history of the modern subjective consciousness will display a *continuity* that is achieved and guaranteed by a "limiting principle,"[31] the selection, across the self-contained cohesiveness of particular discursive unities, of statements that have verbal similarities with one another. If, for example, we find the "same" statement on a point of doctrine in Calvin that we find in Augustine, we think that we have found proof that Calvin's idea is the same as Augustine's idea, or that Calvin must have been influenced by Augustine. Instead of referring the statement to the complex network of discourse within which it occurred and analyzing its meaning within this discourse, instead of trying to identify the problem it addresses or the insight it formulates, we trace the transmission and development of the idea from Augustine to Calvin. We posit a single tradition, whether philosophical or theological, that guarantees the homogeneity, across time, of statements related to this tradition; we never explore the uniqueness of a statement and the particularity of its formulation within a concrete discourse replete with "interests." [32]

The systematic study of historical ideas proceeds by "freeing" a theological or a philosophical statement from its position within a particular discourse so that it can be recognized as the identical concept in a new discursive structure. It ignores the extent to which statements are always formed in discursive practice, "in accordance with specific laws." [33] In a different discourse, they occupy a different position, respond to a different situation, and are governed by a different structure and different laws of discourse. No statement can be abstracted from its position within a particular discourse and retain its meaning:

Even if a statement is composed of the same words, bears exactly the same meaning, and preserves the same syntactical and semantic identity, it does not constitute the same statement if it is spoken by someone in the course of a conversation, or printed in a novel; if it was written one day centuries ago, and if it now reappears in an oral formulation. A statement must have a substance, a support, a place, and a date. And when these requisites change, it too changes identity.[34]

The search for the continuous existence of modern subjective consciousness in the great ideas of the past may be informed not only by the educated perspective of western academic intellectuals but also by a much more subtle perspectival bias. Male physical experience, unless interrupted by serious illness or accident, features continuity, as women's physical experience does not. For women, the continuity of physical existence is secondary to the interruptions of that continuity caused by different physical conditions, which in turn carry different social identities and personal relationships. First menstruation, first sexual intercourse, childbearing, menopause — all these events are primarily irreversible alterations in a woman's body and secondarily changes in social identity. Change, the difference from one day to the next, the different body, perspective, and values of different times of life — these experiences of discontinuity, of being physically, mentally and socially other than one was, characterize women's experience. Change is featured in women's experience; change is figure, while continuity is ground.

This is not a point I want to argue at length; it is a genuine suggestion, which I would not know how to prove. Nevertheless, it indicates the nonverbal influences that may lie beneath our knowledge-producing interests. We need to find ways to factor in different physical experiences as well as different intellectual experiences when we evaluate claims for the universality of subjective consciousness. These claims have led to historical study that uncritically assumes the perspective of a particular human group — with infinite minor variations, of course — white, male, western academics, while claiming to be simply "the history of man." The pursuit of historical continuity is just one point at which the perspective of male experience is revealed, a perspective that denies women's experience of discontinuity.

The third characteristic of historical study that originates in the historian's interest in the antecedents of modern subjective consciousness is its quasi-religious commitment to the fundamental coherence of the ideas that occur in the time and the place the historian explores:

If [the history of ideas] happens to notice an irregularity in the use of words, several incompatible propositions, a set of meanings that do not adjust to one another, concepts that cannot be schematized together, then it regards it as its duty to find, at a deeper level, a principle of cohesion that organizes the discourse and restores to it its hidden unity . . . But this same coherence is also the result of research . . . In order to constitute it, it must first be presupposed.[35]

Contradiction, so prominent a feature of contemporary experience that it might easily be projected in historical inquiry, is, however, too hurriedly denied in the search for the unity of a particular culture. Contradictions are handled either by showing their resolution in a higher or more profound unity or by describing those contradictions as a fundamental tension that energizes the discourse.[36]

The historian's commitment to coherence has resulted in historical description that never acknowledges real and irresolvable conflict. For example, the much-plowed ground of the classical doctrinal controversies of early Christianity inevitably yields a winner and a resolution. The resolution of Christological controversy at the Council of Chalcedon in 451 is usually presented as the happy solution to a long struggle. If the Monohysite empire that resulted from Chalcedon's conclusions is mentioned — an empire which by the beginning of the sixth century was larger geographically than Roman and Orthodox Christianity put together — it is mentioned in another chapter, thus allowing, if not actually fostering, the impression of a conflict overcome.

It is important in our attention to visual evidence from the past to preserve the contradictions we identify, to notice the existence of conflict between various individuals or groups within the communities we examine. We must anticipate that the use of a different kind of historical evidence, visual images, may reveal the presence of even more fundamental contradictions and conflicts than are identifiable with the exclusive use of verbal texts. Our interpretation must not be committed to reconciling these contradictions nor to arguing the productivity of the pressure they bring to bear on the community. Our effort should rather be directed at mapping them, determining their extent and their limits within the discourse, and attempting to identify whom they engaged. If even the cohesiveness of verbal texts has been overdrawn, it is likely that the elements of discontinuity and contradiction will be even more marked when nonverbal evidence is also taken into account.

A Hermeneutics of Visual Images

We have looked briefly at some of the problems with historical study that uses only the linguistic evidence of the past in the reconstruction of a history of ideas. But surely this evidence is the material for a history of ideas, is it not? It is, I acknowledge, the history of philosophy, the history of the governing principles and logical exposition of discursive thought, an exciting and valuable study in itself. But exclusive attention to the history of philosophy has given generations of students the idea that philosophers are the only human beings who organize their lives according to ideas. Yet all people live with and by ideas, whether or not their ideas are ever articulated.

The attempt to understand the structure and content of the discourse of historical christian communities has understood itself on the model of a history of philosophy. It has focused on the great organizing ideas of christian history and the development of these ideas across time, just as the history of ideas has focused on the breakthrough of ideas that have led thought to its "culmination" in ourselves. The study of historical Christianity is therefore vulnerable to the criticisms Foucault has leveled against the history of ideas. It too has, to a great extent, assumed the validity of abstracting theological and doctrinal statements from the particular discourses in which they occurred in order to locate their origin, their continuity and development, and their coherence with other statements.

"It is not necessary to be theologically self-conscious to be religiously sophisticated," Clifford Geertz wrote.[37] Because of its methodology, historical theology has usually concentrated on the theologically self-conscious and has denied, or at least ignored, the possibility that religious sophistication — the fruitful use of a complex of ideas and images conducive to imagining and living a happy and productive human life — does not require, although it certainly may include, the ability to verbally articulate one's religious ideas. Historical theology betrays its origins and historical content when it presents as normative the history of the ideas of an intellectual elite that culminates in the ideas of the academic philosophical theologians of our time.

If historical theology is to become the study of the ideas and images of the people of christian communities rather than an analysis of the ideas of a few great thinkers, however, we need to shape our historical method to the kind of historical understanding we want to obtain. If our assumptions and goals change, our methods must also change. We need evidence that is simultaneously more superficial and more profound. We need, in short, to identify the "media" of the cultures with which we work, the modes and the content of public communication and exchange of verbal and visual ideas.

The media of predominantly illiterate people was not, of course, entirely visual; valuable work is now being done by social historians in recovering the sermons, extraliturgical drama, and popular literature through which ideas were made auditorily available to whole communities. This work is important; it must eventually be understood in relation to the visual media of the christian communities. But before relations between verbal and visual media can be fully understood, before the complexity of the discourse can be reconstructed, we must patiently gather its components. I concentrate in Chapters 3–5 on images as evidence of the messages that were likely to have been received by various persons and groups within medieval and Renaissance communities. We will "read" images for a specifically theological life-informing content, that is, for messages *received* rather than messages *given* by the commissioners and creators of the images.

Moreover, the examination of historical imagery involves exploration of cultures that are fundamentally different from our own, despite similarities between contemporary religious language and images and those of historical Christianity. Clifford Geertz cautions the explorer of an alien culture to approach that culture with humility and to acknowledge the incompleteness of the picture she formulates:

Cultural analysis is, or should be, guessing at meanings, assessing the guesses, and drawing explanatory conclusions from the better guesses, not discovering the Continent of Meaning and mapping its bloodless landscape.[38]

I do not claim, therefore, that images are the key to understanding historical people, but only that they are a significant piece of the discourse of christian communities that has not been systematically incorporated in the study of historical christian ideas. They are, however, a piece that is capable of changing our understanding of the whole discourse.

I have suggested that the study of historical images deals with evidence that is simultaneously more superficial and more profound than the evidence of theological texts. Images are more superficial in the sense that they were more available to historical people, more on the surface of their daily lives. Images are more profound not necessarily in the difficulty or complexity of expression but in their importance at the center of the affective life of the whole community. They provide what Geertz has called "thickness"; they do not help us to "codify abstract regularities" [39] but rather to recognize and perhaps to understand the richness of life's mixture.[40] Even the attempt to interpret the message received from religious images forces us to enter the imaginative worlds of people who have not often been the object of historical study. We must overcome our "flattened view of other people's mentalities." [41]

Images and Texts

In some ways, the interpretation of texts and of images involves similar skills and methods; in other ways it involves quite different methods. Historical study of communities must "stay rather closer to the ground" than the history of ideas has usually been content to do. "Only short flights of ratiocination tend to be effective . . . longer ones tend to drift off into logical dreams, academic bemusements with formal symmetry." [42] We must be careful, however, not to contrast the modesty of claims for the interpretation of visual historical evidence with the far more ambitious claims to knowledge of the history of ideas. Evidence, whether verbal or visual, can be interpreted only by relating a particular text to the discourse that gives it significance, weight as a symbol, and intensity value as language — in other words, meaning. In this sense, interpretation of images is similar to interpretation of texts.

Moreover, in the hermeneutics of images as well as in textual hermeneutics, the perspectival bias of the interpreter must be recognized. As we have seen, the universalizing tendency of language, in combination with the claim of verbal texts to speak to and for all human beings, has led traditional hermeneutics to claim that the history of ideas is universal human history. Will a hermeneutic of visual imagery claim the universality of images?

The claim to universality of language resides primarily in the possibility of abstracting a statement that contains a meaning in itself, a meaning that can — rightly or wrongly — be lifted out of the discourse in which it occurs and used in exactly the same way in another discourse. We have been critical of this aspect of the claim of universality for language; a statement thus freed from its original discourse necessarily takes a different meaning when placed in a new discourse.

In what sense can an image claim universality? An image may be removed from the public discourse in which its range of meanings is acquired. It may be taken "bodily" from its original place — most frequently from a church to a museum. Or, left in its original location, it inevitably acquires new meanings; over time the changing discourse of the community stimulates different

◆ 29

interests and therefore changes the messages received. The image's universality rests not on its potential for abstraction — that is, on a "detachable conclusion" [43] — but on the capacity of the viewer to grasp in the concrete particularity of the image a universal affectivity. The image defines a particular constellation of affective energy that is not foreign to the viewer but that has not, until her encounter with *this* image, been formulated in quite this way. The universality of the image thus depends on an act of recognition by each viewer. The universality of an image lies in its potential affective availability to everyone who contemplates it with generosity and self-reflection. On the other hand, it is always possible that, from the interested perspective of a particular viewer, an image's formulation of affectivity may be seen and interpreted as inaccurate or oppressive; its potential for universality will then be understood as threatening or dangerous rather than emancipatory.

Whether an image is experienced as dangerous or emancipatory will be a function of the interest of the viewer. An image may seduce a viewer to a certain message, but it will not bully him to that message. From the side of the image, there is multivalence, a range of possible interpretations. The viewer chooses, often not consciously, from the range of interpretations permitted by the image one or several interpretations that relate, negatively or positively, to his interest.

Recent hermeneutical philosophers have argued against using the intention of the author as the key to the interpretation of texts; the intention of the artist or donor is even less definitive for the interpretation of images. The creator of an image had, we may assume, a message in mind — political, didactic, or religious — and this message may be more or less forced to the viewer's attention by visual conventions that carry strong connotations for the viewer. At the furthest extreme of limiting the range of messages received, the designer of an image may gloss it with a verbal message, usually a name or a short text. Even then, the viewer of a historical religious image can ignore the message and substitute a meaning quite different in accordance with his interest. The interpretation of an image tends to be more susceptible to and dependent on personal interest than is the interpretation of a theological text. Limited only by the skill of the author, texts attempt to draw the reader into acceptance of a persuasive logic.

The operation of the viewer's interests in the interpretation of an image are evident in contemporary discussions of historical images. The multivalence of the image, its susceptibility to various interpretations, is apparent in the following description of a now badly damaged eighth-century painted icon, originally in Santa Maria in Trastevere in Rome:

Mary is seated on an imperial purple cushion, stiff with jewels, with her feet resting above the ground, on a subpendaneum; *a great arcaded diadem crowns*

her head and a huge nimbus irradiates about her. But the most important
aspect of the icon is the presence of the reigning pope at the Virgin's feet.
For this mingling of the living and the dead plucks the Virgin out of an
inaccessible heaven and brings her within the reach of the one appointed
emissary on earth who, like an emperor's minister in Constantinople, can
grasp his master's foot and be assured his wishes will be granted. In conse-
quence, the legitimacy of the pope as the channel and interpreter of the
divine will on earth is affirmed.[44]

This interpretation is political, emphasizing that the direct proximity of the
pope to the Virgin stresses the immense power of the pope. This contemporary
viewer interprets the painting through her interest in exposing "the Church"
as domineering, oppressive, and self-aggrandizing.[45] The message intended by
the donor of the painting, Pope John VII (705–77), "the first pope to have
himself painted during his lifetime in the Greek ceremonial attitude of pros-
tration . . . at the feet of the Virgin in majesty," [46] may have approximated this
interpretation, or it may have been quite different.

If one interprets the painting in terms of its visual content — bodies, gestures, garments, and so on — the splendor of the Virgin and total abasement
of the highest earthly spiritual power is an explicit message. No humbler attitude could be assumed than that of John VII; had he left himself out of the
painting entirely, the painting could not have conveyed the radical relativiz-
ing of his power as it does. He did not have himself painted, as did other
medieval popes such as Paschal I (817–824), standing in the presence of
Christ and the heavenly court and presenting to Christ a model of the church
building he commissioned.

These clashing interpretations are both permitted by the same image; one
either receives a message based on the pope's proximity to the Virgin or one
receives a message based on the pope's degradation before the Virgin. But these
two interpretations do not exhaust the possibilities of messages received. At
least one other message could well have been uppermost in the perception of
a medieval viewer. The dominating figure is that of the resplendent Virgin
who completely surrounds the tiny child in her lap. One may grasp the magnificence of the Virgin, her power and significance, without reference to the
prostrate pope or even to the child whom she overwhelms both in size and in
splendor. Two angels are on the same upper level as the Virgin, but slightly
behind her; the child is in the middle level, and the pope is off to the lower
right. Why not, in a society so interested in earthly and heavenly hierarchies
of power, interpret the painting as depicting a dramatic reversal — almost certainly not intended by Pope John VII — of earthly social arrangements in
which the subservience of women testifies to the corruption of true values? [47]

In this painting, social arrangements of dominance and subordination as well

◆ 31

as of spiritual and political power are not merely equalized but reversed. It is the Virgin's foot, not the child's, that the pope grasps, and the Virgin both gives blessing to the viewer with her right hand and protects the child with her left. The painting can be interpreted as "iconoclastic" in the broad sense of the word: It judges and shatters human trust in sinful social and political institutions. It substitutes for political or ecclesiastical power the queen of heaven and for social inequality a powerful woman. Would not this have been the primary message received by at least some medieval viewers?

Interpretation of a medieval image by a modern historian interested in emancipation from a past understood as oppressive to women, then, often makes its point at the expense of neglecting the multivalence of visual images and the extent to which the message received depends on the interest of the viewer. It neglects to try to determine the spectrum of meanings that would have been likely or possible within the imaginative universe of a historical viewer.

Even if a medieval viewer was likely to receive from the eighth-century image a message concerning the earthly power of the pope, it is not at all clear that this message would have been experienced as oppressive rather than reassuring. In the circumstances — barely imaginable to a modern North American — of the social and political instability of early medieval Rome, a pope's power, both temporal and spiritual, may have had a highly comforting effect, perhaps on everyone in the city except a rival!

Our example, however, has raised a further difficulty with the interpretation of images; the multivalence of an image means that we can never definitively interpret it. The difficulty of understanding even the message intended, to say nothing of the far greater tentativeness with which one must suggest the spectrum of messages received, has been one of the major objections to the systematic use of visual images as historical evidence. How can images be used as evidence for the existence of certain attitudes, values, feelings, and ideas in historical communities if we must conclude almost as tentatively as we began by guessing at meanings?

Surely visual religious images are susceptible to an even more bewildering range of understandings and misunderstandings than are written theological formulations. If, as the eighth-century iconophile Nicephorus claimed, the function of images is to convey theological information,[48] must not the "information" given and received from an image be even more obscure than the written word? What kind of theological knowledge is more aptly conveyed by an image than by a theological proposition?

The transcendence, the majesty, and the silence of God, Gregory of Nyssa said, are more readily presented in images. Because these qualities of God are, rightly understood, not intellectual concepts but primarily sensory experiences, the mind must boggle; a person grasps God's transcendence by the perception of an image that dizzies and before which her or his breath is taken. God's majesty is more easily and accurately expressed by the gold leaf and rich, strong colors, the unapproachable gaze, the position in the heights of the dome, of a Byzantine Christos Pantocrator than by verbal descriptions. God's impenetrable silence becomes an event and an experience in the contemplation of an image.

While there is a sense, then, in which an image conveys theological knowledge for the trained eye, this does not answer the objection concerning the imprecision, the fuzziness, of the expression. The response to this objection must be to acknowledge the inability of an image to clarify a point, to present a concept, or to dictate a certain activity. Images do not stimulate the mind to greater precision of thought and expression. On the contrary, the contemplation of a religious image is more likely to rest the mind and to correct its busy craving for articulate verbalization:[49]

The image speaks to the sight as words to the ear: I have not many books nor time for study and I go into a church, the common refuge for souls, my mind wearied with conflicting thoughts. I see before me a beautiful picture and the sight refreshes me and induces me to glorify God.[50]

The coordination of intellect and senses in verbal and visual expressions results from a worship and devotional practice that engages the whole human being, in which the senses as well as the intellect are engaged and affirmed.[51] The use of images in worship modifies the tendency of words to exclude people who cannot subscribe to a precisely defined concept. Images also challenge the tendency to confine ourselves religiously to intellectualizing activity.[52]

Thus, although it is easy to defend the use of images in worship and devotional practice, it is not possible to claim that images yield precise information addressed to the intellect. The contemplation of an image does not—to put it another way—yield a "detachable conclusion," [53] either in the form of a single correct interpretation or in constraining or even suggesting particular conduct or activities. The "yield" from the contemplation of an image is not translatable into action to correct social injustice; an image does not direct the viewer either to love his neighbor or to kill his enemies.

This lack of a detachable conclusion, however, can become a basis for criticism of the use of religious images only when we demand that they perform functions that have never been claimed for them in christian tradition. In addition, the lack of a detachable conclusion can be understood in a positive light if we consider the extent to which verbal texts are susceptible to reduction to their conclusions. Reduction of a text to the conclusions it presents, ignoring the particular discourse within which it spoke and from which it was formulated, makes texts peculiarly vulnerable to misunderstanding and misrepresentation. Detachable conclusions can be applied in situations in

◆ 33

which they are the worst possible answer, in which, for example, they may operate to reinforce and support destructive power institutions or in which they oversimplify and thus wrongly prescribe for a situation.

It is not at all clear that the greater capacity of language to direct its own interpretation, to present a detachable conclusion, and to direct activity is an unambiguous benefit. Nor does the greater precision of a theological text necessarily represent a difference in quantity of precision. What *is* decisive in the virtually exclusive use of verbal texts in historical interpretation is the greater skill and training of historians in the interpretation of language than in the interpretation of images. If this imbalance between verbal and visual training were redressed, we could begin to learn the language of images, a language that compensates in affective richness for what it lacks in intellectual exactness.

The problem of the ambiguity of images, then, is not different in kind from that of the ambiguity of texts. If we were to place particular texts and images on a scale of less to more denotative capacity, words and images would have similar spectra. It is possible, but admittedly rare, for a religious image to direct its own interpretation as firmly and decisively as a text. A theological text, on the other hand, can be written in evocative poetic language that invites almost as great a range of personal interpretation and application as does an image. On a scale of more to less denotation, religious language may be creedal, carefully honed to a single meaning exclusive of other meanings; it may be sermonic, an informal language of affirmation; it may be devotional, purposively evocative, inviting the personal content of the pious individual; or it may, at the furthest remove from denotative religious language, be the abstract language of philosophical theology, minimally designating its content in experience — antipositivistic.

Similarly, religious images may, at their most denotative, be iconic, that is, organized according to a traditional depiction whose every detail — position of the figures relative to one another and to the viewer, bodily posture and tension, gesture, color of garments — may be "read" by the worshipper in terms of a particular content of scriptural or historic significance.[54] Or a religious image may be representational, in the customary sense of reproducing a visually accurate scene which strongly encourages the viewer to relate the sacred content to ordinary visual experience. At a further remove from denotation, the religious image may be impressionistic, featuring the feeling-toned impression of a particular content on the artist. Finally, at the furthest extreme of ambiguous presentation, a religious image may be abstract, minimally designating both its sacred content and its content in experience — antirepresentational.

The interpreter of images, like the interpreter of texts, must determine the denotation of the image as a preliminary step to suggesting the spectrum of meanings it was likely to have had for the different members of its historical community. For the viewer, an image is interpreted according to the viewer's interest, as informed by her or his physical experience, status within the community, education, and spirituality. The image offers a "floating chain of signifieds," [55] a wide but finite range of possible meanings.

Theological texts and religious images have a similar structure for interpretation. Both have legitimate claims to different kinds of universality; both are inevitably interpreted on the basis of the perspective, values, and interest of the interpreter. The problems of interpretation are also similar; neither theological texts nor religious images can provide information about the cultures in which they were formulated apart from a reconstruction of the part they played in the verbal and nonverbal discourse of their time and place, in the totality of messages intended and received.

Images and the Life of the Body

We can now sketch an alternative perspective on the relation of images to verbal texts, using a different pair of spectacles to look at the significance of visual images for historical people. As we have seen, the traditional perspective so laboriously drawn in the phenomenon of modern subjective consciousness locates its antecedents and pieces together a tenuous and fragile history, sometimes skipping centuries in tracing the development of a theme. The alternative perspective I suggest is also fragile, easily discounted or ignored, unsupported by great books written by great men, and seldom formulated. Like polarized glasses, my "alternative spectacles" cut the glare of the fore-understandings, assumptions, prejudices, and interests associated with the perspective of subjective consciousness. Why not — as with glasses that are tinted for light-sensitive eyes — try on a pair that is tinted to make other colors, shapes, and dimensions of human experience pop into our eyes?

Attention to the visual imagery of historical communities involves a willingness to entertain the perspective of human beings who were not primarily organized by and who did not understand themselves as primarily constituted by subjective consciousness, in any of its historical antecedents as mapped in the history of ideas. This alternative perspective is not grounded in self-identification with a classical *hegemonikon*, soul, reason, ego, or subjective consciousness, but on the primary connectedness of human beings to the natural world by fragile and transitory bodies. It is possible to lead a life of amazing beauty and richness that understands itself as based on physical existence and its exigencies. From this foundation one can gather, as maturation and physical conditions constellate different life-informing interests, visual symbols that interpret, actualize, and enhance the life of the body.

From the perspective of a life organized by physical existence, subjective consciousness is understood as an epiphenomenon of body. One can extrapolate a world of relationships that receive their origin, their structure, and their energy from physical existence — kinship and social relationships, the "body politic." Attitudes, values, and concepts can also be based on physical existence; Christianity, understood not primarily as a nexus of ideas but as concrete participation in a body — the "body of Christ" — provides a strong formulation of the centrality and significance of physical existence, in which human life itself is understood as given in physical existence — creation — and fulfilled only in physical existence — resurrection of the body.[56]

The perspective I have sketched, or one similar, is closer to the perspective of most historical and contemporary people than is the perspective which posits subjective consciousness as the individuating and universal aspect of human being. Training to reflect on oneself as constituted by subjective consciousness is training in linguistic agility; as we have seen, self-identification with subjective consciousness cannot be accomplished without a comparatively high degree of linguistic training and skill, a level inaccessible to all but a few historical and contemporary people. Thinking of human life as organized by physical existence, however, does not imply a life either limited to or focused on biological functions. Language develops one's identification with subjective consciousness; linguistic activity is the exercise that establishes and strengthens this identification. Visual images, however, are primarily addressed to comprehending physical existence, the great, lonely, yet universal preverbal experiences of birth, growth, maturation, pain, illness, ecstasy, weakness, age, sex, death.

If the texts of the educated provide a history of the antecedents of the modern subjective consciousness, visual images provide a history of the ways by which the nonprivileged understood and coped with physical existence.[57] Only by attention to visual evidence can we begin to reconstruct a history of people — for the medieval period, most men and nearly all women — who identified themselves primarily with physical existence. It was to reveal and interpret the universality of physical existence that visual images existed; this was the reason for their ubiquity and popularity.

Moreover, the recognition of an alternative perspective based on the primacy of physical existence has important implications for the recovery of women's history. I have suggested that when subjective consciousness is seen as primary, historical work recounts a historical development of ideas that strangely resembles male physical experience in its uninterrupted continuity. One of the underlying reasons that women are not willing to accept traditional political history and history of ideas as our history is that a history of continuous development does not resonate with our physical experience of irreversible change and discontinuity.[58] The implicit model of the history of ideas and the predictable continuity of male physical existence have permitted and encouraged male intellectuals to ignore the absolute dependence of human beings on the body, its exigencies, and its natural environment in favor of attention to the nurture and training of consciousness.

Few historical women or men had the luxury of this perspective. In societies before the industrial revolution, labor was directly connected to the acquisition of food, clothing, and shelter; most of the energy of men as well as women was engaged in the reproduction and maintenance of physical life. Before the modern world, we do not find many writers advising the "cultivation of embodiment";[59] physical existence was, for medieval people, a potentially overwhelming and consuming aspect of human being. In conditions that forced continuous attention to the precariousness of life, historical authors consistently attempted to compensate for or overcome the hegemony of the body by language and images that posited a spiritual orientation. Modern authors, on the other hand, from the relative security of an established identification with subjective consciousness sometimes acknowledge their need of reestablishing a relationship with physical existence. For example, the contemporary philosophical theologian Robert Neville writes: "People can learn to increase their sense of embodiment through training their sensual awareness and disciplining their attention to relevant feelings." [60]

From the perspective of subjective consciousness, urging the cultivation of embodiment makes sense to balance exclusive attention to cognitive activity. From the perspective that identifies with physical existence, it makes no sense, however. Although statements are often presented as universally descriptive, they are, in fact useful only insofar as they are accurately prescriptive for those they address. From the perspective based on physical existence, exhortations to "disdain" the body and cultivate the spiritual life call attention to an aspect of human being that people are in real danger of neglecting. From the perspective of subjective consciousness, a reminder that one should recognize a grounding in "natural processes" [61] is needed.

Statements that are rooted in a particular life experience — experience tied to sex, education, or economic and social class — and that are presented as universal can be irrelevant or dangerous to persons who do not share the perspective. Universal prescriptions are problematic. Advice to "cultivate embodiment" is not fruitful for a person who has never conceived of herself in isolation from — or perhaps even as differentiated from — her relationships, her education, her social class, and her body. Although it is not impossible for language to specify for whom it is prescriptive, the process of specifying is laborious, and therefore it is tempting to assume the universality of one's own diagnosis and prescription.

Visual images, however, as presentational rather than discursive and as inherently multivalent, can offer formulation and expression simultaneously to a wide variety of persons with different perspectives. Images can also reflect the discontinuity featured in women's physical existence; religious imagery delights in themes specific to the stages of women's life experience. The universality of physical existence, articulated by images, is different from the universality of the subjective consciousness, articulated by language. While language necessarily begins with a universal expression that it imposes on the particular, images begin with an expression of the particular and evoke the universal, inviting the viewer to participation in a symbolic expression that gives universal significance to the particular experience of human beings.

The antagonism of a few theologians to visual images and their injunctions to "spiritual" — that is, verbal — worship of God reveal a fundamental disdain for the vast majority of human beings, women and men, whose perspective was based on the exigencies of physical existence, in other words for the educationally underprivileged who had not been trained to identify themselves with intellectual activity. The arrogance of the following sixth-century statement finds an echo in the history of ideas and its claim for the structuring hegemony of language:

We ordain that the unspeakable and incomprehensible love of God for us men and the sacred patterns set by the saints be celebrated in holy writings since, so far as we are concerned, we take no pleasure at all in sculpture or painting. But we permit the simpler people, as they are less perfect, to learn by way of initiation about such things by sight which is more appropriate to their natural development.[62]

One of the large issues involved in historical criticism of images was the antagonism of a few men, who identified themselves with their ideas, to the perspective of most people of western christian communities. Most people valued the symbolic imagery of christian faith precisely for its capacity to offer fruitful messages about the value and dignity of physical existence in the present and in the world to come.

It would be a mistake, however, to exaggerate a few men's antagonism to images. Most critics objected not to all use of images but to exclusive attention to images. Typically, they urged the critical appropriation of images, a balance between language and images.

I am urging an analogous juggling of texts and images in the method of historical hermeneutics, a balance based on a respect for an interest in not only historical language users but also historical image users. We must understand the extent to which the linguistic bias of modern historians has foreshortened our historical imagination in favor of historical evidence that yields the history of a highly uncharacteristic historical person and serves the interests of an educationally privileged modern person. Then we can and should develop corresponding skills of informed and disciplined vision for the use of a different kind of historical evidence. We will seek evidence that reveals the presence of whole communities in all their lively diversity.

The limited and complementary claims of language and images will become evident only when we have developed the ability to explore both texts and images in their full nuanced complexity. When we have developed the requisite skills in the interpretation of images and texts, perhaps we will recognize the validity and beauty of a perspective other than that of identification with subjective consciousness. We will become fascinated by the singular effectiveness with which human life, the life of the body, has been represented, expressed, and interpreted by visual images, just as language formulates, articulates, and communicates human life as the life of the mind.

◆ 3 ◆

"The Evidence of Our Eyes":
Fourth-Century Roman Churches

*The evidence of our eyes makes instruction through
the ears unnecessary.*
EUSEBIUS

As a result of the search for historical literary evidence related to antecedents of the modern, individual, autonomous subjective consciousness, modern historians have divided historical people into two camps: the few individuals who "think" — those educated to identify themselves with ideas, the "life of the mind"; and the uneducated "masses," characterized by "popular credulity" and "naive animistic attitudes." [1] This historical vision, however, is often at odds with the actual discoveries of historical research. People of the same historical time had much more in common with each other than they have with us, a fact that becomes apparent in a study of the fourth century.

An examination of the role of vision in fourth-century christian worship reveals a common excitement with the triumph of the church and the reflection of this triumph in visible splendor. If we organize our study of Roman Christianity in the fourth century not around literary evidence but around visual evidence, a different paradigm emerges from one in which the intelligentsia, disdainful of images, is eager to worship spiritually — verbally — and the common folk belligerently defend the use of images, a carryover from paganism. If we begin with the images available daily to the whole community instead of with texts written by a few educated men, we can reconstruct the major interest of fourth-century Christians.[2] Instead of focusing on the great debates over political alliances and theological language carried on by bishops, priests, and emperors, instead of identifying the fourth-century struggle to define and delimit christian ideas as primary, we will be struck by the great excitement of fourth-century Christians with a *via universalis*. In contrast with Gnostics, philosophers, and the devotees of mystery religions,[3] Christians were fascinated with a universal salvation for any and all who, without the intellectual qualifications required by philosophy, without the wealth required for full initiation in the mystery religions, and simply by the affirmation of an unquantifiable faith, could be brought onto the path of salvation by membership in the christian church.

Fourth-century Christians wanted to make the accessibility of their faith visually apparent in the churches that sprang up across the empire. The attitude of "come one, come all" was so prominent a feature of visual evidence, if not of verbal sources, that Christians were criticized by pagans for a lack of standards and requirements, moral and intellectual.[4]

If we begin with visual evidence of the fourth-century Roman christian movement, the political and doctrinal struggles usually so prominent in theological historiography appear as reactions to attitudes of indiscriminating christian salvation. Seen in this perspective, doctrinal debates represent an instinct to define, preserve, and clarify what is essential, precious, not to be diluted by slenderly christianized floods of converts. Doctrinal debates should not be featured, in our historiography, as the primary interest of fourth-century Christianity; they are a response or reaction of discomfort to a high degree of intellectual imprecision. They are comparable, in this respect, to the ascetic movement that gained momentum during the fourth century as a reaction to a high degree of moral "variety" within the christian churches.

At the end of the century and the beginning of the fifth century, problems related to the sweeping universalism of the earlier fourth century came into focus. It is not accidental that at the end of the fourth century, more than a hundred years after the death of Origen of Alexandria, Origen's idea of a cosmic universal salvation, eventually to include even the devil, came to be criticized and roundly rejected. The concern with what to exclude from the ideas and practice of christian faith intensified throughout the fourth century and came to a head at its end. This concern must be seen in the context of the sweeping, uncritical, and inclusive momentum of Constantinian Christianity. In the first decades of the fifth century, Augustine examined and reinterpreted the idea of the christian *via universalis,* both to preserve what was valuable in the idea and to correct abuses, which large groups within the churches by then questioned. Against the moral rigorism of Pelagius and the cultic purity of the Donatists, Augustine insisted on the accessibility of salvation for all people.

Literary evidence from the fourth century focuses on theological debate, creedal definition, and political repercussions, but visual evidence provides material for reconstructing the larger context within which these struggles took place. If we begin with visual evidence we notice, when we subsequently examine literary evidence, the implicit prominence, even in texts, of the theme of a *via universalis*. This theme highlights the communal aspect of christian faith in contrast to the impression given by literary texts that Christianity was defined and developed by independent individual thinkers.

We will examine the idea of a *via universalis* as expressed in its primary communication, the architecture and imagery of fourth-century church buildings. But before we do, we must untangle some common misapprehensions that prevent the construction of an accurate picture of fourth-century worship and practice. We will then discuss evidence of continuity in the use of images before and after the Peace of the Church in 313. Finally, we will look briefly at the late-fourth-century reworking of the concept of a *via universalis* as a reaction against its earlier overwhelming popularity.

Images in the Early Church: Two Unusable Approaches

Sister Charles Murray, in her air-clearing article "Art in the Early Church," has persuasively shown the inaccuracy of the frequently repeated opinion that "responsible ecclesiastics" of the early church displayed an "absolutely monolithic opposition to imagery." [5] Her careful examination of each of the prooftexts that had seemed to support this opinion reveals the use of inaccurate presuppositions, little attention to context, and in the case of an often-quoted letter, allegedly but not surely written by Eusebius of Caesarea, the use of a text for which there is no critical edition. [6] "No protagonist of the hostility theory has yet been able to produce one single clear statement from any Christian writer which says that non-idolatrous artistic representation is wrong," Murray writes. [7]

Nor would early Christians have had to make a break with their predominantly Jewish roots to represent scenes from scripture in their places of worship. The prohibition contained in the second commandment of the Decalogue was apparently not interpreted, either in Judaism or in early Christianity, as completely forbidding images. This has been amply demonstrated by archeological evidence from the mid-third-century orthodox Jewish community of Dura Europus as well as from Jewish and christian catacombs near Rome. [8] Both in the public and the private spheres, representations of animals, flora, sun and moon, and the human form appear repeatedly. The hypothesis of a contradiction between early christian literary evidence that condemns and monumental evidence that reveals the existence of images in places of worship will not stand.

Another reason that we have not recognized the significance of early christian architecture and imagery is that we have often failed to distinguish later events and debates from fourth-century concerns. Ever since the iconoclastic Council of Hiereia in 754, fragments of the fourth- and fifth-century discussion of the use of images have been gathered as support for the argument that the leaders of the early churches were antagonistic to images. The iconoclastic florilegia compiled for the council contain some quotations that survive only in this eighth-century collection.[9] The variety of fourth-century concerns is concealed by removal of the quotations from their context — both textual and historical — and by Byzantine iconoclasts' definition of idolatry as "the making of material objects themselves." [10] Fourth-century authors did not use this definition; they were concerned about pagan idolatry, about extravagantly luxurious decoration without symbolic content or religious meaning or about the trivializing of religious imagery by its use in ornaments for personal dress.[11] In no extant text do they interpret the existence of religious images as automatically idolatrous.

Modern scholars have tended to treat the relatively few patristic statements, collected by Byzantine iconoclasts, that seem antagonistic to imagery as legitimate antecedents to the Byzantine struggle. The iconophile council of 787, the Second Council of Nicaea, exposed the falsifications of the 754 florilegia; it questioned the willingness of participants of the earlier council to accept the selected extracts that were circulated on loose sheets rather than within their original texts. Modern scholars, however, have usually followed the Council of Hiereia in accepting the quotations as accurate indices of educated fourth-century opinion.

If we examine the statements of fourth-century authors about the role and value of images, we find, not surprisingly, that none of the developed theological rationales of later centuries exists. Controversies over the use and abuse of religious images in later centuries forced analysis and explanation that no fourth-century author felt called upon to make. The careful defense by Pope Gregory I of the inspirational value of religious art was written more than a century later to the iconoclastic bishop Serenus.[12] Fourth-century rationales for religious images are few, brief, and unsystematic; the role of religious images was seldom questioned and therefore did not need systematic defense.[13]

The statements we have from the fourth century refer rather to the usefulness of images for the worshipper. Images provided a mnemonic and didactic aid without which many new converts could not participate in a directly meaningful way in christian worship. But images were not condescendingly permitted for the sake of the "simpler sort." [14] Gregory of Nyssa, one of the most skilled language users of the late fourth century, related without embarrassment that he could not contemplate a particular depiction of the sacrifice of Abraham without tears.[15]

Gregory of Nyssa's description of the powerful capacity of images to excite emotions is personal but not idiosyncratic. Fourth-century people were aware of the unique capacity of images to arouse strong emotions and to concentrate the will.[16] The instructional value of an image consists not of the communication of information but of the power of the image to engage and train the will through the perceptions.[17] The immediate emotional response to a powerful image, according to Evodius, bishop of Uzala at the end of the fourth century, is "stupor . . . amor, admiratio, et gratulatio." [18] Augustine's theory of physical vision, a popular version of Plato's theory, supports and explains this phenomenon. The visual ray, the strongest concentration of the body's animating fire, is projected from the eye to touch its object. In the act of vision, viewer and image are connected in a dynamic communication. Images instruct by attraction; in the activity of seeing, the life energy of the viewer goes out to and takes the shape of the object contemplated.

The viewer provides the energy for and initiates the act of vision. Clearly, vision was not understood as passive. The object does not "catch the eye": The eye catches the object. Often this insistence on the activity of the viewer was contrasted with the greater passivity involved in hearing; the ear requires no focusing for it to hear sound — anyone in the vicinity of a sound of a certain loudness will hear it. Moreover, the soul is affected in fundamental and structural ways by its imprinting by objects of vision.

If we look for attitudes toward images not in texts but in the artistic evidence of fourth- and early fifth-century Christianity, our perspective widens immediately. Both the distinction between educated and popular opinion and the temptation to read fourth-century statements as antecedents of Byzantine iconoclasm disappear as we recognize the excitement of fourth-century Roman Christians with the *visible* triumph of christian faith.

Across the Roman empire the appearance of ancient cities was gradually altered by newly erected church buildings that engaged the skill of the best architects, stonecutters, and mosaic craftsmen. Simultaneously, christian congregations changed, if not overnight, at least in living memory, from minority,[19] semisecret, sporadically but persistently persecuted groups to the multitudes who strolled and worshipped in the new basilicas. As the churches were built, flooded with light,[20] and filled with beautiful and precious tapestries, vessels, sculptures, and decorations, the numbers of worshippers increased geometrically. Before Constantine, "Christianity had left no visible trace in Rome"; after the legitimation of Christianity, "the leading features of Constantinian church building: hugeness, a simple plan and exterior, and a gorgeous interior," [21] were designed for maximal visual engagement.

It is impossible to believe that the wealth of art and furnishings from fourth-century churches was produced in spite of the opposition of church leaders. Nor were these lavish buildings constructed either at the insistence or at the expense of the "uninformed masses." From the emperor Constantine to the humblest Christian, highlighting the triumph of Christianity with monumental architecture and exuberant furnishings and decoration seems to have been a unanimous desire.

The paucity of verbal statements concerning the legitimacy of the use of visual images in christian worship and the lack of any theology of images in the fourth century has led to the approaches we have criticized. If, like fourth-century Christians, we open our eyes to visual evidence, our understanding of fourth-century practice and attitudes will benefit from the loudest and most detailed evidence available. Sister Charles Murray writes:

> What has happened is that the materials of church history have been mistaken for the history of the Church itself; because church history, in this matter, has been regarded primarily as based on written documents. The material remains, ignored by church historians, have been left to the analysis of art historians, Roman and Byzantine social historians, or sub-departments of classical anthropology. Yet the purpose of all this art was religious and therefore it is the theological dimension which in the end is paramount . . . Perhaps, therefore, it may be pleaded that the monuments of the Church should be put back into the context of church history alongside the literary remains in order to arrive at a more rounded estimate of matters of fact in the early church.[22]

Architecture and Images Before the Peace of the Church

There is no evidence of a radical disjunction in the use of imagery before and after the Recognition Act of 313, a disjunction which, in Paul Finney's words, would make "the earliest Christians come out looking like Quaker iconophobes, the earlier in time, the plainer their dress." [23] Neither the hypothesis of a "fall of the church" under Constantine nor that of a gradual slipping away from the earliest "spiritual" worship into dependence on material visual aids matches the evidence that, by the middle of the third century — our earliest instance of a well-preserved christian chapel — images were used across the Roman empire in places of worship.

The buildings in which christian images were painted in the church's first three centuries were, by necessity, externally inconspicuous, undifferentiated from normal private dwellings.[24] Interiors were adapted for christian worship simply by the placement of an altar at one side of the largest room.[25] The loss of all intact aboveground house churches in the Roman empire except one at the Syrian edge of the empire at Dura Europus[26] makes it very difficult to reconstruct the full repertoire of images that these churches contained. But fragments of fresco paintings in house churches and catacombs reveal consistencies both in subject matter and in treatment. The christian house at Dura Europus, covered with a series of wall paintings, showed its modern discoverers the following images:

Next to Adam and Eve hiding their nakedness we see Christ carrying the lost sheep on his shoulders. Farther on, the Holy Women are making their way to the tomb carrying torches . . . Then some miracles are depicted: the paralytic, healed by Christ, carrying away his bed; and Jesus walking on the water in the storm, stretching out his hand to St. Peter. We also find the woman of Samaria at the well, and David, who has just slain Goliath.[27]

It was in buildings like these, and not in the catacombs, that Christians worshipped.[28] The small size of catacomb chambers — the largest, the so-called Room of the Popes in the catacombs of San Callisto, would hold fifty people at the most — as well as the distance of the catacombs from the city makes it highly unlikely that they were used for worship very often.[29]

Similar themes and a similar treatment of subjects are evident in the various material remains from before 313.[30] Some themes that we might consider of obvious relevance were never treated directly in early christian images. We have, for example, no surviving depiction of the resurrection or the ascension of Christ, and the Eucharist cannot be positively identified in pre-Constantinian art. There are no portraits of Christ[31] and no depictions of the crucifixion. Scenes of the Last Judgment are also conspicuously absent. Human figures are depicted praying in the customary position, standing with raised arms (Fig. 1), and there is at least one depiction of a seated woman holding an infant, most likely a portrait of the deceased (Fig. 2).[32] Numerous symbols appear again and again, such as a fish, loaves of bread and the chi-rho monogram.[33]

Much more imagery of the pre-Constantinian period, it may safely be conjectured, has been destroyed by time and by human carelessness. Not until the nineteenth century was "exploration of the catacombs carried out in a scientific manner." [34] Until then, barbarian invasions, the removal of inscriptions and sculpture, and disastrous efforts to remove paintings persistently damaged catacombs near Rome. Many faint outlines and partial figures in the catacombs are possible to reconstruct only with a great deal of imagination.

The style of early christian art, like its subjects and themes, is surprisingly standard from Dura Europus to North Africa. The mood is consistently peaceful, even in rare depictions of martyrdom.[35] As the art historian Emile Mâle expressed it, "In those tragic years when the blood of the martyrs was flowing, christian art expressed nothing but peace." [36] The serenity of lines and colors is not placid, however, nor are postures without inner tension. The art of early Christianity has been called expressionistic, but its expression is of inner experience rather than current experience in the world. As such it represents an insistent relocation of normative human experience.

In this art, bodies are expressive; the bodies of the catacomb orantes strain to enter their prayer (Fig. 1); as Clement of Alexandria, a third-century contemporary, described:

For this reason also we raise the head and lift the hands in the closing outburst of prayer, following the eager soaring of the spirit into the spiritual world: and while thus we endeavor to detach the body from the earth by lifting it upwards along with uttered words, we spurn the fetters of the flesh and constrain the soul, winged with desire of better things, to ascend into the holy place.[37]

The eyes of these orantes are large, and already we can see the beginning of the style, common by the fourth century, of gathering the expressiveness of the whole body into the face and especially into the enormous upraised eyes.

What is the relation of third-century christian art to the third-century texts in which imagery is discussed? Sister Charles Murray concludes that, in the third century, "the general question of artistic representation" was never addressed.[38] Texts on church order, the Syriac *Didascalia*, the Pseudo-Clementine *Church Order*, and the Egyptian *Didascalia* require that sculptors and painters of idols — a major business in the later Roman world — renounce their profession before entering the christian church. In Tertullian's *De Pudicitia*, an image of the Good Shepherd associated with a christian group whom he accused of moral laxity is violently condemned — but religious art in general is not.[39] When individually analyzed, the often-quoted passages in Clement's writings that seem to support iconoclastic attitudes yield a range of interpretations, none of which reveal undifferentiated hostility to images.[40] In spite of a certain testiness on questions of images and sculptures, probably caused by an eagerness to distinguish christian from pagan practice, none of these texts supports an interpretation of wholesale or unambiguous iconoclasm. Third-century visual and verbal evidence is not in disagreement; both reveal an early and generally accepted use of images in the settings of christian worship.

The Fourth Century: Architecture, Images, and Liturgy

By the beginning of the fourth century, there were at least twenty-five christian *tituli*, or house churches, in Rome.[41] They now survive only in more or less decipherable ruins, usually under later church buildings. Many of these semipublic house churches continued to be used for worship even after the building of larger churches in the fourth century. Just before 312, the first buildings built specifically for christian worship were constructed in Rome. These are San Crisogono, which lies alongside and below the extant twelfth-century basilica, and San Sebastiano, which still stands, in reduced size and much reconstructed condition, over the spot venerated from 258 as the graves of Saints Peter and Paul on the Via Appia.

New shapes and types of ecclesiastical buildings appeared in the decades after Constantine's victory at the Milvian bridge.[42] Eusebius, bishop of Caesarea, an enthusiastic supporter of Constantine and his programs,[43] saw in the imperial foundation and furnishing of church buildings the most startling possible contrast to the times of persecution still alive in the memories of Christians:

Above all for those of us who had fixed our hopes on the Christ of God there was unspeakable happiness, and a divine joy blossomed in all hearts as we saw that every place that a little while before had been reduced to dust by the tyrant's wickedness was now, as if from a prolonged and deadly stranglehold, coming back to life; and that cathedrals were again rising from their foundations high into the air, and far surpassing in magnificence those previously destroyed by the enemy.[44]

The church buildings, most of them constructed outside the city walls rather than within the already crowded city, were responsive to new liturgical requirements and reflected local customs. In Rome and its vicinity alone, the following churches were erected before 330: the Lateran basilica and its octagonal baptistry of Saint John (c. 324), Santa Croce Gerusalemme (begun 326–328), the funerary basilicas of San Lorenzo, Ss. Marcellino e Pietro, and San Pietro, begun in 324 and consecrated in 326. San Sebastiano and San Crisogono, already mentioned, must be added to this list. Only the Lateran and its baptistry and Santa Croce in Gerusalemme were inside the city walls.

We will not analyze the designs of these buildings in detail, nor will we try to determine their architectural precedents or prototypes in secular buildings, synagogues, or imperial structures. Rather, we will focus on what was likely to have been the experience of worship in one of these buildings, the messages received by an ordinary worshipper from spatial relations and visual engagement in the service and its setting.

Eusebius's description of one of the new cathedrals, the cathedral at Tyre in northern Palestine, given in Book X of the *Ecclesiastical History,* is an emotional rather than a technical description. It is hard to visualize the building as Eusebius describes it; his description runs to superlatives instead of architectural analysis: "The cathedral is a marvel of beauty, utterly breathtaking." [45] Within the cathedral, Eusebius remarks, "the evidence of our eyes makes instruction through the ears unnecessary." [46] For the new Christians of the Constantinian period, visual evidence of the triumph of Christianity — against all odds — was convincing, moving, and cause for praise.

Eusebius's extended metaphor of the cathedral as literally constructed of the people of God, a "building" in which every individual has a place and a role, is indicative of the significance of the first monumental christian churches for fourth-century people. After listing architectural "roles" — some people compose the outer court, some are doors, some "under-props," some columns, some benches within — Eusebius emphasizes that the visible cathedral is symbolic of the invisible.

The function of his metaphor is to demonstrate the inclusiveness of the church. It is inclusive, Eusebius says, both in the sense that *whole* human beings are engaged in the building and support of the church and in the sense that *all* human beings are needed and useful:

from end to end of the building [God] reveals in all its abundance and rich variety the clear light of the truth in everyone, and everywhere and from every source [God] has found room for the living, securely-laid, and unshakeable stones for human souls. In this way [God] is constructing out of them all a great and kingly house, glowing and full of light within and without, in that not only their heart and mind, but their body too, has been gloriously enriched with the many-blossomed ornament of chastity and temperance.[47]

Further interesting evidence of early fourth-century christian inclusiveness, the practical result of excitement over a *via universalis*, is Eusebius's discussion in the *Vita Constantini* of the attempts of Constantine's rival Licinius to destroy the christian church before Constantine became sole emperor in 324. After describing the continuing persecution in the eastern empire, ruled by Licinius, even after the Peace of the Church, Eusebius interprets a sexist edict, effective temporarily in the eastern empire, as deliberately divisive. The edict stipulated, Eusebius writes,

that men should not appear in company with women in houses of prayer, and forbade women to receive instruction from the bishops, directing the appointment of women to be teachers of their own sex.

Eusebius comments, "These regulations being received with general ridicule, he [Licinius] devised other means for effecting the ruin of the churches." [48]

Eusebius has often been read as an uncritical promoter of Constantine. His suspect enthusiasm for the immanent happy marriage of church and state has been frequently interpreted from hindsight as opportuntistic and shortsighted. Eusebius has frequently been discredited as an accurate observer and interpreter of his own time. Nevertheless Eusebius's reports give evidence of the interests of fourth-century Christians even though his scholarship often does not meet the standards of modern historians. It is Eusebius who most clearly reinforces our impression of the number of church buildings erected during Constantine's reign, their size, and their locations in the major cities of the empire. When we discuss the furnishings of these churches, our impression of the significance of visual evidence for fourth-century Christianity will be even stronger.

The contrast between the inconspicuous house churches of pre-Constantinian days and the resplendent churches of the fourth century must have been one of the most prominent features of fourth-century Christianity. Consider the dramatic visual evidence for the triumph of Christianity: in 303 or 304, the razing of the church at Nikomedia began the last great persecution in that city;[49] twenty years later, Constantine inaugurated the building of Saint John Lateran in recognition of and in token of his support for the papal office.[50]

The earliest examples of Constantinian church building are not extant in east or west. But the examination of still-decipherable ruins, some with indications of where columns stood, some with floor mosaics, some with walls erect or traceable, together with eyewitness descriptions and recorded inventories of items donated by emperors and bishops, gives us a roughly accurate picture of these churches' appearance when they were new.

Externally, the new churches were unexceptional; they looked like ordinary Roman assembly halls, "the usual type of secular public building." [51] Inside, however, from the perspective of the worshipper, the eye was engaged and delighted wherever it rested. Fourth-century Christians, worshipping in one of the new basilicas, must have prayed as the orantes of the catacombs are pictured and as modern Italian Roman Catholics pray, with open eyes.

Worshippers stood in the nave, the strong longitudinal orientation of which focused on the altar, which might be placed between the clergy, seated in the apse, and the congregation, as in the cathedrals at Tyre and Aquileia. The bishop sat on his throne and spoke ex cathedra, that is, from his throne, to the standing congregation. Only two features are common to all the Constantinian churches that can be reconstructed: the shift from the transversal orientation of house churches to the longitudinal axis[52] and an apse, marked by choir screens and benches for priests.[53]

By the fourth century, a more or less standard liturgy had developed across the Roman empire.[54] For this liturgy, in addition to an altar, an apse, and a nave, side rooms were needed in which catechumens, those receiving instruction in the Christian faith but not yet members of the church, could be curtained off from the part of the service called the Mass of the Faithful. They attended the first part of the service, the Mass of the Catechumens, which contained the scripture readings, prayers, and homily, and then retired to side rooms where, significantly, *they could hear but not see* the offerings, Eucharistic prayers, and communion.[55] To see, apparently, was to participate in the mass; to hear without seeing was merely to be allowed to eavesdrop, to overhear. Visual participation made the difference between outsider and member.

The christian liturgy was markedly peripatetic,[56] full of processions and of reading, praying, and celebrating from different pulpits, altars, and desks. The offertory procession that joined the Service of the Word to the Mass of the Faithful was in the fourth century very concretely and literally inclusive in that every member of the congregation was expected to participate, bringing to the altar a gift at once symbolic of the offering of herself or himself and useful for the support of clergy and the charitable work of the church. Gifts like bread, wine, oil, olives, wax, cheese, and poultry are listed as appropriate for the offertory procession.[57]

Our understanding of the worship of fourth-century Christians is immeasurably enriched by attention to its setting. It would be rewarding, for example, instead of repeating the well-worn opinion that the basilica form was the result of the requirements of Christian liturgy, to examine the variety of fourth-century church plans as a basis for asking how the liturgies in these buildings were shaped by the architecture. How were the messages received by the worshipper likely to have varied according to whether the building was oblong, like the fourth-century Saint Peter's or Saint John Lateran in Rome, intersecting rectangles, like the cathedral at Aquileia, or quatrefoil, like San Lorenzo in Milan? How would the Eucharistic celebration have been experienced according to whether the altar was placed in the middle of the nave, in front of the apse, or at the rear wall of the apse? How did the liturgical prayers, the mosaics, and the frescoes mutually interpret and reinforce one another while scenes of God's historical intervention, visible on walls, were cited in prayers?

What was there to see in fourth-century churches in addition to the actions and movement of the liturgy? We should first note the management of light, the basis of whatever else is seen. Preference for bright light was a marked feature of fourth-century sanctuaries.[58] The crepuscular dusk of later baroque churches, and with it an atmosphere of close and scanty air, was far from a desideratum of fourth-century Christian architecture.[59] There was, however, no standard plan for the placement of windows. The cathedral at Tyre, on the Syrian coast, had an amply lit nave; at Saint John Lateran in Rome, the aisles were strongly lighted, whereas at Saint Peter's, the aisles were dark but the transept was filled with light from sixteen huge windows. Most Constantinian basilicas had a western orientation, and services were timed to make the most of the natural light throughout the day. Especially in buildings associated with the emperor, Constantine "the Invincible Sun, the Sun of Justice," [60] strong light was a priority. The management of light can itself be interpreted as an inclusive feature in fourth-century worship: Constantine's commitment to the cult of the sun, never renounced during his lifetime, was brought more or less explicitly into the christian churches of the first half of the fourth century.

Second, Krautheimer writes of a "new visual approach" that characterized the interiors of fourth-century churches. Architectural structure is "subordi- nated to coloristic design which encompasses the whole wall." [61] "Color and light, more than anything else, brought this architecture to life." [62] Mosaics and wall paintings — like the double tier of Old Testament scenes in the nave of Saint Peter's — both instructed and delighted the worshipper. A stun- ning array of colors, textures, and materials met the eye everywhere. At Saint John Lateran, for example, a huge silver fastigium was placed across the opening of the apse. Supported by a double row of columns, it was composed of statues of silver beaten or hammered over a wooden core. Christ the teacher, seated among the apostles, faced the congregation, while Christ resurrected, enthroned between four angels, faced the clergy in the apse.[63] The play of daylight, or at night the play of the candles on sixty or seventy gold and silver candlesticks, on these silver statues must have been dazzling. In addition, gold foil and mosaic adorned the roof of the nave, and yellow, red, and green columns stood in the nave and aisles. Seven gold altars were placed in the sanctuary and sacristies.[64]

Fourth-century churches were as lavish as they could possibly be made. Just as crowds of the more or less christianized converts who flocked to them in the fourth century, when it became increasingly politic to affiliate with the christian church, were accepted by the church, so these immense churches were evidently considered capable of accepting and containing artistic works of an enormous range of styles, materials, subjects, and themes. Excitement with a *via universalis,* a way of salvation for all people could not have been more strongly and directly reflected and communicated than it was in the archi- tecture, the images, and the statues of Constantinian churches. Constantine's dream of unifying the empire under Christianity provided the impetus as well as the funds for making the universal way visible and tangible as an integral part of christian worship. The inclusivity of fourth-century christian architecture and art is startling when we think of it as contemporaneous with fourth-century theological debates in which insistence on verbal precision in creedal statements excluded significant numbers of Christians from the Roman church.[65]

We must go to the fourth-century catacombs for detailed information about the images that fourth-century Christians associated with their faith. In the fourth century, "the great period of the catacombs," [66] the anonymous painters of catacombs[67] achieved an effective expressionistic[68] art with an expanded coloristic scheme and range of subjects. In 1955 Old Testament scenes that had not been seen before on any extant catacombs were discovered in the chambers of a series of mid-fourth-century catacombs near the Via Latina outside Rome. The standard scenes of deliverance so popular in third-century sites — stories of Moses, the patriarchs, Jacob's vision, Lot's escape from Sodom, Samson killing the lion — appear along with numerous other scenes,

◆ 53

including the healing miracles of the New Testament.[69] In addition, scenes with doctrinal significance are depicted — banquets, formerly not clearly distinguishable from similar depictions of Jewish and pagan meals, now specify their unambiguous allusion to a Eucharistic celebration by the presence of a chalice and symbolic fish.

By the fourth century, the expressiveness of the figures of catacomb art is strongly concentrated in the eyes, which are large, dark, and characteristically raised to heaven or staring directly at the viewer. The figures are presented frontally.[70] In the small chambers of the catacombs, frontality "spoke" to the viewer, *facie ad faciem,* the better to communicate a strong message of hope and comfort in the face of the ever-present threat of physical death. This popular style was taken up in monumental churches because of the "realization on the part of the artist that in a distant view of a group . . . only those figures shown in full face would have sufficient breadth and carrying power to impress themselves upon the spectator." [71] The frontality of fourth-century images, in vivid contrast to classical images, which are self-absorbed and indifferent to the viewer, originated in catacomb art.

Writing at the end of the fourth century, Jerome described Sunday afternoon meditational walks through the catacombs. Here, in the presence of a strong concentration of reminders of death and of the Christian and Jewish heroes of the past, the mind was concentrated on one's inner life. In fact, the art of christian catacombs can be closely linked with contemporary prayers — in which Old Testament figures are cited, sometimes listed, as examples of God's trustworthy protection, deliverance, and guidance. In the pseudo-Cyprianic prayers collected in about 400, the miracles cited coincide often with stories depicted in catacombs.[72] The two kinds of expression — prayer and painting — used parallel subjects and themes and apparently were understood as mutually reinforcing. Paintings provided an aid to memory for prayer.[73] The *orans* figure, frequently encountered in fourth-century as in earlier catacombs, was the self-image of the individual Christian, concentrated in body and mind on petition and thanksgiving, eyes and hands raised to heaven.[74]

Finally, our rapid survey of visual images of fourth-century christian art must briefly describe the developing technique and style of mosaic decoration. Mosaics, placed on floors, on walls, and in apses, represent an important source of orientation and information for the worshipper in a christian cathedral.

The development of mosaic decoration is itself a fascinating study.[75] From its humble origin as black figures on a white ground — called linoleum — on the floors of seventh- and eighth-century B.C. homes, mosaics came to be used in brilliantly colored apse imagery in the fourth century. Still predominantly used on floors at the beginning of the century, mosaic techniques displayed their full capacity for nuanced depiction on the apse of Santa Pudenziana by the end of the century. During the century the full range of possibility for the placement of mosaics was explored:

On the floor of the cathedral of Aquileia are representations of subjects from the Old Testament such as Jonah thrown to the whale, a picture of the Saviour as the Good Shepherd, and the Eucharist made manifest as bread and wine — and crowned by an ancient goddess of victory! ... it is important to note that in the earliest churches the floor mosaics also played a prominent part in the manifestation of religious ideas.[76]

But soon "the whole pictorial program was transferred to the walls and vaults." Accompanying the transfer of religious imagery to walls and vaults, a "coloristic renaissance" occurred in the Constantine period. Floor mosaics became decorative and neutral, consisting of geometric patterns, vine scrolls, and general symbols without specific christian content, such as peacocks and chalices.[77] In apse imagery, however, the use of brightly colored glass tesserae, set at angles to catch and reflect light, opened a new range of artistic possibilities for mosaics. Since they did not need to be as smooth and durable as mosaics that were to be walked on, these tesserae could be arranged for effects previously unseen.

Closely integrated with architectural features, the whole arrangement of imagery could be designed to lead the eye of the worshipper to the altar. Images, no longer used merely to remind the viewer of a scriptural episode, were now also used to give the viewer delight, both in their narrative content and in their own embodiment of what must surely have been seen as a supernaturally shimmering display of light and color. Only two large-scale examples of fourth-century mosaic work are extant in churches in Rome: the mausoleum church of Santa Costanza, with a mid-fourth-century example of mosaic ceiling decoration (Fig. 3), and the basilica of Santa Pudenziana (Fig. 4), whose mosaic apse dates from the last decade of the century. Since not many of the wall and ceiling mosaics of the fourth century are extant, we do not know which themes and subjects were most frequently treated. However, the few remaining Roman mosaics permit at least a description of their style.

Fourth-Century Images and Theological Language

This brief survey of the kinds of visual evidence in christian public worship in the fourth century gives a sense of the overwhelming engagement of vision in worship after the Peace of the Church. It was "the evidence of our eyes" that reassured Christians and attracted to the churches an increasing, and increasingly diverse, multitude of converts.

Visual inclusive messages were so effective that groups within the churches came to question the value of a *via universalis* indiscriminate enough to absorb the crowds of new worshippers. The movement of ascetics away from their affiliations with local congregations and into the Egyptian desert as hermits or into monasteries as cenobites was primarily a reaction to the dramatically altered status of the churches in the fourth century. The threat of martyrdom could no longer guarantee that merely nominal Christians would not exist.[78] Rather, the Roman church's visibility,[79] its association with imperial power, and its inclusiveness were causing problems unforeseen in the initial excitement generated by the christian *via universalis*.

Bishops and educated clergy were troubled by the variety of imprecise and unclarified beliefs that were tolerated in the general stampede of converts to Christianity. Under cover of the poetic language and imagery of the liturgy, an unexamined and, in the opinion of these clergy, dangerously wide spectrum of interpretations of God's activity of creation, incarnation, and redemption was tolerated and allowed to flourish.

Only when the young presbyter Arius articulated the philosophical framework within which his idea of God's threefold activity made sense did his bishop realize that the idea was incompatible with other important christian beliefs. And so the debate arose that would engage the language users of the christian churches for more than a century. The debate proceeded toward a cohesive and comprehensive description of the faith by eliminating unsatisfactory descriptions along with those who proposed them from christian fellowship. Doctrinal controversies, so perplexingly filled with linguistic technicalities, personal venom, and what appears to a modern student as willful misunderstandings of other formulations, were not often the focus of popular interest.[80] These debates can provide a modern scholar with fascinating reading, and in their own time they genuinely sought to protect Christianity from uncongenial interpretations. Only by ignoring and neglecting the visual evidence, however, have scholars and historians been able to treat the doctrinal debates as the most significant aspect of fourth-century Christianity.

The inclusion of images in fourth-century churches meant that a variety of interpretations of theological ideas was possible. The various christological positions under debate throughout the century, for example, are not clearly decipherable in imagery. But is the Christ-in-majesty of the Santa Pudenziana apse (Fig. 4), reigning against a naturalistic background of fourth-century Jerusalem, intended as a statement of Christ's simultaneous humanity and divinity? Such an agenda for the mosaic would be impossible to document, and yet its visual effect, both in content and in the naturalistic setting of a supernatural scene, certainly would have made this interpretation possible to a contemporary interested in theological questions.

Moreover, the interpretations given to liturgy are strongly influenced by the setting in which liturgy occurs. For example, the derivation of some baptistries from mausoleum architecture reinforced for fourth-century people, who were familiar with the mausoleums of the Roman world, an interpretation of baptism as death and rebirth. But this interpretation did not exclude others: flaming candles, if not included in the setting of the service, were at least depicted on the baptismal basin, adding the imagery of enlightenment. The action of baptism visually suggests that it is also a washing or cleansing. These interpretations visually work together as adding to and glossing, one another, although they may, if analyzed verbally, seem contradictory. The interpretation of baptism as washing considerably weakens its interpretation as a grave entered by the convert and left behind in rebirth. Yet these interpretations were visually presented simultaneously, enriching one another as aspects of a fundamentally ineffable experience to which each of the symbols had something to contribute.

Doctrinal themes and subjects are not absent from fourth-century imagery, as we have seen.[81] But while trinitarian and, later in the century, christological controversies raged in conferences of bishops, in correspondence, and in creedal documents, and while every effort was being made by those participating in this discourse to determine what must be excluded from christian understandings, the attraction of christian faith for most people had nothing to do with linguistic analysis or creedal definition. Fourth-century pagans-becoming-Christians were drawn to the christian faith by its visible splendor; they were instructed by its imagery, a visual program that deliberately and skillfully included and set in a new context of meaning a broad spectrum of cultural inheritance. The curling vine tendrils of Dionysius adorned Eucharistic chalices, where they symbolized the blood of Christ, the fruit of the vine. Christ rides a chariot across the sky as the sun god in one fourth-century mosaic. The ability of the new churches of the fourth century to provide a vivid new context for ancient symbols, a context that guaranteed their interpretation in ways compatible with Christianity, is probably the most striking aspect of fourth-century visual evidence.

Catechetical instruction, with its strong emphasis on the difference between pagan life and christian life, also needs to be understood in the context of a visual experience of familiarity and inclusiveness. It was the visual experience of the catechumen that reassured her or him that the cultural heritage of paganism was not to be exterminated but to be converted.

The presence of pagan symbols in Constantinian churches has frequently been explained by art historians as a result of the inability of artists to immediately identify a properly christian vocabulary of themes and styles. We need not, however, assume that an awkward stage in artistic development occurred inconveniently just when the new basilicas were being built. Pagan motifs like those in the church of Santa Costanza in Rome (Fig. 3), built close to the middle of the fourth century — putti, bunches of grapes, strutting pea-

cocks, vine tendrils, satyrs, maenads, and panthers — may have been deliberately incorporated into christian expressions of creation, the beauty of the
natural world, and the promise of eternal life.[82]

Moreover, pagan — or at least secular — and christian imagery had long
been combined in catacomb art; art historians disagree, for example, over the
interpretation of banquet scenes in catacomb art. Some write that "no direct
representation" of a Eucharistic celebration occurred before Constantine,
while others see in the earliest banquet scenes thinly disguised renditions of
the Eucharist.[83] Similar banquet scenes are found in pagan and in Jewish
catacombs, so it is likely that, instead of attempting to pinpoint a single meaning, we should think in terms of the multivalence of the image and, on the
side of the viewer, the several connotations that would have blended in her
or his interpretation. *No meanings are excluded*. The proliferation of connotations was used in a deliberate way to present the christian church as capable
of accepting a wide range of meanings.[84]

One feature of fourth-century architecture most prominent to historians
who are primarily interested in determining what messages were intention-
ally given by the architects, builders, and patrons of Constantinian architecture is the presence of imperial connotations in imagery and architecture.[85]
The basilica has been seen as primarily resembling an imperial *palatium
sacrum*,[86] and the architecture and imagery of christian worship has been
described as "monumental propaganda to impress the masses." [87] It is well
documented and indisputably true that Constantine and his successors wanted
to present a strong association between the emperor as earthly ruler and God
as heavenly ruler. The image of Christ as an enthroned ruler, seen in the
building, the liturgy, and the decorative motifs, would doubtless have been
one of the messages received by the worshipper as well as *intended* by those
in authority.

This message, however, must be understood in the context of the larger
message of the inclusivity of the christian church. The prominent inclusion
of images of imperial power, so recently a hostile and persecuting power, must
have been for contemporaries one of the more dramatic aspects of fourth-
century Christianity.[88] The alliance of church and state must also have been
one of the most anxiety-producing inclusions of the fourth century since it
did not become clear until late in the century that it was, in fact, the church
that had included the state, rather than vice versa. For late-classical people,
accustomed to the state's jurisdiction in religious matters, the imagery and
architectural reminders of imperial authority in the forms and context of worship must have produced a strong but exhilarating tension, both because of
the state's recent hostility to Christianity and because of the fear, outspoken
in some circles, that Christianity might become a ward of the state.

Significantly, what is *not* included in fourth-century christian imagery can also be understood as relating to the visual presentation of Christianity as the *via universalis*. No depictions of Christ on the cross are extant from the fourth century. Despite its obvious doctrinal importance, fully explored shortly after the middle of the fourth century by Athanasius in *De Incarnatione*, and despite the potential of the subject for emotional expressiveness, depictions of Christ on the cross would have reminded people too readily of what had recently been the shameful death of criminals; Constantine had outlawed crucifixion only in 314. Similarly, the absence of Last Judgment scenes, so popular later in medieval art, may be explained by the fundamental antagonism of the idea of judgment to the *via universalis* theme.[89]

The Late Fourth Century: Reevaluation of the Via Universalis

Texts and images of the late fourth century give evidence of a reevaluation and reinterpretation of the idea and practical application of a christian *via universalis*. Texts and images, however, give differing pictures of the nature and extent of this reinterpretation, both of which must be taken into account in our reconstruction of fourth-century Christianity.

"Universality" is in itself an ambiguous idea; it may be presented in a way that features and highlights its inclusiveness or in a way that emphasizes its exclusiveness. It may be used to describe the unity of a highly diverse collection of persons or ideas or to claim the exclusive validity of certain ideas, perspectives, or persons. The *via universalis,* understood in the Constantinian period as attracting and inviting all people, was interpreted in the reaction of the later fourth century, in legislation and theological texts, as exclusive. Fourth-century images, however, continued to present an inclusive *via universalis.*

Constantine's aptly called Edict of Toleration was a classically Roman statement: "No one whosoever should be denied the liberty of following either the religion of the Christians or any other cult which, of his own free choice he has thought to be best adapted for himself." [90] Christians before 313 were persecuted not for the practice of their own religion but for their un-Roman intolerance in refusing to practice the state religion in addition to their own.

However reluctantly tolerant Constantine's later edicts were, in the Edict of Toleration, he professed himself "unwilling to constrain others by the fear of punishment." [91] His tone was in marked contrast to Theodosius's edict establishing the official Christianity of the Roman empire in February 380. Theodosius's edict stated:

We desire that all peoples who fall beneath the sway of our imperial clemency should profess the faith which we believe to have been communicated by the Apostle Peter to the Romans and maintained in its traditional form to the present day . . . And we require that those who follow this rule of faith should embrace the name of Catholic Christians, adjuring all others madmen and ordering them to be designated as heretics . . . condemned as such, in the first instance, to suffer divine punishment, and, therewith, the vengeance of that power which we, by celestial authority, have assumed.[92]

With the official "triumph" of Christianity, the coercive exclusiveness of the *via universalis* came to dominate its interpretation.

We can see this vividly in the systematic attempt of Augustine, bishop of Hippo and one of the most skillful and influential language users of the early fifth century, to define and preserve what was valuable in the idea of a christian *via universalis*. Against the ascetic purism of Pelagius and his supporters and against the claim of the Donatists to exclusive liturgical purity, Augustine maintained the inclusivity of the church, a church that accepted all comers. His massive and largely successful attempt to define the function to the christian church of its cultural heritage from paganism and his definition of the role of political power in *The City of God* are aspects of his critique of an idea that by then had lent itself to a new nationalism, an illusion of the invincibility of the team — God and emperor — that had often surfaced in Eusebius's enthusiasm.

Against the nationalistic presumption of Constantinian Christianity, Augustine insists on the global inclusivity of the church; Christianity is "the universal way of the soul's deliverance, the way is granted by the divine compassion to the nations universally." Not possessed by one nation as its special property, "the universal way is open to all." [93] Having renounced Eusebius's nationalism, Augustine has also lost Eusebius's optimism about the possibility of a christian empire. Although he is appreciative of the role of political power in securing peace within which churches can flourish, he insists that the supportive role is the appropriate one for political power.

In spite of Augustine's insistence on the universality of the christian church, however, his interpretation of the *via universalis* emphasizes the aspect we have already noticed in Theodosius's edict: Ironically, inclusiveness has become exclusiveness. Although, like Eusebius, Augustine understands the "royal way" as engaging whole human beings and all human beings, this very universality has become coercive: "This is the religion which possesses the universal way for delivering the soul; for *except by this way, none can be delivered.*" [94] The fourth century saw the movement from a *via universalis* that offered salvation to all to a *via universalis* that required and compelled religious assent. It was a short step from the universalizing of the "one way" to the use of force against the religious alternatives of the later Roman empire.

Late-fourth-century images, however, give a different impression of the messages likely to have been received by Christians more oriented to visual than to verbal messages. If we compare, for example, the decoration of the mid-fourth-century mausoleum church of Santa Costanza, described earlier, with the Roman basilica Santa Pudenziana, built approximately fifty years later, we find differences in the images apparently considered appropriate for Christian worship. In Santa Pudenziana, the smiling putti, Dionysiac panthers, and vine leaves portrayed in Santa Costanza beside scenes from the Old Testament have disappeared. Instead, a scene of Christ, enthroned and seated among the apostles, is set in front of a background that depicts Jerusalem. (Fig. 4)

Foreground and background are given a naturalistic realism that shows a newly literal interest in landscape and figures. In this scene, Jerusalem is simultaneously a heavenly city and a recognizably factual depiction of the earthly city at the end of the fourth century. The Constantinian Church of the Holy Sepulchre stands behind Christ to his right; directly behind him is the jeweled cross erected by Theodosius on Golgotha. A new interest in the interpenetration of the spiritual world and the visible world of daily experience seems to pervade this mosaic. The figures are presented naturalistically. The apostles and two women placing crowns on the heads of Saints Peter and Paul turn, with spontaneous gestures, toward Christ and toward one another; only the enthroned Christ is presented frontally. Neither realism nor a supernatural quality stands out to the exclusion of the other; both are skillfully interwoven. The arena of the supernatural is this world.

It took nearly a century for the images accompanying worship to reflect the attitude of Theodosius and his sons and successors that the monarchy was sacred and the state holy. The Santa Pudenziana apse mosaic contains little suggestion of political themes. Although seated on a jeweled throne, Christ wears none of the insignia of the Roman court but is dressed in the same soft flowing robes as are the apostles. It is important not to conflate images of the late fourth century with the images of more than fifty years later, when Christ and the Virgin are portrayed in San Vitale at Ravenna as the supreme members of a Byzantine court, in full court regalia, accepting the veneration of their subjects. As far as can be deduced from extant visual evidence, late-fourth-century representations had no interest in formal hieratic presentation.[95]

Despite the political and ecclesiastical struggles at the end of the fourth century and despite efforts to reinterpret the christian *via universalis* as exclusive, ordinary worshippers continued to receive visual messages emphasizing the inclusivity of the *via universalis*. In the Santa Pudenziana apse, the scene of Christ and the apostles appears remarkably casual; a worshipper could well imagine himself seated among the apostles.[96] Although this mosaic does not include the "outspoken" pagan imagery of earlier churches, its visual message is still inclusive. Indeed, it brings into the context of worship an aspect of experience not formerly presented, the accurate and literal depiction of a contemporary earthly city.

Our examination of the visual evidence of fourth-century Christianity enables us to give a more nuanced description of the messages received by the christian community than that which we glean from verbal sources alone. Theological debate appears in the light of visual evidence as the preoccupation of a relatively few ecclesiastical leaders. Important as the attempt to define and clarify theological understandings was, its major significance can be grasped only when we place it in the context of the indiscriminate inclusiveness of the visual aspect of christian worship. The messages received by a host of new converts as well as by pagan onlookers emphasized throughout the fourth century the capacity of christian churches to accept and place within a christian context a wide variety of Jewish, pagan, and imperial themes and imagery. Even the radical reinterpretation of the *via universalis* of the end of the century, so evident in legislation and theological texts, is only partially reflected in the greater selectivity of christian imagery.

Visual evidence throughout the fourth century, then, corroborates the inclusiveness that is evident in the first church buildings of the Constantinian period. The inclusive *via universalis* continued to be the message received from visual participation in the worship of the Roman church. At the end of the fourth century, Paulinus of Nola described the christian church as a "mother's womb" that "takes all inside it," just as Eusebius, earlier in the century, had seen in the cathedral at Tyre a metaphor of God's activity in building all human beings into the Church of Christ.

◆ 4 ◆

Images of Women in Fourteenth-Century Tuscan Painting

What can I make of church history? I can see nothing but clergymen. As to the Christians, the common people, nothing can be learned.
GOETHE

The frequent lament of feminist historians about the paucity of historical writing by women is echoed by cultural ethnographers. The social anthropologist Edwin Ardener writes of the failure of his own discipline to gather material that represents women: "Ethnographers report that women cannot be reached as easily as men: they giggle when young, snort when old, reject the question, laugh at the topic, and the like . . . Women do not speak." [1] Thus, ethnographers have usually constructed their description of cultures entirely from the perspective of males: "Those trained in ethnography evidently have a bias towards the kinds of model that men are ready to provide . . . rather than towards any the women might provide. If the men appear 'articulate' compared with the women, it is a case of like speaking to like." [2] Ardener criticizes the attempt to "crack the code" of a society solely by males' verbal information and the unexamined assumption that "symbolism is generated by the society as a whole." [3]

The problem of the historian who attempts to understand a culture that is both geographically and temporally alien is even more extreme than the problem of the ethnographer. It is possible for ethnographers to ask the right questions from the perspective of women; women are there to respond if an adequate method of observation or questioning were devised. The historian, however, must work with the evidence she has; she cannot actually question a medieval woman even though she mentally does so through disciplined and imaginative study.

How can historical women, only a few of whom left any words about their ideas of self and world, their interests, and their daily lives, be studied? Historians of women's culture can look at historical images of women, the images that historical women themselves used.[4] There is, however, an inherent ambiguity in medieval images when we investigate them in relation to the culture in which they appear.[5] As far as we can determine, not a single image of any woman — saint, Mary, scriptural or apocryphal figure — was designed or created by a woman. The images we must deal with are images provided for women by men. They formulate and reflect a culture designed by men for the benefit of men. Images of women are men's images of women. They represent a male response to women, a male way of relating to women, and a male way of communicating with women.[6] Toward the end of this chapter we explore the idea that images of women represented a way by which men could deal with women by relegating them to visual objectivity. Simplified thus, the strong and sometimes threatening women of fourteenth-century culture became manageable for men, and not just manageable but inspirational; a danger and threat had been converted to an advantage.

We will not assume, however, that the meaning received from an image or group of images was the same for men and for women. How did women make use of images? Is it possible that women could have received positive and fruitful messages from images of women that were "figures in the men's drama"?[7]

To discuss these questions, we need first to understand the role of vision in fourteenth-century life and worship. Then we will consider the styles and subjects of images that were available in public buildings and churches, focusing our attention on Italian Tuscany. We will then proceed to examine two enormously popular subjects of painting: the life of the Virgin and Mary Magdalene. Finally, we will look at the spectrum of meanings of images of women for men and for women.

The Importance of Vision in Fourteenth-Century Italy

Examples of conversions that were prompted by the hearing of a phrase, ordinary to most ears but striking to the ear of the convert, abound in the history of Christianity. Saint Antony, the exemplar of fourth-century desert monasticism, on hearing the scriptural injunction "Sell all that you have and follow me," immediately obeyed and embarked on a life of ascetic discipline in the Egyptian desert. Saint Augustine, struck at a crucial time in his spiritual quest by a voice that directed him, "Take and read," opened the Vulgate at random to a passage that precisely diagnosed and prescribed for his spiritual condition. Martin Luther's revolutionary insight "The just shall live by faith" was also a verbal revelation.

There are also numerous accounts of people converted by seeing rather than hearing, and in the fourteenth century, conversions prompted by the seeing of a crucifix, a painting, or a vision predominate. Saint Francis of Assisi was converted while gazing at a crucifix in his local church, San Damiano (Fig. 5); Saint Catherine of Siena joined the Dominican Third Order after having a vision of Saint Dominic "in a certain place outside this world . . . in that form in which she had seen him painted in the church." [8] Lady Julian of Norwich was decisively and permanently changed by visions she saw while staring at a crucifix. Henry Suso, Margery Kempe, Angela of Foligno, and, perhaps best known of all, Dante Alighieri all tell of powerful visual experiences that challenged and altered their lives.[9]

Twentieth-century people find it relatively easy to comprehend the potential impact of precisely accurate words heard at a time when one is psychologically, intellectually, and emotionally vulnerable, but we find it much more difficult to empathize with someone whose spiritual life was initiated by a compelling vision, whether based on a sensible object, a dream vision, or an extrasensory vision. Because we think of vision as a passive experience imposed by the object of vision, we are often incredulous, for example, at another person's account of an event we have both witnessed. Fourteenth-century people did not, like us, need to be reminded frequently of the active component, usually called "interpretation," that governs every visual experience. They recognized fully the extent to which *what* one sees is dependent on one's visual training, spiritual preparation, and active engagement with the object of vision. A miraculous event, for example, might be witnessed by only one or two people although it occurred in a large company in a public place. Thus, fourteenth-century people had no trouble crediting reports of visions because they were aware that another person's readiness to see a vision might well be greater than their own.

The importance of visual participation in worship in the fourteenth century was also differently evaluated than in most twentieth-century churches.[10] Accustomed to spending enormous sums on an organ or even on the rehabilitation of an organ, modern congregations are often horrified at the suggestion that a painting be purchased for the sanctuary. In fourteenth-century Italy, large sums of money were spent on paintings for churches. Enormous bequests from people who died of the Black Death in mid-century gave churches and religious orders an "unprecedented accumulation" of wealth; much of it was spent on paintings and frescoes.[11] The new, painted chapels and churches were in striking contrast to the "stony and dark" churches of the twelfth and thirteenth centuries.[12] By the end of the fourteenth century, walls were covered with frescoes, and church buildings were being designed or modified to ensure adequate lighting of the frescoes.[13] Carved pulpits, free-standing sculpture, painted panels, and frescoes filled the churches. Above the high altar was hung a large painting and over it, suspended from the ceiling or vaults, was usually a great crucifix.[14]

The value of images for worship was largely unquestioned and therefore not extensively defended in the fourteenth century. Three rationales, all articulated before the fourteenth century, occasionally find their way into fourteenth-century texts, not as innovative arguments requiring careful, logical explication but as arguments well known by everyone and therefore quickly referred to. A thirteenth-century text, John of Genoa's *Catholicon*, a "standard dictionary of the period," [15] had summarized three reasons for the use of images:

Know that there were three reasons for the institution of images in churches. First, for the instruction of simple people, because they are instructed by them as if by books. Second, so that the mystery of the incarnation and the examples of the saints may be the more active in our memory through being presented daily to our eyes. Third, to excite feelings of devotion, these being aroused more effectively by things seen than by things heard.[16]

The last of these reasons for the use of images was probably the strongest in the fourteenth century. Bishop Durandus of Mende wrote at the end of the thirteenth century that paintings

move the mind more than descriptions; for deeds are placed before the eyes in paintings and thus appear to be actually carrying on. But in description, the deed is done as it were by hearsay, which affects the mind less when recalled to memory. Hence, also, it is that in churches we pay less reverence to books than to images and to pictures.[17]

According to medieval theologians, the high value of images rested on a pragmatic and experiential argument for the power of images to inspire devotion. By their effectiveness in engaging the emotions, artistic representations were considered capable of affecting the will: "Images were supposed to make men better; active sanctification stands in the place of the modern passive emotion of being 'uplifted.' " [18] In addition, the ontological value of images was urged by more philosophically inclined thinkers. The human mind was capable of grasping supernatural truth through visible objects because visible objects both reflect and participate in the being of their prototypes.

Finally, images could act as vehicles to focus concentration and effect vivid states of contemplative visionary experience. The training of the eye by the disciplined use of images provided a democratic method of participation in the most intense and valued religious experiences. Illiterate people were even believed to have an advantage over those more fluent in the use of religious language. The *Meditations on the Life of Christ*, a popular fourteenth-century devotional treatise, declared:

The heart of one who wishes to follow and win Christ must take fire and become animated by frequent contemplation: illumined by divine virtue, it is clothed by virtue and is able to distinguish false things from true. Thus it is the more illiterate and simple people who have recognized in this way the greatness and intensity of divine things.[19]

Minimally, images instruct; maximally, they are capable of translating the worshipper to ecstatic states of contemplation, and the maximum was not beyond the reach of the humblest worshipper.

Medieval theologians made the most extreme claims for the possibility of mystical vision based on physical vision. In the twelfth century, Abbot Suger of St.-Denis had described a contemplative state induced by gazing at the precious stones embedded in the altar and sacred vessels:

When — out of my delight in the beauty of the house of God — the loveliness of the many-colored gems has called me away from external cares, and worthy meditation has induced me to reflect, transferring that which is material to that which is immaterial, on the diversity of the sacred virtues: then it seems to me that I see myself dwelling, as it were, in some strange region of the universe which neither exists entirely in the slime of the earth nor entirely in the purity of Heaven; and that, by the grace of God, I can be transported from this inferior to that higher world in an anagogical manner.[20]

At the end of the twelfth century, Richard of St. Victor wrote to "those to whom it is given to see face to face, who, contemplating the revealed face of the glory of God, see truth without a covering in its simplicity, without a mirror or an enigma." [21] There is ample testimony that such claims were not overdrawn. People expected to experience visions, and they did experience them.

Even the ordinary worshipper without aspirations to mystical experience could expect that his contemplation of the images surrounding him in his local church would erase the distance between his personal existence and the sacred events and figures of scripture, thus placing his life in the context of the divine scheme of creation, redemption, and eschatology. Images encourage the identification of the life of the worshipper with past and future sacred events by revealing a visually present universe. The medieval worshipper became, through concentrated vision, present at the nativity, the crucifixion, the resurrection, and Last Judgment.

But no fourteenth-century person imaginatively entered the sacred world of a religious painting without an extensive visual training, stimulated by paintings and reinforced by sermons, religious drama, and popular devotional meditations. The new, vivid style of public preaching of the fourteenth century imitated the emotional intensity of religious paintings and devotional treatises. While Giotto was depicting scenes from the apocryphal Gospel of James on the walls of the Scrovegni Chapel, Franciscan and Dominican preachers, in the course of the liturgical year, recounted and interpreted the events depicted on the walls of the church, using the gestures and postures of the painted figures. Late-medieval preachers were "skilled visual performers" who used a repertoire of gestures known to their audiences from paintings. Manuals of such gestures existed, providing a stylized body language that accompanied and heightened the verbal communication.

The dramatic visual intensity of sermons sometimes even threatened to entirely overwhelm their verbal content. A mid-fourteenth-century manual for preachers finds it necessary to urge restraint:

> . . . let the preacher be very careful not to throw his body about with unrestrained movement — now suddenly lifting up his head high, now suddenly jerking it down, now turning to the right, and now with strange rapidity to the left, now stretching out both hands as if embracing East and West, now suddenly knitting the hands together, now extending his arms immoderately, now suddenly pulling them back. I have seen preachers who behaved very well in other respects, but who threw themselves about so much that they seemed to be fencing with somebody, or to be insane enough to throw themselves and their pulpit to the ground, were there not people there to restrain him.[22]

Medieval drama also instructed visually. Plays were often given as interludes in sermons, composed of material from popular devotional texts and directed by preachers. The *cantastorie*, groups of story-singers, performed accounts in the vernacular from the same texts to large crowds in public squares.[23] The content of preaching, religious drama, and painting had common sources, and audiences were also common to all three.

Images and Texts

Popular devotional treatises provided material for drama and painting and examples and illustrations for sermons. Two features common to these treatises and to the early-fourteenth-century paintings of Giotto di Bondone reflected the new interests and values of contemporary people. First, devotional treatises showed the same attention to the emotional content of gospel and apocryphal stories that we can see in Giotto's paintings. Second, the sacred figures of popular devotional texts and images were presented as ordinary people, with whom anyone could identify. The *Meditations on the Life of Christ* emphasized this theme in Christ's calling of the disciples:

They were men of rude circumstances and obscure birth . . . Meditate for Christ's sake on those from whom the Church took its beginnings. The Lord did not wish to choose the wise and powerful of this world, that the deeds they were to accomplish might not be ascribed to their strength, but reserved for His goodness, power, and wisdom to redeem us.[24]

In this illustrated manuscript, the humble scriptural characters were more fully articulated than they were in scripture to bring out their feelings, which the hearer was instructed to adopt in pondering the story:

Oh, if you could see the Lady weeping between these words, but moderately and softly, and the Magdalen frantic about her Master and crying with deep sobs, perhaps you too would not restrain your tears. Meditate on their condition as they spoke of these things. Feel for them, for they are in great affliction.[25]

With the disclaimer "Here one may interpolate a very beautiful meditation of which the Scripture does not speak," the author of the *Meditations* provides connecting incidents that give a novelistic verisimilitude to the events of the gospels. Characters are conflated from several gospels to give them fuller characterization. The character of Mary Magdalene, for example, is composed of women appearing in eight different gospel accounts, so that she appears throughout the narration of the life of Christ as the constant companion of the Virgin. Gospel figures that are unnamed in scripture are given common peasant names to increase the hearer's sense of acquaintance with them: The Samaritan woman in conversation with Jesus at the well is named Lucy, while the woman cured by Jesus of the issue of blood is identified as "Martha, sister of Mary Magdalen." [26]

In the case of the unnamed groom of the wedding at Cana, "we may meditate that it was John the Evangelist" and "the wedding was under the direction of the Lady," the Virgin. But John, never allowed to consummate the marriage, was called by Jesus as soon as the wedding feast was over: "Leave this wife of yours and follow me, for I shall lead you to a higher wedding." Disappointing as this strange conclusion to a wedding may have been to the medieval hearer — and to us — the reason for it is clear to the author:

The wedding shows that he approved carnal marriage as instituted by God, but since he called John from the wedding, you must clearly understand that spiritual marriage is much more meritorious than carnal.[27]

Additions to scriptural accounts in verbal and visual media of the fourteenth century were meant to provide greater emotional accessibility. There were also definite limits to fanciful extrapolation.[28] The devotional value of an image did not excuse deviation from doctrine but only allowed what was seen as the enhancement of doctrine. The obvious emotional value of the following excerpt from the *Meditations on the Life of Christ* is one reason that the extension of gospel stories was acceptable:

Reflect thus and see Him as He calls them [the disciples], with longing, being kind, fraternal, benign, and helpful, leading them outwardly and inwardly and even taking them home to His mother and familiarly going to their houses. He taught them, instructed them, and even cared for them as a mother for her son. It is said that the blessed Peter told how, when they were asleep in one place, the Lord rose at night and covered them; for He loved them most tenderly.[29]

Doctrines such as the incarnation and the resurrection of Christ form the nucleus for clusters of extracanonical stories whose purpose is to give the doctrines not intellectual accessibility but emotional vibrancy.

The intimate interconnection between visualizing gospel events and empathizing with them, of placing oneself within the stories, is continuously reiterated throughout the *Meditations*. No event is too challenging to be visualized and illustrated. The birth of Christ is described thus and illustrated accordingly (Fig. 6):

At midnight on Sunday, when the hour of birth came, the Virgin rose and stood against a column that was there. But Joseph remained seated, downcast, perhaps, because he could not prepare what was necessary. Then he rose and, taking some hay from the manger, placed it at the Lady's feet and turned away. Then the Son of the eternal God came out of the womb of the mother without a murmur or lesion, in a moment; as He has been in the womb so He was now outside, on the hay at His mother's feet.[30]

The feelings of Joseph, despondent at his inability to provide suitably for the birth, are given equal attention with Mary's joy at the birth.[31] The directions, "look at them well," and "feel for them," are sprinkled liberally throughout the narratives of the *Meditations*. Seeing, whether by mental visualizations or by the lively illustrations that accompany nearly every page of the stories, generates feeling.

The *Meditations*, in making the figures both more literally visible by illustration and more emotionally accessible, helped the medieval viewer/hearer to think of herself as a participant, connected through her own emotions to those of the sacred characters. The major device that achieves this accessibility is the heightened realism of the narration. The homely additions to scriptural accounts, for which the authority of Bernard or Jerome or the revelation of "a trustworthy holy brother of our order" is invoked, always enhance visibility and empathy simultaneously.

Furthermore, the "carnality" or concreteness of the meditations, the author writes, is neither temporary nor dangerous to spiritual advance:

Even those who ascend to greater contemplation ought not to renounce it,
at the right time and place. Otherwise it will seem to be condemned as vile,
which would show great pride. Remember . . . that the blessed Bernard,
the highest contemplator, never renounced it. As appears in his sermons,
he esteemed and praised it beyond measure.[32]

The fourteenth-century consensus on the religious value of visualizations and images was apparently universal.[33] What is revealed in the *Meditations* and other popular works that were available even to illiterate people through public readings and dramatizations is the training in visualization received by medieval people. These "private exercises in imaginative intensity and sharpness"[34] prepared people to engage fully the visual images that were an inseparable part of public worship:

The painter was a professional visualizer of the holy stories. What we now
easily forget is that each of his pious public was liable to be an amateur
in the same line, practiced in spiritual exercises that demanded a high degree
of visualization of, at least, the central episodes in the lives of Christ and
Mary.[35]

The mutually reinforcing effect of popular devotional treatises and the imagery and liturgy of the fourteenth century is apparent in another highly popular collection of saints' lives, Jacobus de Voragine's *The Golden Legend*, written about 1260 and extant in about five hundred manuscripts from the fourteenth century. Jacobus, theologian and archbishop of Genoa, organized his work as a "layperson's lectionary," a *lectio* of saints' lives that followed the saints' days of the liturgical year.[36] Replete with extrascriptural material, it is a treasure trove of medieval lore and attitudes. Its consistent agenda, like that of the *Meditations,* is the humanization of the saints and scriptural figures. We speak of this treatise again when we discuss paintings of Mary and Mary Magdalene. For now, we simply notice the specifically liturgical context to which these popular devotional stories related.[37] Embellishments in the popular writings were designed to give the familiar religious figures of the liturgical year heightened visual and emotional characteristics. These creative extensions of scriptural accounts in turn inspired new content for painting.

Occasionally it is possible to document the appearance of a particular motif in paintings before it appears in extant texts. More frequently, as is the case with many of Jacobus's legends, a text can be shown to precede painted depictions. No consistently one-way influence can be demonstrated, but ongoing mutual inspiration and influence are evident.[38] This reciprocity of interest and mutual stimulation is perhaps most evident not in transpositions of stories to images, or vice versa, but in the dramatically heightened realism of both popular religious literature and painting in the first half of the fourteenth century.

The lifelike realism of early-fourteenth-century painting was remarked by contemporaries with amazement, and a single master was credited with this innovation. Boccaccio, writing the *Decameron* about 1353, said:

Giotto was able to paint all natural and artificial subjects in a completely lifelike manner, so that many persons considered them to be real. In this way he brought to light again the art that had been buried for centuries through the fault of the painters who painted to please the ignorant rather than the cognoscenti.[39]

In the frescoes of Giotto di Bondone, the scenes of mystery plays came to life on the walls of the Franciscan churches in which many of them were painted. They surrounded the worshipper with crystallizations of the most dramatic actions and moments in the lives of Christ and the Virgin. The medieval viewer, accustomed to religious drama, would have seen in the paintings a moment of an ongoing action — the movie camera suddenly stopped, as it were, so that one frame can be studied. To see these frescoes was to see actions momentarily suspended so that each detail could be savored. The content of Giotto's paintings is provided by the Gospel According to the Pseudo-Matthew, itself based on the apocryphal Gospel of James.[40] These paintings, like the literary works, emphasize the human qualities, emotions, and activities of the scriptural figures.

The images and the texts that inspired the paintings have in common a realistic presentation to convey strong emotion. Giotto, fascinated with French Gothic sculpture, painted bodies with bulk, weight, and three-dimensionality. These statuesque bodies, rather than their facial expressions, primarily express the emotion of the figures. Giotto's Crucifixion, in Santa Maria Novella, has been called the first fully realistic portrayal of the crucifixion of Christ in the history of western painting (Fig. 7). In this depiction, Christ's dead body is pulled downward by its own gravity and is given naturalistic flesh tones and shadings. The centuries that separate the viewer from the event are obliterated, and the viewer is made a spectator at the cross; the viewer sees the scene that he had visualized while hearing a recitation from the *Meditations* of the passion story as seen through the eyes of the Virgin:

Behold, then, the Lord hangs dead on the cross; the whole multitude departs . . . But you, if you will contemplate your Lord well, will consider that from the sole of His foot to the crown of His head there is no health in Him:

there is not one member or bodily sense that has not left total affliction or passion . . . Study devoutly, faithfully, and solicitously to meditate on all this.[41]

In the paintings of Giotto and his successors Taddeo Gaddi, Bernardo Daddi, Maso di Banco, and Pietro and Ambrogio Lorenzetti, the posed iconic frontality of thirteenth-century figures yields to supple figures absorbed in events selected for their powerful emotional quality. A new relationship is created between viewer and painted figures: The viewer is placed *within* the depicted event through the intensity of feeling he or she shares with the human beings of the painting.

We have examined several aspects of the meaning and importance of vision for fourteenth-century people, and we have seen that sermons, plays, and popular devotional texts share the subject matter and themes of painting. Both texts and paintings were more accessible than ever before to medieval people; texts were narrated, sung, dramatized, and preached, and the new paintings attracted so many worshippers to the churches adorned by them that neighboring churches had cause for complaint. Millard Meiss writes:

Within a few weeks after Duccio had set up his Maesta in the cathedral or the Lorenzetti had completed their frescoes on the scala, every Sienese writer, poet, and priest, indeed simply every Sienese had seen them.[42]

A marked increase of interest in vision,[43] either as imaginative mental reconstruction of scriptural and apocryphal events or as painted versions of the events, characterized what has been called the new communal and secularized culture of the first half of the fourteenth century.[44]

The embellishments to the gospel stories that were woven together in popular meditations, plays, and paintings cannot be dismissed as products of popular credulousness, zealotry, or naiveté. In spite of their fanciful or even playful quality, the stories were understood to promote love for the sacred figures and to provide practical help toward moral improvement. Only an eye that has lost a sense of religious gaiety can fail to discern a profoundly devotional spirit in these lovable holy figures. They represent a translation of the hieratic solemnity of medieval religious ritual into a daily life of humble holiness. In visualizing what such a life might feel like and look like — what words might be spoken, how emotions might be expressed — fourteenth-century people constructed models for an ideal spiritual life. In turn, these verbal and visual conceptualizations inspired movement toward the goal. Fourteenth-century people wanted not only to worship but also to imitate, to speak and feel and act like their models. The iconic style and themes of earlier medieval painting did not promote imitation; the formally posed Virgin and Child of thirteenth-century painting did not inspire the worshipper to identify with the sacred figures but rather to worship from a distance.

But did illiterate people immediately enjoy the new naturalistic painting? Michael Baxandall discusses a distinction made by fourteenth-century humanist authors between their own intellectual appreciation of the skill and "form" of paintings and the crude visual pleasure of the "ignorant" who perceive only the "matter" of painting. The humanists taught that "resisting the charms of matter, one is to enjoy the subtlety of form and skill bestowed on it, and the capacity to do this is, in turn, characteristic of the informed, as opposed to the uninformed, beholder." [45]

These humanist authors were the educated language users of their time. They undertook to purge Latin of "monkish words" and to recover classical words; they also changed the meaning of many words.[46] Their attitude to painting was correspondingly self-conscious; it can be characterized as aesthetic in the modern sense that implies a psychic distance that significantly modifies the immediate emotional effectiveness of a work of art. By the beginning of the fifteenth century, these commentators had a large and precise vocabulary for analyzing paintings.[47]

But aesthetic attitudes, although developing throughout the fourteenth century in a few humanists, were exactly the opposite of the attitude toward painting of illiterate, or less thoroughly educated, women and men of the fourteenth century. For these people, the unexamined emotional impact of a painting was of paramount importance. Hence the ill-concealed scorn of the humanists for the *ignorantia;* hence also their eagerness to distinguish themselves and their artistic appreciation from that of most people of their culture. Uneducated people, Boccaccio tells us, were bewildered by the startlingly lifelike quality of Giotto's figures, which, he says, they could not distinguish from living people.

Boccaccio exaggerates to underline the difference between the aesthetic appreciation of men of letters and the naiveté of the uneducated. Still, there may be some truth in his statement; a public accustomed to the authoritative and powerful figures of the thirteenth century must have been initially dismayed at Giotto's simplified, humanized, and humble figures. When the style and content of painting change, a new relationship must be formed between viewer and painting: Something is gained and something is lost. Lost, perhaps, would have been a sense of the powerful protection of a divine cosmic ruler. Gained would have been a sense of the sacred figures and events as contemporary, accessible, imitable.

But before the gain could be experienced, a vigorous training was necessary to define and establish the new relationship of viewer to painting. This training was accomplished by preaching, religious drama, stories of saints' lives, and meditations addressed to popular audiences. One need not demonstrate the temporal priority of naturalistic painting or the explicit acknowledgement that verbal media were attempting to train in order to argue that the effect of preaching, religious drama, and popular devotional works was to train the new relationship of medieval viewers to naturalistic painting.

The constant demand for mental visualization in private devotions, alternating with the visibility of sacred scenes in public drama and painting, trained wide, popular audiences to value the greater ability of naturalistic art to express and excite emotion.[48] There is too marked a correspondence between literary, sermonic, and dramatic interest in the human emotions of the sacred figures and the naturalistic bodies and gestures of Giotto's figures not to conclude that Giotto had an especially sensitive appreciation of the interests of fourteenth-century people.

A similar sensitivity to the emotional augmentation of gospel stories permeates the Deposition of Giotto's contemporary Duccio. The Virgin leans toward the body of Christ as it is lowered from the cross, caressing his beard and gazing into his face. The same emotion, the anguished love not of the king of the universe but of a human son and mother, is expressed in "Donna del Paradiso," the popular poem of the Franciscan Jacope da Todi. In the poem, the Virgin comes to the scene of the crucifixion as Christ is being nailed to the cross. Christ speaks to her:

> *Mamma, why did you come?*
> *You give me a mortal wound*
> *Your crying pierces me*
> *And seems to me the sharpest sword.*[49]

These words and gestures, sentimental only to those who have ceased to invest personal experience and emotion in sacred figures, as medieval people did, served as strong stimuli to the fourteenth-century viewer's response of identification and love.

The Virgin and Mary Magdalene

One result of the presentation of sacred figures in both texts and paintings as humble people with no claim to power, education, or wealth was the proliferation of new images of women. We will examine, with more brevity than this complex material warrants, only two of the most striking female subjects in fourteenth-century painting, which emerged in the course of the century and continued to attract the imagination of painters and a wide, popular audience for centuries. The two sacred women most fascinating to fourteenth-century women and men, if we are to judge by frequency of depiction, were Mary the Virgin/Mother and Mary of Magdala.

Images of the two Marys raise some problems of interpretation that are fundamental to the use of visual images as evidence in historical research. We must ask and try to answer several complex questions: First, what relationship to actual women of the fourteenth century did these images of women have? How were women affected, both in their self-images and in their treatment and esteem by medieval communities, by the images of women that played so continuous a part in secular and religious community life? Second, to understand the messages received from these images, we need to analyze not the monolithic values of the medieval community but the widely differing values of groups within medieval communities, based on differences of perspective related to sex, class, wealth, education, and power. Finally, does the use of images as historical evidence enable us to differentiate perspectives, interests, and values within communities in a more nuanced way than if we were to use only texts?

By the beginning of the fourteenth century, the cult of the Virgin was at its height in central Europe. For a century and a half, great cathedrals had been built and dedicated in her honor. The best-loved hymns of the twelfth and thirteenth centuries extolled her virtues and her purity: "Regina Caeli," "Ave Maria Caelorum," "Salve Regina." The Virgin seemed to become light itself as light filtered through the brilliant blues and reds of her stained-glass images in Gothic cathedrals. She gleamed in pure gold at Amiens, where the Vierge Dorée dominated the central portal of the cathedral.

From the twelfth century onward, she had been depicted as the Queen of Heaven, crowned by Christ in sumptuous apse mosaics and surrounded by apostles, angels, and whirling stars. Crowned, earringed, and dressed in a jewel-encrusted robe in the apse of Santa Maria in Trastevere in Rome, she sits with Christ on a wide couch (Fig. 8). Christ's left hand holds a book that reads "Veni electa mea, ponam in tu tronam meam." [50] Mary gives blessing with her left hand, while her right hand holds a phylactery that reads "Leva eius sub capite meo et dextera illius amplexabit me." [51] Christ's right hand is around the Virgin, and he clasps her right shoulder.

The Virgin as Bride of Christ and Queen of Heaven appears in this twelfth century work as a young Byzantine empress, not kneeling in worship before Christ but seated beside him, crowned and slippered while Christ is bareheaded and barefooted. Countless apse mosaics, tympana, and small ivory statues echo this presentation of the Virgin as crowned Bride of Christ.[52]

Surrounding the apse of Santa Maria in Trastevere, a series of scenes from the life of the Virgin, dated 1291 and done by an exact contemporary of Giotto, Pietro Cavallini, vividly anticipates a contrast between the visual images of thirteenth-century and early-fourteenth-century people. In these colorful mosaics full of lively activity, Mary as the heavily jeweled Byzantine empress is no longer the central figure. A naturalistic treatment, unposed gestures, and a simply clad Virgin give an explicitly humble context to the scenes of Mary's life. Even within the series there is a contrast between the nativity of Christ and the birth of the Virgin in a comfortable home with elaborate wall hangings and a carved bed, attended by four maidservants. The nativity of Christ occurs in a hillside cave, surrounded by animals, a despondent Joseph, and three angels (Fig. 9). From the annunciation scene to the deathbed scene, Mary is dressed in the same unornamented blue cape over a brown robe (Fig. 10).

Although the Virgin's Byzantine facial features — large eyes, aquiline nose, and tiny mouth — are similar to those of the Virgin of the apse, the contrast between the backgrounds, clothing, and gestures of the two mosaics, separated in time by more than a century, could not be more dramatic. Instead of Mary's intimate connection with divinity, her poverty, simplicity, and humanness are emphasized in the Cavallini work. Even the conception of a series of scenes from the Virgin's life anticipates a characteristically fourteenth-century interest. In the choice of these particular scenes[53] is a sustained interest in the physical events of Mary's life — birth, stages of growth, childbirth, and death. There is surprisingly little interest in the gospel stories with which she is associated. The marriage of Cana — Christ's first miracle, instigated by Mary's urging — and even the crucifixion and resurrection scenes are omitted in favor of the scenes from Mary's physical life cycle.

Cavallini's interest in the physical events of Mary's life was modified in Giotto's series on the life of the Virgin in the Scrovegni Chapel in Padua (1303–1304). Interest in physical events is subordinated to fascination with the emotional quality of the events. The cycle begins long before the birth of Mary, with the suffering of Saint Joachim and Saint Anne because of their childlessness. The expulsion of Joachim from the temple, an episode from the apocryphal Gospel of James, gave Giotto a vehicle for depicting the focused longing of the Virgin's parents, a foil for exaggerating the joy with which they later separately received the annunciation of the Virgin's birth. Six paintings precede the birth of the Virgin and give this physical event emotional articulation.

The human figures of the sacred characters dominate these frescoes. Architectural settings are abruptly abbreviated to provide a minimal backdrop for the actions of the scenes. Looking very much like cardboard stage settings — a house with no side walls, a half-shell temple, a corner of the Virgin's home — these pieces of architecture do not compass or contain the actions but are firmly subordinate to them (Fig. 11). Whenever possible, events are portrayed outdoors, unlimited by designed space. Stylistic devices do not limit the human emotions of the scenes. The restrained gestures and solid bodies of the figures carry all the impact. Frontal presentation, the traditional device for indicating divinity and engaging the viewer, is relinquished; figures are absorbed in one another, and the viewer is engaged simply by her or his ability to "read" and experience the emotions of the sacred figures. No luxurious clothing, sumptuous halls, or cosmic setting hinders this empathy. The viewer is not encouraged by the frescoes to seek the protection of the powerful ruler of the spiritual and material universe; rather, she or he is invited to enter directly the inner world of the gospel figures.

Emotions are heightened by juxtaposition with their psychic opposites: The indifference of the soldiers haggling at the right of the cross exaggerates the anguish of Mary Magdalene's wild grief at the foot of the cross and of the figures clustered around the swooning Virgin on the left (Fig. 12); the frenzy of the darting angels in the sky about the pietà emphasizes the catatonic immobility of the huddled figures surrounding the body of Christ.

The physical life cycle of the Virgin is subordinated in Giotto's frescoes to her emotional life, a range of human emotions from joy to the most intense grief, from fear to the glory of the ascension and the exhilaration of Pentecost. Giotto gave pictorial articulation to as many points of this emotional spectrum as he could, ignoring gospel incidents that did not lend themselves as readily to such expression and taking from extracanonical sources incidents that could be exploited for their emotional content.

Throughout the fourteenth century the religious images of central Europe continued to demonstrate an interest in the physical and emotional aspects of Mary's life. New themes appeared, such as the Madonna of Humility, the Madonna with a Cradle, and the Holy Family, that present the Virgin as a simple peasant woman whose emotional life is immediately accessible to the Christian. Madonna of Humility paintings depict Mary seated on a cushion on the floor, often with bare feet, suckling the infant Jesus, who twists around from the breast to look directly at the viewer.[54] Both the eye contact of the figures with the viewer and the image of the nursing child admit the viewer to a scene of unparalleled intimacy that underlines the relationship of physical and emotional conditions.

The nursing Virgin achieved wide popularity as an image and underwent continuing development and variations through the fifteenth century. It allowed a range of interpretations, the most explicit of which focused on the Virgin's milk as a nourishing and cleansing substance through which nourishment passed not only to the infant Christ but to all humankind. Mary was known as *Mater omnium* and *nutrix omnium*.[55] Her milk was also the material basis of her power to intercede for sinners. In startling contrast to the hieratic power of the thirteenth-century Byzantine empress, the humble Virgin claimed a physical and emotional power. A Florentine painting of 1402 shows Mary pleading with Christ on behalf of a group of sinners who huddle within her cloak. The inscription reads "Dearest Son, because of the milk I gave you, have mercy on them." Christ, displaying the stigmata, turns to God the Father, who grants the salvation of the sinners by releasing the dove, the Holy Spirit, which flies toward Christ.[56]

These images of the humble Virgin formulated images of divine power and influence no less than did the earlier image of the Virgin as Queen of Heaven and Bride of Christ. The power of intercession attributed to the Virgin is enhanced and personalized. Rather than power based on a queen's prerogative, it is now the irresistible personal power of a human mother to influence her son. Similarly, Giotto's Last Judgment, which covers the entrance wall of the Arena Chapel, shows Mary, in a mandorla of light, turning toward a kneeling woman and placing her arm on the woman's shoulder. Mary appears not as a legal counsel or mediatrix but standing in a "physical and personal relationship" [57] with human beings.

The Virgin not only is powerful in these new images of the fourteenth century, but she is also prototypical, the model of all Christians in her participation in the life of Christ. Parallel events in the life of Christ and the life of the Virgin are emphasized. Christ's passion is narrated through the perspective of the Virgin and *becomes* the Virgin's passion. In the *Meditationes* also, Christ's passion and the Virgin's passion are concurrent:

She hung with her son on the cross and wished to die with him rather than live any longer . . . she was in anguish like his . . . and the Son prayed to the Father for her and silently said, "My Father, see how afflicted my mother is. I ought to be crucified, not she, but she is with me on the cross." [58]

In addition, Mary's birth and Christ's birth are related, and Christ's ascension is paralleled by the Virgin's bodily assumption. Dormition scenes from the life of the Virgin, such as Cavallini's mosaic at Santa Maria in Trastevere (Fig. 10) and Torriti's mosaic at Santa Maria Maggiore, show Christ standing behind the recumbent, dying Virgin and cradling in his arms her tiny "astral body" — a strong visual parallel to Madonna and Child scenes.[59]

The figure of the Virgin and the events of her life did not, however, exhaust the religious longing of fourteenth-century people for sacred figures with whom they could identify, whose emotions they could feel, and whose attitudes and actions they could imitate. Despite the new images of the humble Virgin, identification with her was limited by the unusual degree to which she was divinely privileged. Perhaps the new devotional writings and images limited the Virgin's accessibility even more explicitly than did the gospel stories. Giotto's use of the apocryphal story of the conception of the Virgin by the sexless embrace of Joachim and Anne at the Golden Gate is an example of the way in which the new stories and images may have removed a crucial point of contact between the Virgin and ordinary human beings.[60] An entirely sexless Virgin was also difficult or impossible for most medieval people to fully identify with. Jacobus de Voragine wrote: "Such indeed was

Mary's innocence that it shone forth even outside of her, and quelled any urgency in the flesh of others . . . Although Mary was surpassing fair, no man could ever look upon her with desire." [61]

Woven throughout Giotto's pictorial account of the life of Christ in the Scrovegni Chapel is the figure of another woman, whose flowing red hair and extravagant gestures identify her immediately as Saint Mary Magdalene (Fig. 13). The Magdalene of the fourteenth century was a composite of women from eight different gospel episodes,[62] conflated at least since the sixth century[63] and unquestioned until 1517, when Jacques Lefevre d'Etaples published a critique of the traditional Magdalene, *De Maria Magdalena et triduo Christi Disceptatio*.[64]

The cult of the Magdalene reached its zenith in Italy, after an earlier peak in France, in the fourteenth century. Her feast day, July 22, was listed in all Roman Catholic missals from the beginning of the thirteenth century; liturgies were composed in her honor, sermons were filled with exempla from her life, and in 1226 an Order of Penitentes de Santa Maria Magdalena was established.

Mary Magdalene, who according to Jacobus de Voragine was the sister of Martha and Lazarus, also anointed Christ's feet with precious ointment, was liberated from the seven devils by Christ, and, according to St. Jerome, was the first to see the risen Christ, who said to her, ("Do not hold me.")[65] On the basis of these scriptural stories, apocryphal and devotional treatises embellished a fleshed-out sacred character whose uninhibited and histrionic gestures provided both the perfect foil for the dignified restraint of the Virgin and a model with whom most people could readily identify. It is Mary Magdalene who breaks away from the huddled group of mourners surrounding the Virgin in Giotto's Crucifixion and kneels weeping, touching the foot of the crucified Christ, the foot that she had once before covered with tears and dried with her hair[66] (Fig. 12).

Mary Magdalene's repentance was presented in fourteenth-century popular texts and images as the dramatic symbol of the possibility of conversion from great sinfulness to great sanctity; tradition, without scriptural warrant, makes Mary Magdalene a prostitute before her conversion. Her conversion, the *Meditations* emphasize, was the result of her single-minded love for Christ:

The Magdalen, who perhaps had heard Him preach a few times and loved him ardently, although she had not yet revealed it . . . was touched to the heart with pain at her sins and inflamed by the fire of her love for Him.[67]

But in the final analysis it was not the Magdalene's capacity for love that secured her place in medieval stories and iconography. The Virgin was cer-

1. *Orans, Catacomb of Peter and Marcellinus, Rome*

2. *Woman and Child, Catacomb of Priscilla, Rome*

3. *Putti, Santa Costanza, Rome*

4. *Christ and the Apostles, apse mosaic, Santa Pudenziana, Rome*

5. St. Francis praying at San Damiano, Giotto, Upper Church, Assisi

dime dgno difere, il fle to pefo dhi fuffeuo reuelate
effeto uenuta lora dl phto ifulla megza nocte fo-
pia ladnuca. Li ugine leuadofi ricta ao poggiofi ndu

maria dume ac gil
tuuen

Iofeph

6. *Birth of Christ, Meditations on the Life of Christ*

7. *Crucifixion, Giotto, Santa Maria Novella, Florence*

8. *Christ and the Virgin Enthroned, apse mosaic, Santa Maria in Trastevere, Rome*

9. *Nativity, Pietro Cavallini, Santa Maria in Trastevere, Rome*

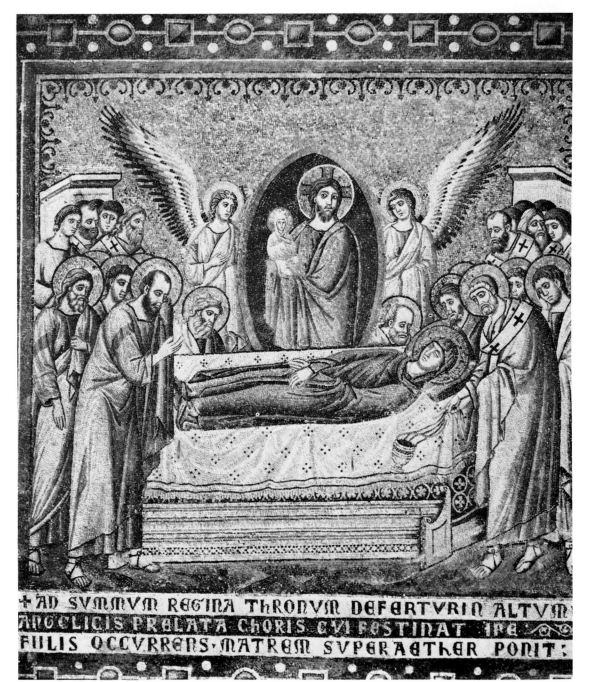

10. *Dormition of the Virgin, Pietro Cavallini, Santa Maria in Trastevere, Rome*

11.   Meeting of the Virgin and Elizabeth, Giotto, Scrovegni Chapel, Padua

12.   *Crucifixion, Giotto, Scrovegni Chapel, Padua*

13. *Lamentation, Giotto, Scrovegni Chapel, Padua*

14. *Mary Magdalene communes with the Angels, Giotto,*
     Lower Church, Assisi

15. *Slaughter of the Innocents, Giotto, Scrovegni Chapel, Padua*

16. *Interior, Grossmünster, Zurich*

17. *Interior, Chiesa del Gesù, Rome*

18. The Triumph of the Name of Jesus, *nave vault, Gesù, Rome*

19. *Interior, Schloss Chapel, Torgau*

20. Adam and Eve, *Lucas Cranach the Elder, Uffizi, Florence*

21. St. Teresa in Ecstasy, *Bernini, Cornaro Chapel, Santa Maria in Vittoria, Rome*

22.   The Triumph of Faith over Heresy, *Pietro Le Gros,*
Ignatius Loyola Chapel, Gesù, Rome

tainly capable of tenacious love. But the Virgin could not represent shame and sorrow over sinfulness; nor was she capable of the extreme gratitude of the forgiven sinner. Mary Magdalene's emotional repertoire was much broader than the Virgin's, and thus her figure more readily evoked the heightened emotional response so valued in fourteenth-century piety. Her confession to Christ articulates the emotional intensity every medieval Christian wanted, and her image helped each person to feel uninhibited gratitude:

O my Lord, I know, believe, and confess firmly that you are my God and my Lord. I have offended your majesty in many and important ways. I have sinned against your every law and have multiplied my sins above the number of sands in the sea. But I, the wicked sinner, come for your mercy; I am grieved and afflicted; I beg for your pardon and prepare to make amends for my sins and never to depart from obedience to you. I request you not to drive me away, for I know no other refuge, nor do I want any other, as I love you above all things.[68]

The significance of Mary Magdalene in fourteenth-century paintings must be evaluated in the light of the connection of vision and love discussed earlier. The power of a visual image to evoke love in the viewer is at its height in the figure of the Magdalene. "Watch her carefully," the *Meditations* instructs, "and meditate particularly on her devotion, which was singularly loved by God . . . Meditate with diligence and make an effort to imitate so much love which is here praised highly in deed and word by the Lord." [69]

Mary Magdalene, the sinful woman, the sexual woman, is singularly loved by Christ, and so every sinner can hope for a similar forgiveness and acceptance. Moreover, her conversion does not require a change of personality. Mary Magdalene is quite as flamboyant, uninhibited, and sensual — though not sexual — as a great saint as she had been as a great sinner. She is portrayed as touching Christ — even in Giotto's crucifixion scene — or wanting to touch him ("Do not hold me") throughout the fresco cycle (Fig. 12). She does not become bland, restrained, or polite after her conversion, nor does she cut or cover her flaming hair (Fig. 14). And she was prized, in painting and stories, by fourteenth-century viewers precisely for her lack of restraint.

Mary Magdalene thus provides a balancing symbolic image to that of the Virgin Mary. These two figures must be interpreted together, as their iconography consistently presents them together, juxtaposing and sometimes contrasting their lives, their personalities, and their actions. The *Meditations* describes Mary Magdalene after her conversion as remaining close to the Virgin for the rest of her life, even living with the Virgin in some stories.[70] Paintings depict the two Marys as leaning on one another for support in their anguish at the crucifixion, and it is the Virgin who persuades the risen Christ to visit and comfort Mary Magdalene.[71]

Images of Women in Fourteenth-Century Italian Communities

We can predict that any particular image is vulnerable to interpretation by different people at the same time or by the same people at different times — not to speak of different people at different times — in widely, but not infinitely, various ways. An image that conveyed the greatest possible fruitfulness to one group could be overwhelmingly counterproductive for another group in the society or in another time or culture.[72] We must try to determine, at least hypothetically and conjecturally, which of the possible interpretations of an image or group of images might have lent themselves to use by various groups within the culture. Our method will be to reconstruct a range of possible interpretations of fourteenth-century images of women for two groups within fourteenth-century Italian communities: women of the increasingly important and prominent middle class and ruling-class men, that is, men from the guilds of great merchants, bankers, and shippers. These were the men who commissioned and controlled the public images available to middle-class women.

But first we must make some assumptions explicit. The first task of any culture is to formulate and make available to its members effective symbols, whether verbal, visual, or a combination of the two, for comprehending and taking an attitude towards bodily experience: birth, growth, maturation, kinship, sex, life cycle, pain, death. Religion, as a prominent aspect of culture, must provide ideas and images that "keep body and soul together," that is, that enable individuals to manage — though not necessarily to articulate — a unified psychophysical process. The secondary task of culture is the articulation of the role and significance of particular individuals within the culture. Values relative to the interaction of people in work, commerce, families, and politics must be communicated in a way that attracts the support of a large part of the community.

The symbolic complex of every community accomplishes these tasks, either in ways that distribute power to the myriad points at which it must operate if the community is to function optimally or in dysfunctional ways such that large segments of the community are oppressed and the community is forced to squander a significant amount of its positive energy in the repression of some of its members.

In our examination of the role of fourteenth-century images of women, these preliminary points must be kept in mind: A symbolic system will not necessarily function in the same way for all members of a community; and a symbolic complex must primarily formulate the personal meaning of biological necessity for human beings and secondarily must present an intelligible social structure that organizes all public and private relationships.

A bewilderingly vast spectrum of images of women existed in fourteenth-century Italy. Among them, as we have seen, were idealized images of Mary, the "perfect" woman at each biological stage of her life. Thus a series of images was available with which a medieval woman might identify and in which she might find articulated the interests and values peculiar to her stage of life. Yet the clear message of these images, both verbal and visual, is the freedom of the Virgin from biological necessity at every stage of her life. She was conceived in a "special" way and was physically and religiously precocious in childhood. Her betrothal was attended with supernatural signs. She conceived without sexual intercourse and experienced childbirth without discomfort or loss of virginity. Only in motherhood, in her human pain over the death of her son, does Mary become a "typical" woman. Even her death was not a real human death; from the twelfth century on, she is shown ascending bodily on clouds into heaven. Mary, the Virgin/Mother, has a characteristic female life cycle but does not experience the biological life of human women. Even the Magdalene, although she is sexually experienced, has turned away from sex and repents ceaselessly for the sinfulness of her former life, which apparently consisted solely of sexual promiscuity. On the one hand, women's experience and life cycle are articulated in a sequence of nuanced and profound images. On the other hand, women's sexuality and biological experience are pointedly rejected.

This perplexing medieval ambivalence about women has been noticed and discussed by many scholars. The following discussion analyzes the medieval ambivalence in which women were at once insistently idealized and systematically deprived of the physical ground of female experience.

Both men and women valued religious images of women in fourteenth-century Italy. Unprecedented amounts of money were spent on painting, indicating that complex religious and psychological factors made these images interesting to the fourteenth-century male community leaders. Let us acknowledge that there were probably overlapping interests between ruling-class men and middle-class women; men and women alike were visually trained and emotionally educated by the sacred figures of scripture and tradition. They shared a lively interest in the stock characters of Christian tradition. This broad area of interest in visual images as they created and stimulated strongly felt piety has been discussed.

What was men's particular interest in the religious images in which women were so prominent? If we try imaginatively to adopt the perspectival vantage point of an educated, privileged, socially powerful man of fourteenth-century Florence, Rome, or Siena, the sheer quantity of images of women in the new naturalistic style must have been very striking. Since it was these men who commissioned, approved, and paid for the images, one must assume that they wanted them. They wanted them, no doubt, for the devotional reasons we have discussed, but it seems that, in addition, the visualization of women was itself compelling. Fourteenth-century texts also testify that the ideal woman was the totally visible woman. For example, deprived of both biology and speech, Dante's Beatrice neither speaks nor touches him until they meet in the visionary sphere of the *Commedia*. In the *Vita Nuova*, Dante's account of their relationship, Beatrice is unattainable and silent, and she dies prematurely, before her visual attributes fade.

Were women threatening to fourteenth-century men? There is a good deal of evidence that in the fluid commercial society of late-medieval Italian towns, a woman was able to exercise economic independence,[73] to own and to manage business enterprises,[74] and to dispose of her own property "even without her husband's consent." [75] Some women also exercised a great deal of personal power. Angela of Foligno, burdened by her duties toward her husband, old parents, and children and kept from the contemplative life for which she longed, prayed for freedom to pursue a spiritual life. Within a year all the members of her family were dead — a blessed miracle! [76] We will look at other examples of fourteenth-century women who exercised formidable power in commerce, politics, and ecclesiastical affairs. The spiritual autonomy of such women may have been deeply frightening to patrician men. The device of simultaneously distancing women and informing them of the role within the community that men preferred them to play made images of women attractive to men.

For men, the totally visualized and spiritualized — silent and bodiless — woman was manageable; thus, the closer real women came to approximating this ideal, the better. Painted images of women provided ways for men to conceptualize and thus to relate to the actual women they found so threatening. Fourteenth-century verbal descriptions of real women, in turn, could often as easily be the description of a painting:

Nine times the heaven of light had revolved in its own movement since my birth . . . when the woman whom my mind beholds in glory first appeared before my eyes . . . She was dressed in a very noble colour, a decorous and delicate crimson, tied with a girdle and trimmed in a manner suited to her tender age. The moment I saw her I say in all truth that the vital spirit, which dwells in the inmost depths of the heart, began to tremble so violently that I felt the vibration alarmingly in all my pulses, even the weakest of them.[77]

The tremendous influence of Beatrice on Dante's life and work — even, he says, on his salvation[78] — was entirely the result of Dante's visions of her, both actual and in dreams. Petrarch's Laura also appears as valued primarily for her visual qualities. In addition, a very revealing spotlight is thrown on our understanding of this poetic evidence by some Venetian laws of the fourteenth century that stipulate sexually differentiated punishments for petty crime. Punishments for men appear to be designed to prevent them from earning a livelihood — a rather counterproductive design; an eye is put out or a hand amputated. Punishments for women focus on disfigurement; the nose or one or both lips are cut off. Punishments for both men and women are posited on their preventive effectiveness. Both aim at removing the criminal from the sphere of their most significant participation in the community — for men, work; for women, visual objectivity or beauty. The unsightly woman, the woman who cannot become an inspiring image, has lost her most precious role in the community, according to the powerful men who made the laws.[79]

It would be a mistake, however, to understand male images of women as formulating accurate descriptions of social experience. Images may either express or compensate experience. The beautiful, silent women of fourteenth-century paintings apparently do not express men's experience of actual women but attempt to compensate their often threatening experience of actual women. Tension between groups within a society is at its height not when one group is successfully kept in severe repression but when the oppressed group very nearly matches — in social class, independent wealth, and ability — the oppressing group.[80] The formulation in visual imagery of the qualities men would have liked women to emulate was "a way of mastering" what was otherwise too immediate, too threatening, too intense.[81]

In pre-Renaissance Italy, a significant number of middle-class women had economic power; some women were in self-created positions of nonecclesiastical religious authority, such as Catherine of Siena (d. 1380) and Bridget of Sweden (d. 1373); some women were well educated; and the cost of dowries had never been higher, indicating the importance to patrician men of advantageous marriages for their sisters and daughters — advantageous to the men, that is, whose power often depended to a large extent on such marriages. Yet the legal position of women did not match their importance within their communities.[82] One fourteenth-century Venetian inheritance law, although stating in its preamble its prejudice in favor of women "to take into account the fragility of woman," nevertheless went on to rank men as heirs before women of the same degree of kinship.[83]

A frequent subject of painting and sculpture in Tuscany at the turn of the fourteenth century may express the tension between ruling-class men and middle- and lower-class women. The popularity of the theme of the Slaughter of the Innocents, King Herod's massacre of male children under one year of age in a desperate attempt to destroy the infant Christ, is puzzling unless it formulates some conflict close to the concerns of fourteenth-century men and women. Giovanni Pisano's pulpit (1301) for the Pistoia cathedral shows a chaos of scrambled figures of weeping women and impassive men struggling over the naked, doll-like bodies of infants. In the lower right, directly under the throne of King Herod, who directs the massacre, a woman and a man engage in a tug-of-war with an infant whose legs are stretched taut in the tension.

In Giotto's fresco on the same subject in the Scrovegni Chapel (Fig. 15), the men, not dressed as soldiers but as ordinary civilians, appear on the left under the throne of Herod. A heap of waxy-gray dead children is in the bottom foreground, and on the right, weeping women huddle while the last infants are killed. A tug-of-war over a child between a man and a woman occupies the center of the picture space. The bodies of the children, although presumably the point of the struggle, are curiously underpainted. One cannot even see whether the large body being pulled at the center of the picture is clothed or naked; when stabbed, the bodies of the children do not bleed but remain a uniform yellow-gray. The clothing of the men and the women, on the other hand, is bright — purples, reds, blues, and gold — and their faces express cruelty and anguish. The pictorial interest of the painting is on the struggle between the men and the women rather than on the infants who are being slaughtered. The image of a life-and-death tug-of-war between men and women may have been expressive of a strongly felt and thus strongly visualized social tension.

The rejection of women's biology was, as we have seen, a prominent aspect of painting cycles that treated the life of the Virgin. The spiritualizing of physical events was an important part of the message given by these paintings. Medieval medical theories of the female body help us understand the investment of men in this aspect of images of women. The classical opinions of Aristotle and Galen were considered unquestionable throughout the medieval period. In addition to Aristotle's infamous view of women as misbegotten males[84] and Galen's arguments that women's bodies are less perfect than men's "by as much as she is colder than he," [85] Galen's description of women's sexual organs as identical with those of males but turned outside-in, emphasized the oppositeness of women to the standard human being, the male. These theories of woman's body expressed and reinforced medieval men's fear of the mysterious biology of women.

Moreover, medical care of women was probably carried on primarily, if not exclusively, by other women; even male physicians did not understand female biology.[86] Ignorance and fear thus led to fantasies of evil women whose most prominent feature is their physicality and sexuality and fantasies of good women that emphasized their disembodied spirituality.

The evil woman, the witch, was, of course, everything that the Virgin, saints, and scriptural figures were not. She was described as sexually insatiable, loud, and smelly. She was in cahoots with the physical world and could cause impotence and infertility, illness, death, and damnation, just as the Virgin, in league with the spiritual world, could effect health, cure, and salvation. The witch combined all the personal characteristics that real women were expected to shun; the most emphasized feature of the witch in the 1484 *Malleus Maleficarum,* second only to her ability to pervert the smooth functioning of nature, was her physicality.

Male anxiety concerning the physicality and sexuality of real women, in addition to the threat of women's changing social roles, was translated into fantasies of women as purely spiritual and purely visual. These images did not, however, promote a transfer of esteem, affection, and acceptance by men from the images to actual women but emphasized the inferiority of women in comparison with the images.[87]

But it was not only privileged medieval men who felt a great attraction to images of women. Why were medieval women, not otherwise known for their docility, willing to tolerate images designed to criticize and denigrate their bodies, their personalities, and their accomplishments?

Catherine Benincasa, twenty-third child of a Sienese dyer and an illiterate woman,[88] modeled her spiritual journey and her energetic life after the images she knew in local churches — those of Saint Dominic, Saint Francis, and especially of her namesake, Saint Catherine of Alexandria. Images of Saint Catherine's mystical marriage to Christ, of Saint Francis's stigmata, and of Saint Dominic's call to monastic dedication gave shape and content to the early spiritual life of Saint Catherine of Siena.[89] Especially interesting is the extent to which Catherine's active life was informed by possibilities available to her through the popular iconography of Saint Catherine of Alexandria. Catherine of Alexandria was a learned woman, depicted in both story and image arguing philosophy and theology against the most accomplished masters of fourth-century Alexandria and the emperor Maxentius himself. Jacobus reports that she was able to argue "according to the divers modes of the syllogisms, by allegory and metaphor, by logic and mystic" and thus "demonstrated the incarnation." [90] Catherine of Siena, despite her lack of education, was able to use this model to picture herself a competent "language user" like Catherine of Alexandria, and her native intelligence coupled with commitment and study supplied the rest. She preached to Pope Gregory XI "with such a wonderful grace, eloquence, and authority, that the Pope himself and all that were about him were astonished to hear her." [91]

As Saint Catherine of Siena's life is one of the better documented lives of illiterate women, it is difficult to know whether the crucial role of images in her life was typical of illiterate fourteenth-century women. It is always dangerous to extrapolate from women whose careers show them to be anything but ordinary. Yet we must also ask whether the ability to use, learn from, and sometimes pattern themselves after religious images of women did not to a large extent determine the effectiveness of extraordinary women such as Saint Catherine of Siena, Julian of Norwich, Margery Kempe, Bridget of Sweden, and many more.

That many or most fourteenth-century women were attracted by images of the Virgin, women saints, and scriptural figures does not seem to be in doubt.[92] How are we to understand the attractiveness of the images we have just discussed as serving the fantasies of the privileged men who commissioned and paid for them? Having identified the "message given" by religious images of women, may we not be content to claim that it is in fact the meaning?

One of the prerogatives exercised by historians is the choice of a particular perspective within a historical community from which to interpret the evidence of that community's life. A historian can align himself with the perspective of privileged males even when historical images are used as evidence. When feminist historians adopt this perspective, for example, they understand quite rightly the repressive aspect of images of women, the gap between the experiences of actual women and the male values promoted by images of women.[93] But is this the only legitimate perspective? It is undoubtedly important to understand the "message given," but that is only a part of the task of historical understanding.

We have been exploring a general and a particular hypothesis; the test of a hypothesis is its capacity to make intelligible more of the historical evidence than an alternative hypothesis does. The general hypothesis is that the same spectrum of images can be understood and interpreted by different persons or groups within a culture in different ways, so that, for example, it is possible that the same image can be seen and interpreted as repressive from the perspective of one group and as productive and enriching from the perspective of another group.

The particular hypothesis is that it was possible for fourteenth-century Italian women to receive messages from religious images of women that expanded and enriched their lives. These images provided models of a spiritual life liberated from immersion in the potentially overwhelming biological contingencies of childbearing and the physical and environmental necessities of household, farm, or business, of nursing infants, of caring for old parents, and so on. Saint Catherine of Siena, for example, vowed virginity when her favorite older sister, Bonaventura, died; the visual images with which she conceived her life offered an alternative to the marriage her parents were pressing her to enter, that is, to a life ordered by biology.

Religious images of women provided for fourteenth-century women the primary resource for conceiving their lives as something more than biologically determined, as containing potential for spiritual growth, meaningful rather than arbitrary suffering, and a degree of individuation. By identifying with whichever of the rich spectrum of images articulated her particular momentary and changing situation, a medieval women could achieve some distance from, and therefore a genuine response to, her own life and circumstances.

Moreover, it is possible for a person to select not only the image that gives intelligibility to her experience at any particular moment but also the precise features of a particular image that are useful to her at a particular time. An image that to many modern women has come to carry a repressive content may have meant something very different to medieval women. The idealization of the virginal woman, for example, may have symbolized to medieval women freedom from the burden of frequent childbearing and nursing in an age in which these natural processes were highly dangerous.

The images themselves substantiate this interpretation. The Virgin is not merely the passive, receptive, visible woman. She is also a powerful woman. In iconography, she scolds the boy Jesus for distressing her when he stays behind to dispute with the elders in the temple at the age of twelve — an image that was banned by the sixteenth-century Council of Trent as exaggerating Mary's power. It is her importunate urging that prompts Jesus' first miracle at the marriage of Cana, and she appears continually through Jesus' human life. She remains with him in iconography in his heavenly life, crowned, dispensing blessing, and interceding for the sinners in her care. In image and story, the Virgin was so powerful that, in a popular story, even a bandit who seeks her protection continues to receive it until the day he forgets to pray to her. No medieval woman would have missed the strong implication that the power of the Virgin was related to her freedom from subjection and obedience to a husband and the cares of a home — a freedom contingent in the fourteenth century on virginity. The power of the Virgin came from her virginity as surely as it came from her motherhood.

Historical Images of Women and Hermeneutics

Great care and a good deal of generosity must be exercised when we attempt to understand an alien symbolic system. And western Christian historical visual images are, even more so than texts, alien to modern western Christians. A greater problem for interpretation, however, is that the content of historical images is not alien to western Christians; in fact, the content seems all too familiar in that it has often been used to condition modern women to the role that contemporary western societies assign them. It is difficult for many twentieth-century women to restrain their impatience with historical images that may have become genuinely counterproductive for them. The meaning or range of meanings these symbols were likely to have held for persons in a very different world of physical realities and spiritual values can be obscured by modern projections. The images are alien, but not alien enough to promote dispassionate historical interpretation.

The corrective agency of images is not sufficiently acknowledged when we seek to assign an ultimate meaning — our own meaning — to a particular symbol. In a culture in which women were biologically bound, the pursuit of spiritual and political freedom required the rejection of the main link in the chain by which women were held in captivity — sex. The perpetual virginity of Mary and the rejection of sex of Mary Magdalene may, however, have an opposite meaning in a culture like ours, founded on instinctual repression, delayed gratification, and the pursuit of success — however success may be understood by a particular person.

If we try to inspect these images without prior assumptions from twentieth-century experience, the plays, paintings, and popular devotions that deal with the life of the Virgin reveal a woman who was able to experience the events of girlhood, young womanhood, motherhood, old age, and death without being overwhelmed by their physical aspects. Through all biological changes she pursued a life of spiritual intensity and personal power. That this spiritual autonomy was even possible, medieval women would have known from no other source. The Virgin's biology was ancillary to her life cycle, a spiritual process that must have reversed — and compensated — the experience of actual medieval women.

If this hypothesis seems fruitful for making us aware of other messages than the "message given" by fourteenth-century paintings, it does not negate this message; it does not ignore in the message a page from the history of the oppression of women. But it also honors the creativity and ingenuity with which visual images can be and were used by women. The same symbols, approached from different perspectives, can appear to convey or contain amazingly different "obvious" contents. Part of the value of the hypothesis is its attention to the creative intelligence of medieval women and their ability to work for their own advantage with images they did not control. The alternative interpretation — to read in these symbols nothing but a history of oppression, understood and interpreted from the perspective of modern feminist interest — forces us to find fourteenth-century women self-destructive, stupid, or lazy in their willingness to cooperate with their oppressors, to be helpless victims.

What is it about images that makes them even more susceptible than texts to alternative and even conflicting interpretations based on personal interest? Texts, assuming a literate, more or less educated readership, can count on the reader's trained capacity to understand language in the way the author of the text intended it. Images can assume no such educated subjective empathy of author and viewer. Their message, once drawn, is, within limits, up for grabs. Even the heavily symbolic/scriptural universe of a medieval person, in which the image of a particular sacred figure was to some extent denoted by liturgy, by drama, and by popular devotional material, only partially and incompletely governed the message received from a painting.

The distinction between message given and message received, in addition to the different ways in which the symbols themselves can be interpreted, is related to a difference between the symbolic aspect of a painting and its semiotic quality. If the symbolic aspect is the story line or narrative content of a painting — that which relates it to a public universe of meaning[94] — then the semiotic aspect is everything about the painting that is not a part of its narrative content, that is, the painting as it would be seen by a viewer who knew nothing whatsoever about Christianity or western history. The colors used, the style of the painting, including the treatment of the human figures — whether representational or tending to abstraction — the textures of paint and the painted textures of garments, buildings, or the natural surroundings of the figures are all aspects of the semiotic quality of a painting. Also, the mobility of the figures is part of the semiotic aspect: Are we looking at a snapshot that catches the figures in the middle of a motion, a gesture, a struggle? Or are we gazing at a timeless moment in which, like Byzantine iconography, the figures seem to hold their precise characteristic poses eternally?

The semiotic factors of a visual image are everything that cannot be reduced to words. All the semiotic factors communicate, beneath and around the symbolic content, a world of signs that cannot be articulated apart from reference to the symbolic factors — and without a specialized aesthetic vocabulary — but that profoundly alter the viewer's relation to the symbolic content of the painting.[95] Semiotic factors expand the range of possible interpretations according to the interest of the viewer even beyond the possible interpretations of the symbolic content. Will the figures in a Byzantine Madonna and Child be construed as haughty and inaccessible, or will a particular viewer experience the figures as positively powerful, guaranteeing help and salvation? Will the betrothed Virgin in a Giotto painting be seen as a perfectly docile and passively obedient woman? Or will she be seen as untouched by physical weakness, grinding labor, and the biological necessities so continuous and costly to most medieval women? Answers to these questions depend largely on the coordination of the culturally trained visual conditioning of the viewer and the semiotic qualities of the image.

For fourteenth-century Italian women, both the new symbolic subjects of painting and the new representational style provided the possibility of identifying themselves with the image of the Virgin, the nonbiological woman, and thus of beginning to conceive themselves as constituted by a subjective consciousness. The possibility of correcting the weight of the biological, of modifying unindividuated immersion in a chain of physical processes and living conditions, was given primarily by visual images with their capacity for eliciting and informing the emotions. These images educated fourteenth-century women to subjectivity and in so doing corrected — as one corrects a seasoning by balancing it with another seasoning, rather than as one corrects a mistake, from wrong to right — potentially overwhelming physical experience.

Identifying oneself as constituted by subjective consciousness, we have said, requires training. No one "naturally" learns to identify herself or himself with a centered consciousness. Subjectivity, the habit of differentiating oneself from the world, the community, and natural processes by awareness of an inner unified activity, cannot be achieved without the cultural availability of a spectrum of models within which one can recognize and appropriate objectifications of one's inner process. Either texts — stories, metaphysical or philosophical explanations, devotional exercises, and so on — or images can provide the models for a differentiated and unified consciousness.

The difference between a sense of self based on language and one based on visual images is that only language can provide the tools for analytic activity. That is why I had to write a book about images rather than simply present a picture book or a series of picture essays[96] which would show what cannot be said. Analysis of the visual as well as the verbal ideas that inform subjectivity requires language. A person whose education to subjectivity is predominantly visual can identify a complex of images that provide models for an inner process, but he or she cannot, without linguistic training, evaluate the relative value of particular images or articulate how an image operates intellectually and emotionally. This is why medieval women, an overwhelming majority of whom did not receive linguistic training, did not leave us many verbal indications of the messages they received from images and why we must therefore go to the images themselves to try to determine this.

Nor do non–language users consciously reject images that are counterproductive or contradictory. An extensive linguistic training in verbal analysis is necessary for such conscious rejection, and such a training has been available only to twentieth-century women in numbers great enough that they can ratify and reinforce one another's insights and provide the continuing support necessary for sustaining detailed cultural analysis and critique from a variety of perspectives. To reject, without linguistic analysis, is simply not to see whatever lies outside the interest of the viewer. Persons without linguistic training are sheltered from messages that are counterproductive for them by not receiving messages irrelevant to their interests. Thus we cannot, as language-using reviewers of fourteenth-century images of women, claim that the "objective" content — the message given — of an image was inevitably destructive to non–language users by whom the negative content was apparently not even perceived.

The real tension between men and women in fourteenth-century Tuscany, however, must not be dissolved by our discussion of the usefulness of religious images of women for actual women. The spiritualization of women's bodies and personalities in paintings represented for men a method of "mastering what is otherwise too intense"; in quite a different sense, these same images represented for women an increment of ability to "master" what was otherwise too intense, the "short, nasty and brutish" biologically determined life. No account of the role of images in the religious life of fourteenth-century communities that assumes the perspective of only one group of persons within the culture can even begin to tell us about the complexity of the images and their possible interpretations.

◆ 5 ◆

Vision and Sixteenth-Century
Protestant and Roman Catholic Reforms

The ears are the only organs of a Christian.[1]
MARTIN LUTHER

The Protestant and Roman Catholic liturgical reformations[2] of the sixteenth century brought fundamental changes to the worship of western European Christians. In this chapter we explore some of these changes, especially as they involved the relative importance of visual and auditory participation in worship. We consider how visual evidence from the sixteenth-century can contribute to our sense of the "thickness" of historical discourse, that is, to the totality of verbal and nonverbal communication, the messages given and the messages received, by which a culture is constituted, perpetuated, and rapidly or gradually altered.

Generalizations about differences between the Catholic and the Protestant reformations are often counterproductive because they disregard the variety of local reformations and tend to exaggerate both the rapidity of change and the stability of the opposing positions. At the beginning of the sixteenth century, all the ecclesiastical and secular leaders who were to initiate and cope with the religious, social, and political crises of the reforms were committed and practicing Catholics whose training and education were thoroughly organized by late-medieval content and methods. In addition, the reforming movements of the sixteenth century had common problems and similar creative energy and achieved similar goals in the renewal of a religious interest and in the reform of liturgy.

Within these broad areas of common preparation, common problems, and similar achievements, however, our concentration on the visual experience of sixteenth-century Christians will help us to identify some fundamental differences between Catholic and Protestant reformations. We will approach an understanding of both similarities and differences by comparing the visual and spatial experience of worshippers at a Protestant reform church, the Grossmünster of Zurich (Fig. 16), and the experience of worshippers in the Catholic reform Chiesa del Gesù (Fig. 17).

Vision in Late-Medieval Liturgy: Theory and Practice

The engagement of vision in worship and piety, trained for centuries by instruction and practice, was experientially validated for medieval people by its results in increased love and piety. It was also, as described in Chapter 3, supported by an ancient theory of physical vision that described vision as occurring when a quasi-physical ray is projected from the eye of the viewer to touch its object. An impression of the object, in turn, travels back along the visual ray to be imprinted on the soul and preserved in the memory. In this theory, as we have seen, the viewer is active, both initiating and completing the act of vision in a stored memory of the object.[3]

Vision was thus the strongest possible access to an object of devotion. The culmination of the late-medieval mass was the elevation of the consecrated bread so that it could be seen by the congregation, a practice introduced in the thirteenth century. The sight of the host, the *touching* of the body of Christ by the visual ray of the worshipper, was thought to have a salvific effect.[4] A sermon on the mass by the late-thirteenth-century German preacher Berthold of Regensburg describes what occurs as the worshipper gazes on the elevated host: "See the Son of God who, for your sakes, shows his wounds to the heavenly Father; see the Son of God who, for your sakes, was thus lifted on the cross; see the Son of God who will come to judge the living and the dead."[5] Since the wine, the blood of Christ, could not actually be touched by sight, the practice of elevating the chalice was begun at a much later date, and even then out of formal rather than devotional requirements.

Understood in the context of medieval popular visual theory, the insistence of medieval worshippers on contact by sight strikes one less as "superstitious" and misplaced sensuousness[6] than as a desire by the worshipper to place himself or herself in the most immediate and strong contact with the object of devotion. Viewing the consecrated bread with concentrated attention was considered of equal or superior value to ingesting it, and medieval congregations were often urged by their priests to communicate "spiritually," that is, visually, rather than physically.[7] Vision was considered a fully satis-factory manner of communicating, so that people frequently left the church after the elevation.[8]

The visual ray theory of vision was amended at the end of the thirteenth century by Roger Bacon (d. 1292), who attempted to integrate various the-ories each of which explained some aspect of vision neglected by other theories. It is difficult to evaluate how much of Bacon's revised theory of vision had become known by people other than philosophers and scholars by the end of the fifteenth century. Bacon's theory was inductive, based on methodical observation of the act of physical vision.

In Bacon's description, a quasi-physical visual ray does not initiate vision and unite viewer and object. Rather, vision originates with the object, "which sends its visible qualities through the intervening air to the observer's eye." [9] The visual ray of the observer, however, is still necessary for vision; its role is to stimulate sight by providing the psychological attention by which the object is enabled to communicate its visual properties.[10]

Bacon could well have been describing what he observed in medieval churches. His theory amounts to a revision of the idea that vision is entirely the result of the viewer's activity; it formulates and emphasizes instead the important sense in which the viewer is affected by the object. In Bacon's theory, the object receives an autonomy, while the viewer's role is under-stood as partially — psychologically — active and partially — physically — passive. The viewer's role, then, in contemplating a sacred image is limited to the exercise of a concentrated attention, while that of the object is to reach out to the viewer.

Late-medieval liturgy, so developed visually, was for most participants a minimally verbal experience:

The liturgy from the Middle Ages onwards was looked upon as the exclusive concern of the priest. Hence while the celebrant "read" the mass at the altar with his back to the people, the faithful were busy with other devotional exercises . . . Only at the three main parts of the eucharist: the offertory, the consecration, and the communion, did the faithful, raised by the server's bell, turn their attention briefly to the sacred action that was being performed at the altar, in order that they might make certain recommended "affections." [11]

After about the beginning of the eleventh century, the custom that the celebrant, his back to the congregation, recite the liturgy in a whisper be-came normative for the western church. Auditory participation became al-most nonexistent as the celebrant's words became inaudible.[12] In addition, the service of the word, except for the sermon, was conducted in Latin, a lan-guage that had become unintelligible to laypeople and even to most priests.[13] Even the sermon, delivered in the vernacular and intended, since the emergence of the Franciscan and Dominican preachers, to recover the instructional and edifying aspects of Christian worship, had become a visual as well as a verbal performance. As discussed in Chapter 4, stylized gestures, rhetorical tricks, even costumes and acting out of the narratives became part of the repertoire of the more dramatic and popular preachers.[14]

Nor were liturgical celebrations made more intelligible to worshippers by careful instruction at other times than the services themselves. Commenting on a complete lack of evidence for the existence of confirmation instruction in Italy in the fifteenth century, Francis Haskell writes that this was "true of almost the whole of Christendom and nearly all the later Middle Ages."[15] In the sixteenth century, Jesuits found Christians in Italy crossing themselves without knowing what the sign meant.[16]

In addition to myriad other complaints, contemporary sources on the eve of the sixteenth-century reformations were unanimous in deploring the end of a linguistic christian culture. The "doomed sense of accelerating decline" described in writings of the period, however, must be interpreted with care. As Francis Oakley has cautioned, these writings, taken at face value, may indeed indicate "declining levels of performance,"[17] or they may primarily reveal the mood of ecclesiastics and intellectuals who would have liked to see their linguistic values and tools more widely appreciated. These complaints may also suggest "rising standards of expectation," at least among an educationally and culturally privileged few. Clearly, however, the complaints suggest that a balanced equilibrium between language for instruction and clarification and visual images to direct and increase devotional piety had eluded the late-medieval Roman church.

In dramatic contrast to the verbal impoverishment of worship, the engagement of vision had never been stronger. A reconstruction of the Grossmünster in Zurich in 1518 demonstrates the dominance of the visual aspect of worship in this church. Descriptions and extant building records enable us to visualize the church. Replete with brightly painted pillars and walls, a huge wooden cross, reliquaries, at least seventeen altars, an organ "whose carved wooden case was painted red and blue," elaborately painted and decorated side chapels, the sanctuary also contained an "Easter grave," installed only three years before Zwingli's arrival.

For this sight the pilgrim was prepared symbolically on entering the chapel, since over the portal leading down into it was a wall painting of Christ standing in the tomb with the instruments of His passion on either side. Once the pilgrim had descended, he would have seen a wooden sepulchre under a canopy supported by pillars, likewise of brilliantly painted wood. Surrounding the sepulchre were large wooden statues of Mary Magdalene, Mary, and Saint John, while in it, wrapped in a white coverlet with silken tassels, was laid a wooden replica of the body of Christ, which was removed from the grave on Easter Sunday.[18]

It was not only Protestant reformers who condemned the overuse of images; Erasmus, who remained a Roman Catholic, claimed that even prior to the Protestant complaints he had condemned practices "that images . . . be treated as if they were alive; that people . . . bow their heads, fall on the ground, or crawl on their knees before them, and that worshippers . . . kiss or fondle the carvings." Huldreich Zwingli, people's priest and reformer of Zurich, added to the list of these abuses a catalog of objectionable devotional practices:

Men kneel, bow, and remove their hats before them; candles and incense are burned before them; men name them after the saints whom they represent; men kiss them; men adorn them with gold and jewels; men designate them with the appellation merciful or gracious; men seek consolation merely from touching them, or even hope to acquire remission of sins thereby.[19]

Charles Garside describes the Holy Week practice at the Grossmünster at the time of Zwingli's arrival in December 1518:

On Palm Sunday, in Zurich as elsewhere, [the practice arose] of drawing down the nave of the Great Minster a wooden donkey bearing a statue of Christ. Just as His entry into Jerusalem had to be enacted before their eyes to be fully comprehended, so, too, His agony in the garden. Hence, outside the Great Minster, against either the north or west wall, there stood under a canopy a group of figures representing Christ with His disciples on the Mount of Olives. His effigy in the Easter-Grave enabled them to meditate on His dead body wrapped in the linen shroud. Even the miracle of the Ascension had to be presented to them visually, so that on Ascension Thursday a huge image of Christ was slowly raised up from the floor of the choir until it disappeared from the people's sight through a hole in the vaulting contrived especially for the purpose.[20]

Architecture, Images, and the Reform of Liturgy

An imbalance between engagement of the visual sense and of the auditory sense of the worshipper became a focus of both Roman Catholic and Protestant reformers. Both recognized the need to increase auditory aspects of worship and religious instruction. The common problem of underverbalized liturgy and thus of worshippers not expected or trained to use ears and discursive intellect, but only eyes and emotion, in worship led to different responses by Catholic and Protestant reformers.

We will examine in particular two sixteenth-century solutions to the problem of the relative importance of eye and ear in christian worship. The solutions we will discuss were not characteristic of the whole of the Protestant reformation and of the Catholic reform. Some features of both solutions were explicitly rejected by fellow reformers; but both churches were influential in presenting solutions to a problem common to all reform movements of the sixteenth century — the relation of word and image in christian worship.

Iconoclastic attitudes and activities were one of the least agreed-upon aspects of the Protestant reformation in Germany and Switzerland; the range of convictions was represented early in the reform by the opposing views of Martin Luther and his senior colleague at the University of Wittenberg, Andreas Bodenstein von Karlstadt. Nonetheless, concern over images and efforts to remove them from Christian worship are characteristic of the Protestant reform. There was less agreement on how to accomplish it — whether by violent action, by orderly and legalized procedures, or simply by "removing them from the heart," as Luther advocated.

We consider two Protestant church buildings, one constructed after the Protestant reform had become settled in Germany, the other a medieval cathedral that was stripped of its earlier images and statuary and rendered appropriate for Protestant worship as its congregation and leaders understood it. The first building is the Schloss Chapel, Torgau, Germany (Fig. 19), dedicated by Luther in 1534. The other is the Grossmünster in Zurich (Fig. 16), whose appearance at the beginning of Zwingli's ministry we have already described. We consider the Grossmünster after its decoration was adjusted to the standards of Zwingli's theological principles.

The Catholic reformation building we will explore is the Chiesa del Gesù in Rome (Fig. 17), the mother church of the Jesuit order. The Jesuit order originated in response to the Roman Catholic church's need for support and reform; it was "the most vigorous, militant, and successful" of all the reforming groups within the Roman church.[21]

We will focus on the message received rather than on the theological rationale given by reforming leaders.[22] Instead of concentrating primarily on particular images, except as they contribute to a total spatial and visual experience, we will try to imaginatively reconstruct the messages received from the architectural ambiance of these churches and chapels. If we would like to understand the worshippers' visual and verbal orientation in worship, we must initially determine the *changes* from accustomed experiences of worship that would have jarred a worshipper into a different engagement of energy, a different kind of attention.

Protestant Vision

In the early fourteenth century, Meister Eckhart, the German Dominican preacher and mystical theologian, questioned the visual preoccupation of his contemporaries in liturgy and devotional practice:

Hearing brings more into a person, but seeing one gives out more, even in the very act of looking. And therefore we shall all be more blessed in eternal life by our power to hear than by our power to see. For the power to hear the eternal word is within me and the power to see will leave me; for hearing I am passive, and seeing I am active. Our blessedness does not depend on the deeds we do but rather in our passiveness to God . . . God has set our blessedness in passivity.[23]

The association of hearing with passivity and seeing with activity was traditional. But the relative value Eckhart, unlike earlier authors, gave to each became increasingly emphasized by later authors whose educational training sensitized them to the capacity of language to instruct, to clarify, and to affect not only the intellect but also the emotions.

The most fundamental insight of Martin Luther, and after him the leaders of the Protestant reformations, was the necessity that the Christian be passive, in worship as in salvation, totally dependent on God. Luther's understanding of the activity of the word on the passive worshipper identified simultaneously a different access to salvation and a different source of activity. Moreover, his description of the origin of language in the "bottom of the heart" is nothing less than a rejection of the traditional understanding of the intimate connection of vision and emotion and a statement of the primary connection of language to the human affections:

But when one ponders well his divine works in the depths of the heart, and regards them with wonder and gratitude, so that one breaks out from very ardor into sighs and groanings, rather than into speech; when the words, not nicely chosen nor prescribed, flow forth in such a way that the spirit comes seething with them, and the words live and have hands and feet, yes that the whole body and life with all its members strives and strains for utterance — that is indeed a worship of God in spirit and truth, and such words are all fire, light, and life.[24]

If language can intensify love and piety as well as express it, then the traditional claim that devotional images best concentrated and increased piety loses its persuasiveness. Luther argued against the violent iconoclasm of Karlstadt and his followers; he felt that images need not be combated as dangerous but can simply be disregarded as ineffectual.

It is tempting to interpret Protestant rejection of the efficacy and value of images as a result of perspectival bias of educated language users. The education of Martin Luther in scholastic theology and that of Calvin and Zwingli, who had received thorough humanistic training, were characteristic of the leaders of the magisterial reformation. Zwingli, called by his friends "the Cicero of our age," corresponded with Erasmus and was influenced by Erasmus's ideas concerning the need for reform of the church. Calvin founded the Academy in Geneva, which later became the University of Geneva. For leaders of the reformation in Germany and German-speaking Switzerland, linguistic education was seen as a necessary accompaniment to the reform of the church. The Protestant reforms began with educated leaders who sought to achieve their goals through the education of the communities with which they worked. Luther's high regard for public education grew out of his own involvement in an academic community. Even the publication of the Ninety-Five Theses, which initiated the German reform, was intended to provide concise points for discussion by a community of scholars. Luther's ideas became known throughout Germany in a fortnight and throughout Europe in a month, but how far the public excitement was from Luther's original intention is clear from a 1518 letter:

It is a mystery to me how my theses, more so than my other writings, indeed, those of other professors, were spread to so many places. They were meant exclusively for our academic circle here . . . they were written in such language that the common people could hardly understand them. They . . . use academic categories.[25]

Let us nevertheless resist the temptation to interpret the Protestant reforms as the triumph of an educated elite over a popular, visually oriented liturgy and piety until we have examined some of the nonverbal evidence. A debate among scholars, carried on in "academic categories," could not have effected the landslide of public support for the Protestant reform that occurred in large parts of western Europe in the 1520s. What can we learn from the visual evidence?

The Grossmünster, Zwingli's parish church from 1518 until his death in 1531, was founded in Carolingian times, its main basilica completed about 1215.[26] Gothic towers were added at the end of the fifteenth century. Along with the newer church buildings, the Grossmünster had been decorated in a renaissance of church art in Zurich at the end of the fifteenth and beginning of the sixteenth centuries.[27] "Not a hundredth part of the paintings and statues that Zwingli would have seen in 1518 had been made in 1500." [28]

The methodical removal of all this recently acquired art from the churches of Zurich, from June 20 to July 2, 1524, became a model for iconoclasm in the Protestant territories of German-speaking Switzerland and southern Germany.[29] A committee headed by Zwingli and two other secular priests and comprising members of different guilds entered every church in Zurich and within thirteen days had stripped them of all art.

Every standing altar was removed from its niche or base and, together with the base, taken out of the church. It was then either broken up by the

masons, if made of stone or plaster, or burned, if made of wood. Every
painting was taken down from the altars and burned outside, and all
crucifixes were removed. Even the carved choir stalls were taken up and
burned. Then the walls were whitewashed so that no traces whatever of the
old decorations and appointments might be seen ... By Sunday, July 3,
1524, scarcely a statue, a painting, a crucifix, a votive lamp, a reliquary,
a shrine, or image or decoration of any sort was to be seen anywhere in
the Zurich churches.[30]

A traveler returning home from pilgrimage to Compostela and the Holy
Land after the committee's work had been completed said of the Grossmünster that "there was nothing at all inside, and it was hideous." Zwingli's
evaluation was different: "In Zurich," he wrote, "we have churches which
are positively luminous; the walls are beautifully white." [31] Significantly, some
of the churches that were whitewashed after being stripped were adorned two
years later "at various places with gold gilding and 'lovely inscriptions.' " [32]
In the absence of public museums[33] in which prereformation religious art
could have been preserved, almost nothing is known today about medieval art
in Zurich; "not a single statue has survived" and "scarcely one-tenth of pre-
Reformation painting." [34]

Modern historians, discounting the religious significance of artistic works
and deploring the aesthetic insensitivity of Protestant iconoclasm, often fail
to appreciate that sixteenth-century people — reforming leaders, middle-class
burghers, and "blue-collar" workers alike — understood that the issue of words
and images ultimately and intimately affected their salvation. We, whose
sights are trained to *this* world, can scarcely compensate our own perspective
strongly enough in our interpretations of an earlier age. Sixteenth-century
people, educated and uneducated, Roman Catholic and Protestant, lived in
expectation of a final judgment resulting in everlasting reward or punishment.
The normative event of human life, for sixteenth-century people as for medieval Christians, lay after death: One's life would receive an absolute interpretation and evaluation only at the Last Judgment. Two depictions of the Last
Judgment covered whole walls of the Grossmünster before its dismantling.
A high degree of religious anxiety must have been stimulated and exacerbated
by these vivid visual reminders of an inevitable judgment. Probably not until
Jonathan Edwards's sermons in the eighteenth century — sermons such as
"Sinners in the Hands of an Angry God" — would verbal descriptions rival
these late-medieval paintings of the Last Judgment.[35]

Within the larger context of concern about salvation, reforms that seemed
to serve the specialized interests of educated language users were typically
matched and extended by the interests of ordinary people. Often iconoclastic
activities were instigated by middle- and working-class people who were at

least partially motivated by resentment that not only theological language and access to scripture but even liturgical language had become the exclusive property of those with privileged educations. A vigorous appropriation of language "from below" is evident in the many instances of popular initiative in iconoclastic riots, especially at Basel and Wittenberg and to a lesser extent at Zurich, where town councils were slow to implement the removal of images.

Auditory participation in worship represented simultaneously a new relation to the language of liturgy and an essentially political appropriation of the spiritual equality of believers. A new elitism of the word, cutting across boundaries of class and education, characterized the Protestant reform in Switzerland and Germany. At Strasbourg a group of burghers petitioned the town council to move beyond its initial hesitant removal of some of the art of the churches. Signed by a fisherman, a member of the draper's guild, a carpenter, and three other unidentified men, the petition read, in part:

We see all images as evil, for they appeal not to the perfected Christians but to the weak and those whom the word has not yet possessed.[36]

The focal point of services in Lutheran and reformed churches was the preaching of the word. The Zurich reform began with Zwingli's decision to preach through the New Testament.[37] Using only the Greek text in the pulpit, he expounded verse by verse, with amazing results. For Luther also, it was the spoken word, the word read aloud and preached, that carried the strongest potential for confronting, for exposing, and for justifying the hearer. Luther even said on occasion that ideally the scriptures should not have been written. On paper, the word loses its quality of proclamation: "Christ did not command the apostles to write, but only to preach";[38] "the Gospel should not be written but screamed." [39]

The stripping of altars, and eventually their removal and the substitution of bare communion tables, were also prompted by the desire to focus the attention of the congregation on the words of preaching and liturgy. Like images and statues, the elaborately carved, draped, and decorated altars had distracted worshippers from attending to the language of the service. The traditional retable altars, placed against a wall, did not permit the celebrant to face the people during the mass. The bare communion table permitted the celebrant to face the congregation, no lavish adornment distracting attention from his words.

As at the Grossmünster, the more or less drastic alteration of existing churches was the usual solution for Lutheran and reformed worship. Throughout the sixteenth century the Protestant reform produced little new church building.[40] The earliest example in all Europe of a surviving Protestant ecclesiastical building is the small Schloss Chapel in Torgau, Germany (Fig. 19). This rectangular building with galleries is white-plastered, its only color consisting of moldings and ribs of gray stone. Its furnishings are plain, comprising an altar, baptismal font, organ, and pulpit. The altar, supported by four carved pillars, holds no relics; a painted altarpiece depicting the Last Supper was added after the dedication of the building. The only other decorations in the church are the polychromed carvings on the pulpit by Simon Schröther, depicting three scenes: Simeon and the infant Christ, the child Jesus preaching to the doctors in the temple, and Christ driving the money changers out of the temple.

The extreme visual simplicity of reformation churches was maintained, to a greater or lesser degree, even in larger churches in Protestant territories. Their lecture-hall appearance was created largely by "the care taken to eliminate all pillars and columns and any hierarchical division between one portion of the building and another." [41] In the Schloss Chapel, the galleries, originally designed to separate the rulers from the people, were used by the time the building was completed, simply to contain larger numbers of worshippers. In earlier buildings, space had been broken up into private side chapels from which the nave and high altar were minimally visible, and private masses, or masses for small groups, often went on at the same time as a celebration at the high altar. [42] In the Schloss Chapel, the galleries permitted a greater number of people to hear and see the service. The unity of the worshippers in Protestant places of worship was also reinforced by the removal of the choir screens.

The elimination of the traditional barrier between clergy and laypeople must have been very striking to people accustomed to worshipping in buildings that visually reinforced social, ecclesiastical, and spiritual distinctions wherever the eye turned. Medieval congregations worshipped in churches whose architecture and lexicon of images expressed the subtle yet nonnegotiable hierarchies of the spiritual world. The placement of images of Christ, the Virgin, saints, prophets, and martyrs within the church followed a traditional pattern which immediately told the worshipper the relative significance of the figure. Social hierarchies, reflecting the cosmic hierarchy, were also an integral aspect of church buildings. The ruler, as reflection and representative of God; the wealthy and nobility, with their special relation to particular saints as depicted in the chapels they donated and decorated; and the people, standing together in the crowded apse, all reflected and reinforced the social distinctions of everyday life in the spatial and visual experience of worship. The spatial relationship of a person's body to the other bodies in the church was, at the most unconscious level, the communication of a message received by the whole community. This message was more than visual; it was the total synesthetic experience of spatial relationships in architecture and images, felt in the relationship of one's body to other bodies and to the architectural setting.

The concept of hierarchy is primarily visual. It is impossible to paint a scene without giving to the various figures, landscape, and buildings of the scene a particular hierarchical relationship. The foreground figure or figures dominate, either in size or in placement at the focal point, the supporting figures and background. Although details of the painting may be beautiful and worthy in themselves of lengthy perusal, the total painting clearly presents a scene in which some figures are more important than others. The organization of a visual space requires hierarchical arrangement. For medieval worshippers, visually engaged in worship, the message received from single paintings or mosaics as well as from the arrangement of the whole visual field must have strongly reinforced ecclesiastical, social, and familial hierarchies.

As reformation churches were stripped of their images, sculptures, choir screens, and altars, they were simultaneously stripped of their nonverbal presentations of spiritual and social hierarchy. The unity of the congregation and the rejection of social and ecclesiastical hierarchies patterned after a carefully graded hierarchy of saints as intermediaries between people and Christ were the primary visual message of Protestant churches. Private devotions, carried on before a particular painting or statue while the mass was being recited inaudibly by a priest, were rejected in favor of the great unifying force of the word, attended to by all members of the congregation. Before the word, each worshipper was simultaneously saint and sinner, without distinction — though not without individuality — in the worship service.

Congregational singing, associated with reforming movements since the fourteenth century, further affirmed the unity of verbal participation, the one voice of the congregation. Luther's complaint about the many activities of late-medieval worship, variously attended to by various persons, demonstrates his sense of the value of a service in which each participates, undistracted, in the same verbal activity at the same time:

Alas, the word "service of God" has nowdays taken on so strange a meaning and usage that whoever hears it thinks not of these works of God, but rather of the ringing of bells, the wood and stone of churches, the incense pot, the flicker of candles, the mumbling in the churches, the gold, silver, and precious stones of the vestments of choirboys and celebrants, of chalices and monstrances, processions and church-going, and, most of all, of the babbling of lips and the rattling of rosaries. This, alas, is what the service of God means now. Of such service God knows nothing at all, while we know nothing but this. We chant the Magnificat daily, to a special tone and with gorgeous pomp; and yet, the oftener we sing it, the more we silence its true meaning and music. Yet the text stands firm.[43]

Suggestions of at least two different, and ultimately conflicting, interests in Protestant reformations arise even from a cursory examination of the iconoclasm of the reform. Leaders of the magisterial reforms, although themselves identifying images as subversive of reformed liturgy — the service centering on the word — only gradually came to understand the connection of the contemporary movements of social unrest and rejection of social and ecclesiastical hierarchies with rejection of images in public worship. As educated language users for whom the powerful messages of the stripped and whitewashed churches were modified by verbal insistence that the equality of Christians was limited to a spiritual equality, they did not initially realize the impact on visually oriented people of the removal of visual reinforcement of hierarchies.

For people for whom the word had been the privileged prerogative of an educated ecclesiastical elite, however, participation in linguistic culture was immediately grasped as a means toward social and political equality. The destruction of the old visual worship by the removal of images, then, was a concrete way of claiming equality. And equality, even though insistently presented by reforming leaders as spiritual equality only, is addictive. People accustomed to receiving from their church a message reinforcing hierarchical social arrangements received from the newly stripped and whitewashed churches an intoxicating sense of this-worldly equality as well.

Sixteenth-century people destroyed images not because they loved them too little or were indifferent to them but because they loved them too much and found themselves too attached to them. The enthusiasm of recent converts is evident in the popular iconoclasm of the Protestant reformation. Images in churches reinforced social and spiritual hierarchies and subliminally persuaded people to accept their place in hierarchical arrangements. Sixteenth-century people who had been primarily image users could rid themselves of their conditioning only by ridding themselves of images.

"Whether I will or not," Luther wrote, "when I hear of Christ, an image of a man hanging on a cross takes form in my heart, just as the reflection of my face naturally appears in the water when I look into it." [44] For Luther, this automatic formation of an image was not as distressing as it was for others. Andreas Bodenstein von Karlstadt, Luther's senior colleague at the University of Wittenberg, was more sensitive to the psychological attachment to images that could effectively undermine one's concentration on language. Karlstadt's insistence on immediate and violent destruction of images was one of the disagreements that led to his rift with Luther. He gives a poignant account of his attachment to images, illustrating the wry acknowledgment of the Catholic reformer Johannes Molanus that even scholars are affected by images.[45] Karlstadt's statement is also an insightful description of the frequently unconscious power of images:

My heart since childhood has been brought up in the veneration of images, and a harmful fear has entered me which I would gladly rid myself of, and cannot . . . When one pulls someone by the hair, then one notices how firmly his hair is rooted. If I had not heard the spirit of God crying out against the idols, and not read His Word, I would have thought thus: "I do not love images." "I do not fear images." But now I know how I stand in this matter in relation to God and the images, and how firmly and deeply images are rooted in my heart.[46]

Zwingli's support for rather than leadership in the stripping of Zurich churches provides an interesting example. Zwingli claimed to derive more aesthetic pleasure than others from images: "There is no one who is a greater admirer of paintings, statues, and images than I." [47] But aesthetic appreciation is not the same thing as conditioned attachment. Zwingli's support for iconoclasm came from his realization that images were to others what music was to him — an attraction so powerful that it irresistibly drew attention away from worship.[48] His zeal in excluding all music from worship services was unmatched by any other reformer and entirely uncharacteristic of the Protestant reform.

This kind of attachment is not consciously chosen; it is not aesthetic appreciation; and it is consistently interpreted as "dualistic" by people who have not experienced the "pull by the hair" of a particular art form. For Zwingli, a thoroughly trained musician and composer skilled in performance on the harp, lute, viol, flute, reedpipe, and cornet, it was impossible not to attend to the structure and performance of the music during worship. He continued to enjoy music at other times but prohibited music from public worship in Zurich. The great organ of the Grossmünster was dismantled and destroyed; even congregational singing did not reappear in Zurich until the end of the sixteenth century.[49]

The indifference of educated reforming leaders to visual images often made the physical removal of images irrelevant or of a low priority in relation to reforming agenda. It was not so for people who had been primarily image users, whose self-images and ideas of community, universe, and God had been visually informed.

Catholic Reform

Similar theological ideas, evangelical zeal, and commitment to public education characterize both Roman Catholic and Protestant reforms in western

Europe. There is also evidence of a similar concern with increasing auditory participation in liturgy, preaching, and religious instruction. However, sixteenth-century instances of iconoclastic activity in Catholic territories are isolated and rare.[50] Iconoclastic attitudes, especially anxiety about lavish church decoration, can occasionally be found in the writings of Catholic reformers. But the absence of any significant iconoclastic activity, instigated either by leaders or by the general population, meant that Roman Catholic Christians never worshipped in churches without images.[51]

Although images were not removed from churches, existing churches were frequently modified according to reforming ideas in Catholic territories. In the second half of the sixteenth century, naves were widened, side chapels lost depth, and worshippers were concentrated in the large central area where they were better able to see and hear. Pulpits were also placed a third to half of the way down the nave, among the worshippers, for greater projection of the preacher's voice. Often the choir, which traditionally separated worshippers from clergy, was eliminated.[52] New churches built during the century were designed for greater visibility and audibility. Most frequently they developed the Renaissance central-plan church in which "the faithful are placed in a completely new position ... in more direct and intimate contact with the scene of the religious service ... and with the altar, instead of being cut off from it."[53]

The Chiesa del Gesù (completed in 1584), mother church of the new Jesuit order, became the model for Jesuit churches all over the world (Fig. 17). Johannes Molanus, the contemporary theologian of sixteenth-century Roman Catholic art and architecture, called it an image of heaven on earth[54] and an argument for the presence of God in the mass.[55]

Architecturally, the building demonstrates the concern of Catholic reformers for preaching to large congregations:

The Jesuits cultivated the art of conversion and salvation through preaching, wrote books on how to learn to preach, and became, in fact, the greatest preachers of the time. The Gesù is a great hall for Jesuit preaching and a pulpit is still prominent in the nave.[56]

But the Gesù and the dozens of churches modeled on it could never be mistaken for a lecture hall.[57] Even before the decoration of the Gesù was completed nearly a century after it was begun, an English visitor to the church in 1620 wrote of it:

Wherein is inserted all possible inventions, to catch men's affections and to ravish their understanding: as first, the gloriousness of their Altars, infinit number of images, priestly ornaments, and the divers actions they use in that service; besides the most excellent and exquisite Musicke of the

◆ 109

world, that surprizes our eares. So that whatsoever can be imagined, to express either Solemnitie or Devotion, is by them used.[58]

There was apparently a difference of opinion among the Jesuits themselves on the subject of lavish church decoration.[59] The Jesuit Peter Canisius argued in 1579 that churches could be richly decorated, even though in 1558 a ruling on Jesuit churches had stipulated that they should be "neither lavish nor overly decorated"; they were supposed, rather, "to inspire contemplation of poverty." [60] Protestant iconoclasm had caused Catholic reformers to rethink questions relating to religious architecture and images. In Catholic circles, since doctrines of Mary and the saints as mediators for living Christians were still accepted, the discussion was limited to the legitimacy of the enormous expense of decoration. Even though the Jesuits valued and extolled poverty, they were also educators, and it was the proven capacity of images to inform and train religious sensibilities that decided the issue.[61]

Another factor contributed to an early decision for lavish decoration of the Gesù. The strong influence of early christian architecture in Rome had come, as Battisti puts it, "to symbolize the rebirth of the empire and the religious power that for centuries had dominated the political plans of the Roman Curia and guided it to art patronage." [62] The presence of fourth-century churches in Rome and their association with the hierarchy of the Roman church led to the continuity of a monumental architecture and rich decorations whose essential features predate even Christianity itself. "Probably only the collapse of the papacy could have achieved a wholesale simplification of architectural decoration such as had taken place in northern Europe, where religious edifices came to have bare whitewashed walls and nothing more." [63]

Worship in the Gesù by the beginning of the seventeenth century did not, if we are to believe the impressions of the English tourist quoted above, miss any opportunity, auditory or visual, to engage the senses of the worshipper. The worshipper was placed bodily in relation to a visually articulated spiritual universe. The present earth-bound gravity of the individual worshipper was emphasized by his or her physical location beneath whirling scenes of heavenly bliss in which saintly human beings, angels, scriptural figures, and putti achieved a weightlessness that translated the ultimate goal of the spiritual life into visual terms.[64]

It is only, however, in the liturgy that the building can be adequately experienced. A tourist, wandering around among other individuals and small groups of people, is likely to feel dwarfed, overwhelmed, dizzy, even crushed, ironically, by the weightless spiritual universe surrounding her. In the liturgy three important orienting processes occur which, taken together, form an effective relation between the worshipper and the architecture. First, words — spoken and heard language — balance the potentially overpowering visual engagement. Auditory participation relieves the sense of the visual overload. Second, the role of the celebrant and the priests is to embody, to act out, as well as verbally connect a concrete relation between the worshipper and the sacred world. The procession of vested priests to the altar, the words and gestures of the liturgy of the word, the sermon, which translates into practical challenge and reassurance the words of scripture and the scenes of suffering and ecstasy — all specify the relation of the individual worshipper to the spiritual world.

Third, the Gesù, like the vast fourth-century basilicas, must be experienced in a great crowd.[65] Only in the midst of a throng of other human beings is the body of an individual worshipper adequately related to the spatial dimensions of the Gesù. A tourist cannot escape a voyeuristic relation to the building. Nor can a single individual avoid feeling lost and insignificant in the stronger beauty, energy, and timelessness of the spiritual world made visible. The life-sized human body feels simultaneously gravid and insubstantial in this visible world. Human values, even the ultimate commonsense value of self-preservation, melt in the strength of the spiritual values depicted: self-sacrifice, losing all to gain all, even martyrdom, the ultimate affront to human values. Yet, experienced as a member of a vast throng of human beings, united in the activity of worship, human life recovers its significance, strength, and beauty, not over against but within the spiritual world, and becomes an adequate ballast for the architectural setting. What was initially too much, too vast, too overpowering, now appears intimate, knowable, manageable, and *for the sake of* human beings. The whirling visible environment now becomes an interpretation of the meaning and goal of human life that gives it articulation as well as its most comprehensive scope.

The spiritual world, the unseen world rendered visible in the Gesù, is not, however, a chaotic world. It is, despite the dramatic diversity of the figures, an orderly world in which depicted events are located in the building according to their relative significance. Visual depiction of an orderly spiritual universe implies and necessitates hierarchy. The living worshippers, standing on the floor of the church, are pointedly contrasted with the whirling figures of the vault. But these figures are also contrasted with the figures of the central pair of chapels, the Trinity and Angel Chapels, the "spiritual inhabitants of the heaven of heavens." [66] The accessibility of the spiritual world is perceived simultaneously with the perception of its great distance from the ordinary concerns of human life.

Between the worshipper and the "Trinity worshipped by archangels" stands first the living clergy, then saints — such as Saint Ignatius and Saint Andrew — who have died; then come the apostles and finally the trumpeting angels of the Angel Chapel. This spiritual hierarchy was understood positively as describing the steps by which one could reach the triune center of spiritual power. It was seen as holding together, not holding apart, as a way of making visibly explicit the connection of living human beings with God.

The imaginative reconstruction of the different experiences of worship in the whitewashed Grossmünster of Zurich and the Chiesa del Gesù of Rome indicates profound differences in the messages likely to have been received by worshippers in these churches. In both churches, reform of the liturgy took the form of increased efforts to make the service of the word audible and forceful. In the Protestant church, however, a sense of spiritual autonomy and equality was one of the primary messages received. The absence of a visualized spiritual hierarchy and visible social and clerical hierarchies in this building was combined with a rhetoric emphasizing the immediate access of the Christian, by faith, to salvation. Simultaneously justified and sinful, as were all the saints and scriptural figures, the other worshippers, and the officiating clergy, the Protestant worshipper was subliminally encouraged by the visual context of worship as well as explicitly urged by preaching to look to no other human being — living or dead — for spiritual help.

The sudden removal of visible hierarchies together with the teaching of spiritual equality of all believers caused problems for which the Protestant reformers were unprepared. The Peasant's War in Germany was only the most pointed example of the widespread social unrest that drew strong statements from leaders of the magisterial reforms concerning the necessity for social order and the limitation of the concept of equality to spiritual equality. Despite theological principles that required the removal of images from Protestant churches, reforming leaders soon recognized the relationship between unauthorized destruction of images and popular demands for social and political rights. More fearful of iconoclastic riots than of the danger of images, Zwingli preached against images for nearly a year without advocating the removal of a single image from the Grossmünster. Luther argued that images, once eradicated from the heart, need not be removed from the eyes. Accused of conservatism, if not of hypocrisy, by the iconoclastic Karlstadt, Luther replied in his treatise *Against the Heavenly Prophets in the Matter of Images and Sacraments*: "I seek to tear [images] out of the hearts of all and want them despised and destroyed ... I have allowed and not forbidden the outward removal of images, so long as this takes place without rioting and uproar and is done by the proper authorities." [87]

The distinction between spiritual and social equality so carefully maintained by the magisterial reformers was, however, abolished in another branch of the Protestant reformation, the so-called Anabaptist movement. The two main groups of Anabaptists emerged in areas specifically associated with violent iconoclasm; one of the largest groups came from Zwingli's Zurich, the location of the earliest and most thorough iconoclasm, and the other from the Peasant's War, associated with an iconoclasm encouraged and participated in by Karlstadt. It is tempting to speculate that the rejection by Anabaptists of the authority of secular leaders in religious matters was fostered by worship in locations in which visualizations of spiritual hierarchies were absent. The close association of the experience of worship in stripped and whitewashed churches and the Anabaptists' insistence on spiritual autonomy and equality is undeniable. Both their strict biblicism[68] and their commitment to a confessional church could have been initiated or strengthened by the experience of imageless worship rather than primarily by rhetorical persuasion. The greatest problem of the Protestant reformers, the problem of authority, could have come from the elimination of visual hierarchies as much as or more than from a rhetoric of spiritual equality that was "misunderstood" by the uneducated to imply political and social justice.

Images, Education, and Propaganda: The Protestant Reform

That the message intended by Protestant leaders was not one of antinomian spiritual and social autonomy was one of the most prominent and constant themes of the verbal messages of the Protestant reformers. Each of the Protestant magisterial reformers experienced anxiety about having initiated something, which they could no longer control.[69] They were quickly and increasingly made aware of the potential irresponsibility with which people would translate into concrete action ideas designed for academic discussion. Not trained to discount, modify, or argue against a presented "position," these German peasants, newly converted to formulating and evaluating experience linguistically instead of visually, startled Luther and other reformers who apparently expected to continue to preach against the cult of saints and images in churches loaded with such images.

As would any trained scholar of his time, Luther put his thesis in its strongest and least ambiguous form so that other scholars could then attack, argue, rebut, and finally come to a consensus on a modified statement of the thesis. Popular involvement with reformation ideas, however, meant that the rhetoric of reformers was taken seriously and literally by people whom Luther did not hesitate, on more than one occasion, to call "lawless beasts." Luther, Zwingli, Oecolampadius in Basel, and Bucer in Strasbourg were pressingly aware of the need for education as a form of social control.[70] The somewhat warranted paranoia of Protestant reforming leaders over the difference between messages intended — reform of language in liturgy and piety — and messages received — an invitation to spiritual and social equality — was expressed as a systematic and concerted effort for public education.

Protestant efforts to educate were addressed to both adults and youth; adults were bad, but youth were worse:

Never has youth been more insolent than today — we see how little they obey, how little they respect their parents. On this account, undoubtedly, is the world full of plagues, war, rebellion, and other evils.[71]

The response of Lutheran leaders to the dangerous intractability of the young was efficient education:

Use the knife of God's word to cut off the branches of their contumacious will. Raise them in the fear of God. And when their wild nature comes up again — as weeds always will — and the old Adam sins in them again, kill it and bury it deep in the ground, lest the newly grown good nature once more revert to its wild state.[72]

The new, systematic education of the Protestant reform, in contrast to the earlier education of children in the home and in monastery and cathedral schools, was concentrated on education in language use. A handbook on the education of children, written in 1419 by the Florentine Dominican Giovanni Dominici, had described how fifteenth-century children ought to be taught respect for religion:

The first regulation is to have pictures of saintly children or young virgins in the home, in which your child, still in swaddling clothes, may take delight and thereby may be gladdened by acts and signs pleasing to childhood . . . Make of such pictures a sort of temple in the house.[73]

By contrast, Protestant reformation education emphasized language.[74] Christoph Vischer wrote in 1578:

. . . all parents are obliged on danger of losing their souls to teach the catechism to their children and domestic servants. Every day, let your children recite the main articles of the catechism, taking care that they speak clearly and pronounce distinctly. Ask them also what they remember from last Sunday's sermon, and, if they remember nothing, admonish them to pay closer attention. And if kind words don't help, take the stick to them or give them nothing to eat and drink for supper until they have repeated something from the sermon.[75]

Adults as well as children required, according to Luther, constant badgering: "We must exhort, admonish, and nag with all our power and diligence and care."[76] The means for this barrage of words was provided in multiple media: preaching, pastoral instruction and catechetical examination, written treatises, and the new printed mass media — pamphlets, which early in the sixteenth century replaced the traditional bulletin board on the church door for medieval publicity.[77] The importance of printed media to the reformation in Germany led Luther to remark that printing is "God's highest and extremest act of grace, whereby the business of the Gospel is driven forward."[78]

Steven Ozment estimates that more than ten thousand different pamphlets appeared in the first half of the sixteenth century, about half published anonymously or pseudonymously. They communicated information and instruction in print and cartoons "in a language and style ordinary people could identify with and understand." [79] But could people read? Gerald Strauss cites the Lutheran campaign to promote domestic instruction, which is described in the extant mandate and visitation records in Protestant territories, as evidence for his conclusion that "the ability to read with fair facility was evidently much more widespread in sixteenth-century German society than is ordinarily recognized. General illiteracy would have made nonsense of the Lutheran endeavor to promote domestic instruction." [80] In addition, Ozment points out that pamphlets were "designed to succeed as well when heard as when read"; [81] they were read and their contents discussed in churches, at social gatherings, and on street corners. [82]

Despite the new interest in public communication by means of language, printed images were not absent from pamphlets or from Luther's German Bible, published in 1534. [83] Luther urged the inclusion of illustrative images in the first edition of his translation. Printed images did not carry the same dangers as large, painted images. They did not invite devotional adoration, they did not become part of the liturgy by virtue of being placed in a significant position within a church building, and they could be very decisively denoted to keep idiosyncratic interpretation at a minimum.

Protestant reformers were too interested in education to entirely reject printed images. Luther himself argued from the acceptance of printed images, even by iconoclasts, to the validity of painted images:

I have myself seen and heard the iconoclasts read out of the German Bible . . . Now there are a great many pictures in those books, both of God, the angels, men, and animals, especially in the revelation of John and in Moses and Joshua. So now we would kindly beg them to permit us to do what they themselves do. Pictures contained in these books we would paint on walls for the sake of remembrance and better understanding, since they do no more harm on walls than in books. It is, to be sure, better to paint pictures on walls of how God created the world, of how Noah built the ark, and whatever other good stories there may be, than to paint shamelessly worldly things. Yes, would to God I could persuade the rich and the mighty that they would permit the whole Bible to be painted on houses, on the inside and outside, so that all could see it. That would be a Christian work. [84]

But for most Protestants, this was a highly questionable conclusion. [85] Printed images were unobjectionable for the reasons we have discussed, while painted images, especially in churches, distracted from the spoken word. Moreover, the new techniques of woodcutting and engraving that enabled printed images to be mass-produced were less vividly sensuous and representational forms than was oil painting. Erasmus praised Dürer's engravings as a conceptual or rational art. Dürer, he wrote,

accurately observes proportions and harmonies. Nay, he even depicts what
cannot be depicted; fire, rays of light, thunderstorms, sheet lightning, or even,
as the saying is, the clouds upon the wall; all the characters and emotions;
in fine, the whole mind of man as it shines forth from the appearance of the
body, and almost the very voice. These things he places before our eyes by
most felicitous lines, black ones at that, in such a manner that, were you
to spread on colors you would injure the work. And is it not more wonderful
to accomplish without the blandishments of colors what Apelles accomplished
only with their aid? [86]

The Protestant reformers, despite a diversity of practical attitudes toward images and a more or less adequate appreciation of the power of images to visually mediate religious and social conditioning, were eager to use images for reformation education and propaganda. But they sought to harness the didactic and persuasive capacity of images without permitting them to act directly — that is, without adequate linguistic interpretation — on the unconscious minds of Protestants.

The role of images in the Protestant reformation was to accompany, illustrate, and reinforce verbal education. Images were always to be balanced with verbal instruction, a role understood well by artists affected by reformation ideas. Dürer wrote:

The art of painting is made for the eyes, for sight is the noblest sense . . .
A thing you behold is easier of belief than [one] that you hear; but whatever
is both heard and seen we grasp more firmly and lay hold on more securely.
I will therefore continue the word with the work and thus I may be the
better understood.[87]

Limited to the function of illustration of verbal instruction, printed images flourished in the Protestant territories. "Where the reformation was, and continued to be, accepted, every nation, every region, every sect, every social group, even every artistic personality developed both its own kind of Protestantism and its own kind of art." [88]

New subjects and themes lent themselves to the emphasis of the Protestant reformations on the personal and unmediated appropriation of justification. The saga of Adam and Eve, alone and disoriented in a newly created world, was one of the most popular themes of the sixteenth century in Germany (Fig. 20). Portraits of living reformers,[89] businessmen, scholars, and their wives largely replaced the earlier iconic representations of Mary and the saints. While saints were still painted throughout the reformation in Protestant territories, they were treated in a naturalistic style that augmented their interpretation as "moral and practical examples of christian living" [90] rather than as a means or method of access to salvation.[91] The most popular subjects for altarpieces were the Last Supper and the crucifixion.[92] Scenes of the Last Judgment lost the fascination they had held for late-medieval people; instead, depictions of the suffering human Christ — "ecce homo" — was an often-painted image.[93] "The Last Judgment is abolished," Luther proclaimed in a sermon preached on September 7, 1538, "it concerns the believer as little as it does the angels ... All believers pass from this life into heaven without any judgment." [94]

Nonrepresentational symbols were also used in Protestant art. Luther described in detail his seal, intended as a visual statement of his theology, in a 1530 letter to Lazarus Spengler. A black cross on a white heart was meant to signify that

although this cross is black and mortifies and must also cause pain, it never-theless leaves untouched the color of the heart ... it does not kill but gives life ... However, this cross must be set in a white rose to indicate that faith gives joy, consolation, and peace and, in brief, places us in a pure and joyous rose ... Then the rose is set against a background of heavenly blue ... And around the field there is a golden ring as a sign that the bliss of heaven lasts for eternity and is endless.[95]

The advent of Protestantism, then, was far from the end of the arts in Protestant territories,[96] but its immediate effect was to drastically curtail the quantity of religious images. "The painter's profession is in a bad way," complained Hans Holbein in 1526; in several towns, members of the painters' and sculptor's guilds petitioned the town council to provide them with sec-ular work so that they would not be forced either to adopt another profession or to emigrate.

Protestant public education — education in language use — was, however, largely unsuccessful in the short run. Many people, initially excited with the possibility of appropriating and participating in the linguistic culture, quickly became disenchanted. The difficulty encountered by Protestant educators was not clearly recognized by modern scholars until the 1978 publication of Gerald Strauss's book *Luther's House of Learning*. Strauss studied parish visitation records that give a detailed picture of the passive resistance en-countered by Lutheran pastors and teachers of a "vigorous religious subcul-ture." [97] Parish visits, recommended by Luther, by teams of four territorial and municipal authorities — two to examine the economic and two the re-ligious affairs of the parish — sought to ferret out and punish resistance to the demands of an authoritative verbal culture and creed. The 1528 *Instruc-tions for the Visitors of Parish Pastors in Electoral Saxony*[98] gives a resume of the activities by which reforming leaders thought the reforms were resisted:

Whenever a visitation takes place in our town and villages, respondents shall be required, under threat of severe punishment to report and enumerate to the visitors whether there are to be found among them any blasphemers and adulterers, fornicators, gamblers, drunkards, idlers, or loafers, disobedient sons and daughters, and others of the same sort, leading a wicked life and exhibiting the outward signs of an evil nature. Also any people suspected of Anabaptism or of abusing the holy sacraments by Zwinglianism. Also any who mutter against the government and oppose it as if it were not a power ordained by God. All such are to be reported by name.[99]

Parish visitors were also instructed to be on the alert for "soothsayers, cunning women, crystal-gazers, casters of spells, witches, and other practitioners of the forbidden arts." If an educational program is effective in generating the assent of the large majority of a culture, we can expect to hear little about coercion. If the catechism of Caspar Aquila, *Des Kleinen Catechismi Erklerung*, for example, had done its job of training a child to grasp both her nonnegotiable sinfulness and the extreme conscientiousness with which she must overcome it with God's help and by education, we would not be confronted with the phenomenon of witch-hunting in sixteenth-century Protestant Germany.[100]

Images, Education, and Propaganda: The Roman Catholic Reform

The Council of Trent, which sought to reform and standardize Roman Catholic doctrine and liturgy, took up the question of images in its twenty-fifth session in December 1563. The council defined a proper use of images and proscribed subjects apt to cause or reinforce dangerous dogmatic errors. Such images had been common in medieval art; only occasionally did a medieval theologian question the use of an image with indisputable devotional value on the grounds that it was antidogmatic or unscriptural.[101] Images of the Trinity as incarnate in the Virgin's womb, the Virgin fainting at the crucifixion, the child Jesus carrying a cross, and depictions of the Trinity with a crucified and dead Christ were commonplace, accepted for their devotional effectiveness. All these images were proscribed for churches by the Council. But even after these proscriptions, nonscriptural and antidogmatic images were not removed from churches that already contained them, nor was the dictum of the Council always enforced in the case of new images.[102]

Moreover, the Council was concerned only with images in churches, associated with liturgy, not with private devotional images. No destruction of images identified as antidogmatic was carried out, other than the occasional quiet removal of a painting here or there by clergy. Johannes Molanus, who wrote a 1570 handbook on religious art that became the standard textbook of the seventeenth century, interpreted the Council's reticence on earlier religious images as "proof that none of the existing images in churches were dangerous." [103]

Despite the Council's recognition of the need for reform of images, the value of images in public worship was affirmed:

. . . not that any divinity or virtue is believed to be in them by reason of which they are to be venerated or that something is to be asked of them, or that trust is to be placed in images, as was done of old by the Gentiles who placed their hope in idols; but because the honor which is showed them is referred to their prototypes which they represent, so that by means of the images which we kiss and before which we uncover the head and prostrate ourselves, we adore Christ and venerate the saints whose likeness they bear.[104]

The Council, in its capacity as a reforming body, also recognized the need for the balancing of visual and verbal aspects of worship by renewed attention to effective preaching. Session twenty-four, near the end of the Council's meetings, described the obligations of bishops and priests to preach as their "chief duty." [105] But the attempt of the Protestant reformers to suppress the earlier image-centered worship and to replace it with an exclusively linguistic worship did not have a counterpart in the Roman Catholic reform. There was no sharp disjunction between late-medieval worship and reformed worship in the Catholic church such as occurred in the Protestant territories. Fifteenth-century Italy was used to good preaching, both in and outside of the liturgy. Great preachers like Bernardino da Siena, a Dominican Observant, and Savanarola often preached for hours to spellbound crowds in churches or public squares. The Council of Trent, in requiring a general improvement in preaching, identified and encouraged rather than originated a trend already in process.

Nor did linguistic public education play a role in the Catholic reform similar to the emphasis it received by Protestants. Catholic educational reform came slowly and, in the sixteenth century, did not attempt mass education but primarily sought improvement in the education of clergy.[106] No concerted effort at mass literacy characterized the Catholic reform, and there was no promotion of independent reading of the Bible by lay persons.[107] All attempts to promote the linguistic aspect of Catholic faith and worship were directed at a balance of word and image rather than at the intensification of one to the exclusion of the other.

New uses of images in the Catholic reform for propaganda and education were striking and effective. Sanctuary art, devotional images, and a strongly

◆ 119

intensified inspirational art appeared in the second half of the sixteenth century and throughout the seventeenth century.[108]

We have considered the skillful coordination of painting, sculpture, and architecture in the Chiesa del Gesù in Rome. A similar integration of the spatial and figurative arts to produce a unified visual context for the liturgy characterizes the church buildings of the Catholic reform. As if in answer to the self-consciously imageless buildings of the Protestant reform, these churches exhibit a renewed and refined skill at creating a visual environment. In the Gesù, the vault above the nave (Fig. 18) exhibits flying human and angel figures that intermingle in a radiance of light. In the center of the vault, this light appears to be so intense that separate figures cannot be seen;[109] figures are differentiated only in the outer and lower areas of the vault. Stucco figures on the edges burst out of the gold picture frame that encloses the vault painting and act as intermediaries between the flying figures of the vault and the human worshippers below. Similarly at Santa Maria della Vittoria in Rome, in the Corona Chapel, life-sized sculptured members of the Cornaro family gently lean out into the church from the shallow balcony against the wall, three-dimensional figures that relate worshippers to the events portrayed in free-standing sculptures and paintings. The viewer is no longer simply viewer, but is a participant in Bernini's *Ecstasy of St. Teresa* above the altar (Fig. 21).

Painted and sculpted images of the Catholic reform and the following century exhibit a new intensification of feeling in the portrayal of both new and traditional subjects. Figures in ecstasy — from Mary Magdalene to the recent founders of the Catholic reform orders, such as Saint Philip Neri and Saint Ignatius Loyola — are painted and sculpted with eyes raised to heaven, often even floating above the ground.[110] Nearly every order had a saint or founder who is depicted as permitted by the Virgin to hold the infant Christ, and Saint Bernard of Clairvaux is one of several saints shown receiving drops of milk from the Virgin's breast.[111]

In addition, the time-honored device for the intensification of the present moment, the *memoria mortis,* is ubiquitous in Catholic reform art. Saints are depicted meditating on death in the form of a skull, a motif also thoroughly explored in private devotional art.[112] The meditations on one's own death of Ignatius Loyola's *Spiritual Exercises* have been cited as the inspiration for the Catholic reform emphasis on meditation on death.[113] The *Exercises* are a formulation of Ignatius's own experience of meditation and they describe the tools he found useful. Fr. Bartomomea Ricci, in the *Vita D. N. Jesu Christi* (1607), wrote that "despite Ignatius' exceptional gift for meditation, 'nevertheless, whenever he was going to meditate on those mysteries of our Savior, shortly before his prayer he looked at the pictures that he had collected and displayed around the room for this purpose.' "[114] The powerful stimulus of visual objects and images for concentrated meditation was recognized by Catholic leaders and incorporated in churches as well as in private devotions.

The propaganda aspect of Catholic reform art is at its most pointed in images that affirmed those features of traditional piety criticized and rejected by Protestants. The triumphant church, trampling its heretical enemies, as in the Le Gros sculpture in the Ignatius Loyola Chapel at the Gesù (Fig. 22) is a general statement of the reaffirmation of tradition in the Catholic reform. Purgatory, the cult of Mary, the use of images in worship, and the cults of saints and martyrs are all explicitly affirmed in visual images. The Chapel of Pope Paul V in Santa Maria Maggiore in Rome, decorated in 1611, illustrates Catholic propaganda against the Protestant rejection of images. Two large scenes in the chapel, painted by Baglione, depict the anguished deaths of the medieval iconoclastic emperors of the Eastern church, Leo V and Constantine V.

Honor of the Virgin and honor of her images were bound together in iconographic and in verbal statements. On the hundredth anniversary of the founding of the Jesuit order, a centennial book published by the order stated: "We have resolved to particularly honor the Virgin, seeing that the heretics defame her and destroy her images." [115]

The cults of saints and martyrs were also affirmed by images that expressed the miraculous quality of their lives.[116] One of the earliest subjects of art in Jesuit churches and seminaries selected a traditional — but in the Renaissance underplayed — theme for newly detailed graphic treatment.[117] Depictions of the tortures and executions of martyrs, many of them painted by a favorite artist of late-sixteenth-century Jesuits, Niccolo Circignani — called Pomarancio (1517–1596) — repeatedly compare contemporary Jesuit missionary martyrs with martyrs of the pre-Constantinian persecutions of the christian church.

The sixteenth-century discovery of catacombs near Rome was a factor in promoting interest in martyrdom.[118] However, the unprecedented vividness and detail of Pomarancio's scenes suggest that the style as well as the content was primarily expressive of contemporary Jesuit martyrdoms in England, Asia, Africa, and the New World.[119]

Scenes of martyrdom, characterized by representational accuracy, were painted in the churches of San Vitale, the Gesù,[120] Santa Cecilia in Trastevere, San Lorenzo in Damaso, and others. But the earliest and most forceful use of the subject of torture and martyrdom was in Jesuit colleges for the training of novices. By 1581 the Jesuits had 144 colleges and 5,000 men. The training of these men for lives of sacrificial service, often to the point of martyrdom, was one of the highest priorities of the order. The first decorated Jesuit church in Rome, the Ss. Anunziata of the Collegio Romana, had over the high altar a painting of the Annunciation to the Virgin, but beginning in 1570, the year of the Society's first martyrs, chapels and other buildings of the colleges were decorated with vivid martyrdom scenes of immediate — almost newsreel — significance to Jesuits.[121]

In 1582–1583, thirty frescoes of martyrdom scenes were painted in the church of the German Hungarian College, Santo Stefano Rotondo. This church, still the largest circular church in the world and one of the oldest churches in Italy, was covered with the frescoes by Pomarancio and his assistants Matteo da Siena and Antonio Tempesta. In these lurid scenes of torture and slaughter, the severed limbs of dismembered saints are numbered, as in anatomical paintings of the time. The paintings are carefully described by rather lengthy inscriptions in Italian and Latin. Jesuit novices were instructed to memorize and mentally affix to each scene a short prose piece or poem of devotion. This program of simultaneous visual and verbal exercice was apparently highly effective in training Jesuit novices for a sacrificial life of contemplation in action.

These paintings are universally deplored by modern art historians. They are called "atrocious" by art historians and guide book writers alike,[122] illustrating the perhaps unbridgeable distance between modern aesthetic taste and sixteenth-century ideas of the function of art. Pope Sixtus V (1585–1590), a contemporary relates, burst into tears on seeing these frescoes. It must be remembered that actual torture and execution scenes were well within the common experience of sixteenth-century people, who frequently witnessed executions involving various forms of torture. What was distinctive and thus would have gripped the emotions was not the grisliness of the painted scenes but the sacrificial heroism of the victims.[123]

In the Catholic, as in the magisterial Protestant, reformation the educative, persuasive, or propagandistic techniques of reformers were underwritten by the repressive power of the state, the bottom line of persuasion. The human beings on whom education failed were persecuted as heretics or witches.[124] In spite of the tendency of modern historians to highlight the repressive aspect of the Catholic reform, however, the threatened or actual use of force to compel religious assent cannot explain the voluntary enthusiasm and popular support for the reform of the Roman Church.

The Success of the Sixteenth-Century Reformations

Our survey of the reformation of liturgy by adjustments in the roles of vision and hearing in worship led to a description of Protestant worship as featuring spiritual equality, the equidistance of each Christian from God. The whitewashed churches and lecture halls of Protestant communities did not so much reject visual participation in worship as provide a startlingly new visual experience in the absence of presentations of a hierarchically ordered universe as a setting for Christian worship. For people whose primary orientation to and participation in worship had been visual, the new visual situation was powerfully moving. For those who came to Protestant worship unprepared by preaching and teaching to see the positive implications of the absence of images, the stripped church was ugly; but for those who saw it as cleansed of spiritual and ecclesiastical hierarchies, the result was intoxicating.

The Protestant reform was successful in communicating the visual message of equality to people. As we have seen, the message given by reforming leaders was not intended to convey political and social equality, but this was the message received by many Protestants. Faced with the immediate translation of spiritual freedom, autonomy, and equality into the social and political arena by German people who were prepared to take seriously the messages received in worship locations, Luther was forced, ironically, to turn his powerful command of language to arguing for the centrality in the christian life of the "works" he had rejected as necessary for salvation. "It would be much better," he wrote in 1528, "to teach people to do good works and drop the sharp disputes." [125] The major losses of the magisterial reformation to Anabaptist groups indicate the inability of first-generation reforming leaders to connect effectively a sense of responsibility for a social and political status quo with the heady sense of religious autonomy and equality experienced by congregations in reformed liturgies. In churches whose spatial and visual qualities emphasized the unity of worshippers and their equal and direct access to God, people became impatient with political and social inequality.

In the social and political upheavals of the third decade of the sixteenth century, Lutheran reforms launched a concerted effort of mass education, an effort which, as we have seen, was resisted and which largely failed in the short run. However, people excited and gratified by the acquisition of a new skill had their own reasons for wanting to become literate. The supply of a variety of stimulating reading material on subjects of immediate general interest, provided by printing presses, was in the long run effective in creating a reading and listening public in German-speaking Protestant territories.

The ultimate success of the Protestant reform, then, came with the emergence of a language-oriented religion and culture. As people were gradually educated to attend more to the word than to visual images, as they became habituated to worship in churches in which no images presented spiritual hierarchy, the success of the Protestant reform in the creation of a new linguistic culture was assured. As printing stimulated auditory instruction that covered every aspect of life, the reading eye became the ancillary of the hearing ear; vision lost its centrality to religion as it became only incidentally engaged in worship and devotion. The medieval use of images for the construction of self-images and ideas of community, universe, and God was replaced by language use. Self-images, ideas, and behavior were conceived, formulated, and communicated verbally through pamphlets, by private and public reading of scripture, and by preaching. Over the course of a long and extensive education, attitudes and values could also be instilled or altered.

In the short run, the educational efforts of the Protestant reformers succeeded, if not with the larger population, at least in the training of a Protestant clergy. The Protestant reformation irreversibly established the expectation that a learned ministry was necessary for a proper preaching of Scripture. Preaching, understood as the construal of a text rather than as moral exhortation, made it essential that a pastor be educated enough to be capable of accurate scriptural hermeneutics and application. Protestant Christianity, notwithstanding its limited use of visual images for education and propaganda, became, often abruptly, a religion in which a Christian was trained increasingly to use the ears; if eyes were engaged in devotional piety, it was for reading. Images were no longer used at the points at which self-understanding, relationships within a community, and relationship to God are imagined and formulated.

Catholic reformers did not undertake a comparable alteration of the perceptive capacities of a whole society. In baroque churches such as the Gesù, a stable spiritual world was presented as the context of human life and worship. Architecture, painting, and sculpture achieved a strong message about the worshippers' place at the outer limits of the spiritual world but connected to it by many links in a trustworthy chain. The most characteristic themes of Catholic reform art are also related to the confirmation of celestial, spiritual, and, by implication, ecclesiastical and social hierarchies. Affirmation of the significance of Mary, ecstatic states of saints, and the heroic martyrdom of ancient and contemporary Christians — these subjects brought vividly to worshippers a sense of the varying degrees of participation in the spiritual universe.

The productivity of the Roman Catholic reform can be seen in the variety and prominence of new organizations dedicated simultaneously to spirituality and to committed service. In such a universe, the personal activity of an individual can at once effect change in the world and advance a person's participation in the spiritual life. Moreover, the new charitable and missionary movements of the Catholic reform were frequently originated not by those with a "vested interest" in maintaining and augmenting the Roman church but by laypeople newly inspired to commit themselves to self-sacrificing service. The undeniably youthful vigor of the Catholic reform took much more of its impetus from laypeople than from "attempts to promote reform from above." [126] Like Saint Ignatius Loyola, many of the leaders drew inspiration and nourishment from the powerful images of the Catholic reform. For people trained in the disciplined use of vision, the primary organ of the medieval Christian, the sixteenth-century art of ecstasy and suffering — ecstatic suffering — attracted large numbers of young people to the lives of service that placed them, as the Santo Stefano Rotondo frescoes made clear, on the same spiritual level with the saints and martyrs of the ancient church.[127] The spiritual universe, although hierarchical, was nevertheless infinitely permeable.

The crucial distinction between the reforms of the Roman Catholic Church and the Protestant reforms was not primarily theological but perceptual. The messages received visually by Catholic worshippers reaffirmed and reinforced hierarchical ecclesiastical and, by implication, social arrangements. In sixteenth-century Protestantism, the sacrifice of visual perceptions so central to the activity of worship and piety created a religious culture in which language use became pivotal. Both reforms were undermined as severely by their successes as by their failures; the business of a historian is ultimately not to evaluate but to understand, and discussions of religious change, if they aspire to convey something of the affective tensions of a former age, must always try primarily to formulate the sense of something lost and something gained.

◆ 6 ◆

Image and Language
in Contemporary Culture

We are what we look upon and what we desire.
PLOTINUS

From verbal evidence from the past, political history — man as actor — and intellectual history — man as thinker — can be reconstructed. But the history of people of the past who have not been trained to think of themselves as essentially structured by a verbal nucleus has not been available from the study of historic texts. I have therefore suggested that we must use the visual images of the past as historical evidence for the lives of historical people who were not primarily language users.

We have investigated several historical examples of the use of images for understanding people who themselves used these images to formulate ideas, attitudes, and a sense of relatedness within the community and the universe. In working with religious images available to whole communities in the churches that were the center of community life, we discussed the primary communication media of late-Roman, medieval, and Renaissance communities. In selecting not single paintings, mosaics, or frescoes but repeatedly depicted subjects, we explored images of continuing fascination and usefulness for historical people.

In this chapter we move on from historical examples. We begin by exploring the use of language and images in the media of contemporary North American culture. The traditional function of public media has been to

◆ 127

present ways of conceiving and managing physical existence and to offer ideas and images for the understanding of our relationships with other human beings, the community, and the world.

Our historical examples can give us perspective on our own cultural arrangements. Might our culture offer a more effective equilibrium between language and image that allows each to exercise more fully its capacity to orient and enrich human life? Moreover, although the test of a contemporary analysis is its accuracy and comprehensive treatment of the data with which it works, it must also answer to a further criterion. It must be therapeutic. We must recognize and understand ourselves more accurately by means of the analysis, and we must be helped to take up active attitudes toward a cultural complex in which, formerly, we had been simply immersed.

Two fundamental differences are immediately apparent when we compare the role of media images in our culture with historical religious images. First, contemporary images are secular; they represent secular values based on more or less immediate gratification or individual happiness. Specific reference to the origin or goal of human life is excluded from a secular perspective. Second, the way a contemporary viewer expects to interact with images is very different from the expectations of historical people. The viewer of an advertising image, for example, approaches the image with a conscious resistance to its claim that the product it promotes will make life more satisfying. From a news photograph, the contemporary person expects to receive information about current happenings, not life-orienting messages of timeless significance and value. The historical viewer, on the other hand, expected images to present a world in which reality and values were organized in an absolute, harmonized, and permanent configuration. The historical viewer expected to contemplate the image and be formed by it; he or she did not expect to receive information from it or to evaluate it critically.

Since we have defined media as those communications that are available to an entire community on a daily basis and used for the organization of values, attitudes, and ideas by members of the community, it is clear that modern religious images — museum art or illustrations in religious publications — do not play the role of "media" in our culture. Both of our criteria are met, however, as I have suggested, by press photographs and advertising images; they are available to everyone, and they explicitly present material for the formulation of self-images and for knowledge of the world. It is to these images, then, that we must look for one of the primary means by which a community of values is created and behavior is conditioned and coordinated in accordance with these values.

The first spot news pictures, reproduced by wood engraving and published in *Harper's Weekly*, were Roger Fenton's photographs of the Crimean War. By the end of World War I, tabloid newspapers, crowded with pictures, presented the reader with "a pictorial rather than a literary summary of the day's events."[1] The effectiveness of photographs in selling newspapers was immediately evident; an exceptionally newsworthy picture, prominently displayed, was and is able to increase circulation over normal figures by the thousands.[2] The first mass-media magazine, the photojournalistic *Life*, was started in 1936; it was financed not by sales but by advertising.[3]

There are two reasons for the immediate and continuing success of news photographs; photographs entertain and inform. But does a photograph present uninterpreted information about an event? Does it speak "the truth and nothing but the truth"?[4] A news photograph as we see it in our daily newspaper has gone through a complex process of selection and denotation. First, it has been selected from other photographs of the event it relates and other events. Not all newsworthy events lend themselves to photographic presentation. A meeting of the joint chiefs of staff may be of enormous significance to the nation and the world, but a photograph of it will not stimulate a newspaper's circulation. Accidents, disasters, crimes, and sports provide much of the contemporary daily diet of images, not because these events are more important than a meeting of the president's advisers but because they make more striking photographs.

The scene we see in the photograph also has been isolated from the event in which it occurred. It is taken from a particular angle that inevitably spotlights some features of the event and shades other features in darkness. Moreover, the photograph may have been treated to emphasize aspects not clearly delineated in the original.[5] Finally, a news picture is never allowed to speak simply in its own language as visual image; its caption directs and limits the interpretations that can plausibly be applied to it. Roland Barthes writes of the "repressive value" of the caption to "remote control the reader towards a meaning chosen in advance."[6] A photograph without denotation is not news but art.[7] Only its verbal denotation decisively removes its potential evocative ambiguity. The caption fixes the meaning of the photograph, ensuring that the public will in fact see what the photographer and the editor think it should see.

Accidents, disasters, crimes and sports — these images, severed from the emotions and physical experience of the human beings involved in them become the "devotional" material of millions of secular breakfast tables. In the evening, often in place of dinner-table conversation, another dose of media images, the television news, gives a reassuring sense — no matter how bad the news — that we are responsibly oriented to the real events of our world.

Both the negative images of news photography and the attractive images of advertising are in constant supply on the television screen. In an ironic reversal of the ancient theory of the visual ray, television rays reach out to

passive viewers by an X-radiation of such unknown and potentially dangerous consistency that its voltage has been repeatedly reduced by law.[8] Physio-
logically, television rays can cause eye damage and heart rate changes; psychologically, television is potentially addictive, offering safe and stimulating
surrogate experience.

But, we may protest, for the millions of Americans who participated by
means of television in the events surrounding John F. Kennedy's assassina-
tion or who experienced the exhilaration of the first moon landing, these
images were far from entertainment, and our involvement in the events they
recorded was far from passive. To the extent that television acts as a recorder
of events for those who are involved [9] emotionally and politically in those
events, television extends rather than circumvents engagement.[10] Moreover,
it was media films of the Vietnam War that motivated the demonstrations by
which the American public effectively protested the war. There is an enormous difference, however, between showing real events to which moral response is possible and the daily cumulative display of images to which no
effective emotional response or action is possible. To the extent that response
is stimulated and responsibly directed, press photographs and television can
indeed be a positive force for involving the public in social and political
action.

However, a voyeuristic relation to press images and films is inevitable because of the quantity of images we receive; we cannot respond to this quantity of images in any meaningful way. Instead of images acting as a record
for those involved, they are used as substitutes for experience, as "unexperi-
enced experience." [11] We become accustomed to watching violence and suffering about which we can do nothing and toward which we feel nothing.

It is tempting to identify in the interchange of message given and message
received an active and cynical power on the one hand and a passive, acted-
upon public on the other. However, ultimate responsibility for the violent
images that condition people to voyeurism can be located neither in those who
direct the communications media nor in a public that demands a daily ration
of titillating images. The communication of media images, rather, is organized and demanded by a complex of interests that Foucault described as
operating from a "myriad of tiny points."

The second type of image that is accessible to everyone in our society on a
daily basis is the advertising image. If the press photograph claims to present
uninterpreted and therefore accurate information about the world as it is,
the advertising image portrays the world as we would like it to be — offering
personal attractiveness, success, and happiness.

Advertising images are an example of "control by stimulation." [12] Beautiful models invite the viewer to take advantage of the toothpaste or cigarette
or dress that appears to have made the model's life one of continuous and

obvious bliss. In contrast to press photographs featuring sports, accidents, disasters, and crimes, advertising images offer a vision of unlimited fulfillment. In *Henderson the Rain King*, Saul Bellow writes of a man tormented by a cry within him, a voice that says, "I want, I want" but can never be begged, bribed, or bullied into saying *what* it wants. It is this infinite and undefined longing that advertising images address, parading before our eyes a variety of products each claiming to be the very thing, exactly what we want, the thing we have been missing. Advertising thus directs the inarticulate and unspecific desires of human beings to serve the culture's economy.

A great deal has been written on the sociology, psychology, and methodology of advertising. I will not summarize these studies but will examine the use of words and images in advertising art to analyze what messages are likely to be received from it.

Let us consider first the predominance of images in advertising. Very few advertisements consist simply of a linguistic text. Usually the image is dominant, the primary communication of the advertisement, while the text is in the subordinate role of interpreting the image. Because the advertisement is designed to channel a portion of individual and collective desire toward possession of the advertised product, the attracting image is more central to the communication than is the verbal text. Historical people found images effective in focusing attention and affection, in training desire on the object portrayed. Advertising images act in the same way. As secular images, however, they do not present an orderly spiritual universe of being, reality, and value but rather attempt to capture — to break off — a piece of the infinite longing of a person and disperse it in the acquisition of an immediate satisfaction.

Unlike historical religious images, advertising images are strongly denoted. Very few advertisements use only words, but even fewer use only images. Images are, in themselves, notoriously ambiguous and susceptible to the most various interpretations. Medieval people sometimes received a message or messages quite different from or even opposite to the intended message of a painting. Linguistic anchorage, the "repressive value" of a text or caption, was rare. In advertising, however, the possibility of a wide variety of interpretations according to the particular interests of viewers is firmly limited. The linguistic message is used as "a kind of vice that holds the connoted meanings from proliferating, whether towards excessively individual regions . . . or towards dysphoric values." [13] In advertising, the message given must also be the message received; lacking a verbal gloss, no image can guarantee such univocity.

The linguistically fixed image was an innovation of the sixteenth-century discovery of the usefulness of verbally denoted images in the progressive education of individuals to a predetermined end. In advertising images as in the captioned paintings of Pomarancio, the cartooned pamphlets of German reformers, or the illustrated *Foxe's Book of Martyrs,* the verbal text engages the conscious attention of the reader while the visual message makes its impact on more profound levels of consciousness undistracted by critical evaluation.

Similarly, the verbal text of an advertisement addresses, and therefore establishes the existence of, an autonomous ego, capable of independent choice and self-actualization. It speaks personally, sympathetically, reasonably, often in the form of a question: "Do you have dry skin?" "Are you *sure* your retirement plan is adequate?" "Are you getting as much from life as you should?" The question focuses and articulates a general anxiety as a specific concern. It frequently asks about an unquantifiable factor of which almost no one can be completely sure of having enough. The question makes the reader vulnerable; the image — usually of someone who obviously does have enough of whatever is advertised — offers the possibility of overcoming the anxiety.

A crucial difference between the secular and religious use of denoted images becomes apparent if we consider the political question: Who profits from the successful communication of these messages? Successful communication of modern advertising has as its immediate goal the selling of a product. The gain for the advertiser can be measured quite concretely in money. The gain for the consumer, the recipient of the effective advertising image, is temporary relief from the voice that says, "I want, I want." The religious image, no matter how much it may have on occasion served the power or greed of an ecclesiastical elite,[14] provided an implicit critique of secular values by presenting alternative and transcendent values in images capable of engaging and directing infinite longing to an infinite object.

But the immediate gain, for advertiser or consumer, is only part of the successful communication of an advertising image. Images, we have said, play a role in two primary tasks of culture: They present ways of conceiving and managing physical existence, and they coordinate individual desire to form community. How do advertising images function to fulfill these tasks?

We have discussed the role of advertising in directing and coordinating individual and collective desire. The conditioning of polymorphous desire to socially acceptable objects is crucial to the maintenance of any culture. But power, as Foucault has pointed out, is not primarily concerned with consciousness but with behavior. A more fundamental question, then, concerns "the kind of body the current society needs."[15] If a culture is to perpetuate itself, it must both direct desire and give messages that specify what kind of body is required. That is the primary task of the media images of any culture: to attract its members to develop the body that will perpetuate cultural values.

Foucault's question What kind of body does the present society need? will help us to focus the first cultural task in which images function. Clearly, the body required by contemporary society is not the body presented in medieval media, a body whose physical characteristics, gestures, dress, and stance express emotion, love, and longing. Nor does it recall the tortured bodies of the sixteenth-century Jesuit frescoes, bodies valued for their capacity of sacrifice to the point of death for their convictions. The body essential to our society on the one hand consumes the quantities of food, alcohol, and cigarettes that manufacturers need to sell if the economy is to flourish. But, curiously, the body needed by our society is on the other hand a beautiful body. Incited to eat and drink continuously, we are also supposed to be thin, unblemished, young, and energetic. This body is, however, not so much a contradiction of the consumer body as it is its other aspect. Maintenance of the consumer body requires exercise machines, cosmetics, nonprescription drugs, and fashionable clothing. To overcome the effects of what is put into the body, the body must be doctored, artfully clothed, and treated with moisturizers. A tension between the consumer body and the beautiful body is set in motion by advertising. The economy and the manufacturers dependent on it are the only winners, as the body is alternately indulged and disciplined. If it were not damaged by consumption, it would not seem to require as much cosmeticization and medication; if it were not so fashionably attired, it would not need to consume so much. What do the beautiful people of advertising images do when they are made up and dressed? They go to parties where they eat and drink too much; they get together to look at each other and to consume together.

Finally, how do advertising images function to inform members of the present society of their value and position in the society? Verbal captions of advertisements proclaim, by seeming to address everyone, a rhetoric of social equality. Images, however, usually present young, wealthy, slim, sexually attractive Anglo-Saxon women and men as the satisfied users of their products. The verbal text denies the powerful subliminal message of the image, which promotes sexism, racism, and agism, creating by the endless repetition of these visual clichés "marginal" people who can never realistically aspire to youth, wealth, the right skin color, or sexual preference to qualify for the satisfaction promised by the image. In advertising images the valued and valuable members of the society are clearly identified; cumulative and consistent messages are given by which people measure themselves and formulate self-images.

The images of contemporary culture — most commonly press photographs and advertising images — thus play a highly important role in orienting us to the events of the world, forming our attitudes toward physical existence, self-images, and values, and coordinating our desires.

Language Training in Our Culture

There are at least two major ways in which a proportion of the North American public can receive training in the critical use of language. Education is throughout an increasingly sophisticated training in the use of language, and psychoanalysis and the various psychotherapies provide training in "the language of the self." It is important, however, not to overestimate the practical availability of public education that actually trains a critical use of language. And the individualized, specialized linguistic training of psychotherapy or psychoanalysis is practically available to even fewer people. Nevertheless, these disciplines demonstrate a cultural recognition of the importance of linguistic training and, at their best, provide such training.

The importance of education has itself become a cliché in North American society. Generations of immigrants have recognized the necessity of acquiring a competent use of the English/American language as fundamental to economic success. These immigrants have urged on their children the best available education as the single most important tool for social and economic advancement. Moreover, every schoolchild who has memorized a poem or learned to read and write has been taught respect for the power of language to alter perspectives and train capacities.

Education, however, has largely been understood as training in the use of "technically exploitable" language.[16] The connection of language to self-reflection, that is, to articulation of the "verbal nucleus" of the self, has not often been understood and trained by public education in contemporary society. Psychoanalysis has become important in North American culture as a critique of the application of linguistic proficiency to technical efficiency and scientific knowledge.[17]

The "talking cure" explores the language by which the ego or individual subjective consciousness is formulated in order to establish the points at which this language has become dysfunctional, counterproductive, or destructive. The ego, formed of and delineated by language, is susceptible to linguistic analysis:

The ego's flight from itself is an operation that is carried on in and with language. Otherwise it would not be possible to reverse the hermeneutic process hermeneutically, via the analysis of language.[18]

In the process of analysis or therapy, lacunae in the individual language system are identified [19] that indicate the existence of a delusion "found applied like a patch over the place where originally a rent had appeared in the ego's relation to the external world." [20] Once a diagnosis — a description of the structure and function of the delusion — has been made, the analysand can be trained in a more comprehensive and productive language use. She or he has by then understood her or his freedom from the "seemingly natural restraint" [21] imposed by an uncritical use of language. The hypostatized power of language is overcome in its use as self-reflection.

In making explicit the relationship of language to a person's perspective, self-image, and interest, training in the therapeutic use of language goes a step beyond education. Academic language, even — or especially — at the most sophisticated levels of education, aims at objectivity. To specify one's particular perspective and interest in the subject of a paper or one's emotional and intellectual agenda in the thesis of the paper, would weaken the universal significance of the study, it is thought. In psychoanalysis and psychotherapy, on the other hand, knowledge itself is established only by its recognition by the person who must claim it as self-knowledge. [22]

Education and psychoanalysis thus provide systematic linguistic training; education primarily describes the world of objects, texts, or ideas, and psychoanalysis primarily develops self-reflective language. Neither is practically available to everyone, but both represent cultural recognition of the importance of language and the development of its critical use. A person who has been trained to use language critically understands the capacity of language to describe new experience, to be bent, shaped, and stretched to new meanings that describe, more accurately and more fruitfully, the world and the self. The alternative to the critical use of language in our linguistic culture is to be used *by* language, to be forced to grasp feelings, objects, events, and ideas only in their sloganistic or stereotypical form, to fit one's experience to clichéd language.

We have seen, both in our historical examples and in our discussion of contemporary media, that images play a highly important role in the daily communication of messages given and received. In the modern world, technical skill permits the production and dissemination of images in a quantity and saturation impossible in any earlier historical period. Moreover, the variety of economic, political, and social interests that govern the media images of the North American public make it more important now than at any previous time for us to critically evaluate media images.

Susanne Langer discusses the extent to which individual and collective sensibilities are educated by the arts with which we live. [23] The formulation and expression of feeling is trained primarily by the picture books we looked at and read when we were young, by the music we hear regularly, and by images we look at frequently — the art forms of daily life. These present styles of feeling that form the affective life of individuals. If media images have such potential to shape and limit or to enhance our lives, must we not find ways to evaluate and choose our daily images? What training, then, might we seek out that would help us to become critical of the images we entertain daily?

Would an education in the history of art provide such a critical perspective? Certainly an education in art history gives training in awareness of the use of pictorial space and in the subjects and styles of the visual arts. It is possible also for the paintings and sculptures we see in museums and reproductions to strengthen the imagination and provide valuable visual training. But do these methods produce the kind of training we need to evaluate and use images fruitfully?

Museums offer great numbers of people the opportunity to stand before paintings originally located in palaces, distant churches, and town halls, paintings formerly available only to a few human beings.[24] But simple proximity to great paintings does not automatically confer a training of vision.[25] The quantity of paintings, the modern phenomenon of publicized and enormously expensive paintings, and the artist's name all draw more attention than the visual qualities of the painting. And while we are visually gobbling up the paintings surrounding us, the eye grows weary, having seen nothing of the skillful deployment of visual values in a single painting and having not learned from the painting to see one's own world in a new way. Just as a medieval relic did not often work a healing miracle on a lethargic, indifferent, or infidel bystander, a painting is not likely to impose itself on a person who has not brought to it a trained eye.

It is, we have said, the arts we live with on a daily basis that imprint themselves on us. Compared with the comparatively constant barrage of images from magazines, newspapers, television, and billboards, the artistic images we seek out probably contribute minimally to the overall volume of images we entertain.

Even if a person were to engage in lengthy and expensive training to become an art critic or historian, she would not be likely to receive training in the critical *use* of images, that is, the use of images for self-reflection in a way comparable to the use of language for self-reflection as trained by psychoanalysis.

An example may help to clarify. A chipping canvas on the wall of my rented apartment in a working-class neighborhood in Rome depicts the bust of a Madonna. She is alone, on a dark ground, without any background figures or landscape. The painting looks old, but I do not know who painted it, where, or when. When I come in the door after climbing six flights of stairs from a day spent ransacking the several libraries I use, the painting is the first object I see. The heavily cloaked figure, apparently withdrawn into a world of spiritual values, reminds me immediately of the world of inner activity, a world I have largely forgotten in my reading and my struggle with Roman buses and crowded sidewalks. The image recalls, represents — *repraesentare* means to make present[26] — and corrects the imbalance in my world. The image is simply there, a visual access to the rich healing silence of the world it makes present. I use this image when I allow its values to "speak" to me and to affect me.

Subsequently, of course, I can say quite a bit about the painting's use of space, color, solidity, shape, and so on. But when I talk about it or when I remove it from the wall to see if there is any information about it on the back of the canvas, I am not acting as an image user. I am curious; I want information that is irrelevant to my relation to the painting and to its self-reflective value for me; I am acting as an art historian.

I *use* an image when I choose to allow it to address me. Something about the image strikes me as important, not as a general or universal communication but as a particular message to me, at this moment, during this time in my life. Thus far, however, I have not used the image critically. The critical use of images involves understanding the particular message received from the painting; ultimately it means being able to articulate the relevance of this message to my present affective life.

One must not move too rapidly, however, from the use of an image to the critical use of that image. Articulation of the message received from the image must come as the spontaneous result of living with the image. One must look at the same image again and again until it has attracted, has drawn to the surface, all the associations, memories, and longings that originally gave the image its sense of importance for me. Then the personal message of the image can be articulated. Only in this way will critical understanding of the image not dilute its original visual/affective power. Rather, understanding the precise relation of the image to my self-reflection will enhance the effectiveness of the image for me; its visual qualities can then collect the relevant psychic material — the associations, memories, and longings — more effortlessly when I contemplate the image.

Since we have not found in North American culture a provision for visual training comparable to the linguistic training offered by education and psychoanalysis, we will explore a theory of the roles of language and images in spiritual and psychological development. The theory will enable us to make some concrete suggestions for self-training in the critical use of images.

◆ 7 ◆

Language and Images: A Theory

I will set no worthless thing before my eye.
PSALM 101:3

Plato was the first to demonstrate the therapeutic use of language, in the dialogues of Socrates. In these dialogues, Socrates led his friends through discussions whose primary agenda was to make them aware of their misunderstandings of pivotal words and concepts, misunderstandings that resulted inevitably in a "misrepresentation of reality" by which they were disoriented conceptually and perceptually.[1]

Moreover, thinking they knew what in fact they did not, they were not conscious of the dislocation of values inherent in their misunderstanding. Socrates therefore sought to unravel, by dialectic, the components of the misunderstanding, to expose the linguistic flaw that was the foundation of the false construction of reality.

This was the first step toward a more adequate construction, and it was on this step that Socrates remained, never permitting himself to rush ahead to the work of construction until the dismantling of false conceptions of reality had been completed. By so doing, Socrates demonstrated the potential of langauge to discover and analyze misrepresentations of reality. Language is primarily therapeutic or remedial. Its therapeutic role can be detected as clearly in education as in psychoanalysis and other psychotherapies. Education proceeds from the assumption that without systematic instruction and

◆ 139

conditioning, the individual will "naturally" develop in idiosyncratic ways, that is, along lines that will not support society's claim to reflect and legislate universal values.

The personal self-actualization of any of the members of Plato's utopian republic was far from Plato's mind. Rather, he sought "to discover a cure, a *therapeia* for immoralism and social disintegration." [2] Frightened by the failure of an oligarchic government he had supported,[3] Plato left politics to find a more effective way to promote the cohesiveness of his society. The imaginative society he constructed in the *Republic* and, in his old age, its emendation in the *Laws* were designed to expose and correct the disruptive individualism he detected in contemporary Athenian society. Plato's republic is exactly the opposite of a society that assumes that the pursuit of each individual's self-interest will lead unerringly to the "common good."

Human self-determination and relative autonomy were not only foreign but threatening to Plato's model state.[4] Plato's genius lay in grasping that the coordination of complementary behavior that ensures the functional efficiency of the state was essentially a linguistic matter. The role of philosophy was to analyze and diagnose the disease of the Athenian state and to prescribe the therapy that would cure it.

The therapeutic word was, for Plato, the spoken — the "living and breathing" — word. The spoken word is fundamental both to education and to rhetoric. This word

plants and sows in a fitting soul intelligent words which are able to help themselves . . . which are not fruitless, but yield seed from which there spring up in other minds other words capable of continuing the process forever.[5]

Plato compares the printed word to a painted image; just as the painted image is "an image of an image," so the printed word is "a kind of image" of living speech:[6]

The painter's products stand before us as though they were alive: but if you question them, they maintain a most majestic silence. It is the same with written words: they seem to talk to you as though they were intelligent, but if you ask them anything about what they say, from a desire to be instructed, they go on telling you just the same thing forever.[7]

Neither the printed word nor the painted image can respond to and participate in the dialectical process by which people are instructed and have their queries and objections met so that they are persuaded.

Plato recognized the capacity of language to formulate the universal concepts by which a community is pulled into existence from a chaos of interests and desires. Language, through its universality[8] and its discursive method, is uniquely suited to the analysis of experience, of "what went wrong"; Plato's utopian society is not a fanciful creation *ex nihilo* but a translation into positive terms of his analysis of what went wrong. The *Republic* represents his reordering of experience "so that what is important stands out to the comparative neglect of what is trivial." [9]

Linguistic descriptions of relative import serve centripetal interests, however, by enabling a skilled rhetorician like Plato to promote the values of a particular perspective over other perspectives from which alternative judgments of import may be made. Centripetal forces are, of course, valuable. Every society, to the extent that it is vigorous and productive, must manage to deploy or coordinate the desires of individuals and groups. The cohesiveness and functionality of a society must certainly be a high priority of each of its members. But most of us would not agree with Plato that it is an ultimate goal. A perfectly ordered society, with each member in place and performing certain assigned roles, is not in itself desirable. Such a society is achieved, as in the *Republic*, at the direct personal expense of each of its members.

Language, we have said, is necessary for the identification and analysis of potentially disruptive centrifugal forces of individual interests. Failure to coordinate the desire of individuals sufficiently to elicit support for the values of the society from a "myriad of tiny points" results inevitably in a chaos of contradictory interests that allows takeover of the society by anyone who commands enough physical force to impose his or her interest on the whole society. Language, then, is crucial to one of the constant and continuing tasks of every culture — its own self-healing by analysis and diagnosis. This is what language does best, whether within a culture or in an individual.

But what of images? Our discussion of images must again begin with Plato, the first philosopher to direct philosophy to analysis of human nature rather than physical nature. It is not accidental that Plato, fascinated with the power of language, banished artists from his republic as an unaffordable luxury. But there is in Plato's description of physical vision as the foundation of abstract thought a suggestion, not explored by Plato but articulated in the medieval idea of vision. It is with Plato's account in the *Symposium* (210a–212b), of the generation of knowledge that we must begin to form a theory of the role of images in culture.

Plato's description of the development of knowledge is not a curriculum of subjects of progressive difficulty. It is, rather, a description of the way in which an act of vision — such as the sight of a beautiful body — effectively gathers the energy requisite for initiating knowledge. Fascinated and delighted by the sight of one beautiful body, the student soon begins to notice that other beautiful bodies exist, bodies that have in common the property of beauty. Gradually an ineffable awareness of "the beautiful" grows, and the visual experience of physical beauty is not eliminated as the student becomes adept at recognizing beauty in its abstract form. The somatic experience of beauty, rather, remains as a permanent connection between ideal beauty and the sensible world.[10]

It is important to notice that the drawing power of a beautiful image does not automatically create in its viewer an idea of beauty. The role of vision is to concentrate, through the stimulus of the beautiful image, the *energeia*, the intellectual and somatic intensity of *eros* which is a necessary precondition of learning. Then education — language — must intervene to articulate the inferences of what has until now been a strong but undefined perception. Should education — anticipatory therapy — not occur to interpret visual experience, the viewer/lover will become compulsive in the pursuit of the particular object that seems to him to *be* beauty itself.[11]

Moreover, the existence of visible beauty within the sensible world is the medium in which the divine becomes perceptible. Plotinus, the third-century philosopher who thought of himself not as a Neoplatonist but as a faithful interpreter of Plato, wrote:

I think, therefore, that those ancient sages who sought to secure the presence of divine beings by the erection of shrines and statues, showed insight into the nature of the All; they perceived that, though this Soul is everywhere tractable, its presence will be secured all the more readily when an appropriate receptacle is elaborated, a place especially capable of receiving some portion or phase of it, something reproducing it or representing it, and seeming like a mirror to catch an image of it.[12]

Beautiful images, through participation (*methexis*) in the absolute beauty of the divine, translate into a sensible medium the ubiquitous presence of divinity, thus making divinity continuously accessible through visible objects:

Now beauty, as we said, shone bright amidst these visions, and in this world below we apprehend it through the clearest of our senses, clear and resplendent. For sight is the clearest mode of perception vouchsafed to us through the body.[13]

The idea of accessibility to understanding God and participating in the divine energy through visible objects has also been important in christian theology. Natural objects, created by God, reflect and give witness of their creator. And the strongest and most direct "image of God" is human being, created in God's image. Soon after Aristotle became known in the medieval west, his idea that images formed by perception are an irreducible part of all thought[14] was applied to theological knowledge. Thomas Aquinas said that theology requires the continuous use of images. Aquinas, like Aristotle, corrected the tendency of popular Platonism to regard sensible objects as the first step toward knowledge, but a first step to be left behind as quickly as possible,[15] by insisting on the permanent mediating function of images:

The image is the principle of our knowledge. It is that from which our intellectual activity begins, not as a passing stimulus, *but* as an enduring foundation. *When the imagination is choked, so also is our theological knowledge.*[16]

What part does the artistic image play in the theological imagination? John of Damascus, the authority most frequently quoted by medieval authors on the subject of religious images, wrote:

If, because of love for human beings, the shapeless receives shape in accordance with our nature, why should we not outline in images that which became evident to us through shape, in a manner proper to us and with the purpose of stimulating the memory and inciting the emulation of what may be represented? [17]

The incarnation of Jesus Christ, God entering the sensible world in a human body, decisively ratified the depiction of the spiritual world in anthropomorphic form.[18] It became possible and important for artistic images to represent the incarnation, an effective reminder of the historical event, capable of attracting the worshipper's attention and affection to the figure represented.

In Christianity, the religious image was no longer understood as the heavily diluted "image of an image." [19] The christian image, whether of Christ, Mary, or a saint or martyr, represented — made present to the medieval worshipper by its presence in the liturgy — one who has lived on earth and who continues to live in the omnipresent spiritual universe, participating, along with the presently living, in worship. The image awakened and focused the worshipper's desire to imitate the spiritual characteristics presented by images. Visual beauty, for the Platonist, reminded the viewer of his home in the intelligible world; for the Christian, images recalled the intimate, concrete, historical affinity of the worshipper with the figures of the spiritual world. It was not, however, the idea of transcendent spiritual qualities that attracted the worshipper to imitation of the image. Rather, the endurance, ecstasy, faith, or whatever spiritual quality was embodied by the image came to the worshipper not as an idea but as the embodied experience of a historical person. The image posited the possibility and the fruitfulness, *for embodied human beings*, of the depicted spiritual qualities.[20]

It is not necessary to posit a continuous history of developing ideas from Plato onward to demonstrate the importance of images for the late-Roman, medieval, and sixteenth-century people whose images we have discussed. Few historical people could have identified the conceptual components of their sense of the value of religious images. They just used images; but they used them, and spoke about them, in ways that demonstrate that images formed them by attraction. The ability of images to generate and concentrate emotion and to direct human desire and longing to an infinite object was recognized and acted on. This recognition of the function of images was not the result of Plato's ideas, transmitted across fundamentally different cultures. It was, rather, discovered in daily practice, in the *use* of images by people who felt themselves affected — changed and enriched — by their contemplation of religious images.

Language and images each have an indispensable role in the development of human beings and communities. Images allow the "interested" perception of messages tailored to the viewer's life situation, the individuated, unconscious selection of relevant attitudes and values. The visual "language" of images, although specific and precise to each viewer, is singularly adaptable to a variety of interpretations — whether or not articulated — by a diversity of individuals. As long as images played a prominent role in christian worship, a wide variety of individual interpretations not only was tolerated by necessity but was accepted in christian communities. Images form by attraction those who are drawn to some particular feature by interests determined by their life situation.

The primary role and value of religious language, on the other hand, discovered and rediscovered as people needed to correct or balance potentially destructive centrifugal tendencies, is therapeutic or remedial. Education, instruction, definition, exhortation — all either anticipate or unravel confusions of ideas, values, or emotions that result in individual or communal disorientation.

Neither language nor visual images can appropriate all these functions in human life. Both language use and image use have dangerous characteristic temptations when one is developed to the neglect of the other. Western Christianity has been much more aware of image abuse than of language abuse, perhaps because language users were quick to detect and condemn exclusive devotional attention to images. Thus, careful theological rationales and guidelines for the use of images were, as we have seen, formulated and reiterated. Language users were not, however, so adept at self-criticism; compulsive concentration on religious language — language abuse — has not received much attention in western Christianity.[21]

The repeated attempts of theologians to clarify theological ideas and to make precise statements on points of dogmatic conflict, although they have undoubtedly consolidated christian faith and protected it from local and temporary styles of understanding and speaking, have also led consistently to the exclusion of alternative formulations. Many individuals and groups have realized, when confronted with the newly clarified definitions, that in fact they had not thought of the dogma in question in precisely such terms. They also have found that they had certain intellectual and religious interests in the way they were accustomed to understanding and stating the doctrine. The history of western Christianity is littered with the silent figures of Christians who found themselves excluded by each increment in verbal theological precision.

Moreover, the perennial bewilderment of non–language users about what may appear to us to be theological niceties is apparent in the records of thousands of medieval trials for heresy and witchcraft. "I believe what the church believes" came to be the standard, though far from foolproof, way for the theologically unsophisticated to avoid inadvertent self-incrimination. For a historian, records of doctrinal controversies, like medieval trial transcripts, are fascinating exercises in language use, but, as the novelist Saul Bellow wrote in another context, "for one aware of the suffering, it is appalling." [22] Language becomes coercive when it is used not therapeutically — to examine, interpret, and suggest — but as a standard, in alliance with social, political, or ecclesiastical institutions that require universal assent to particular formulae.

If the characteristic temptation of those who are primarily language users is preoccupation with precise statements and the universal enforcement of those statements, the characteristic temptation of those who are primarily image users is diffusion, the tendency to neglect to understand and formulate the particular power of attraction the image has for the one who is drawn to it. It is not sufficient in these days of easy availability of a variety of contemporary images — from pornography to museum art — simply to recognize that one is drawn to a particular image. Rather, if the image attracts me, it speaks to me in a "significant and definite way." [23] It has, *for me,* a "specific expressive power" that I can come to understand by being attentive to the complex of memories, associations, and longings gathered in me, over time, by the image. This exercise is the only way to overcome the capacity of images to attract one to values one does not, and would not, consciously choose.

From this cluster of historical theories and practices relevant to the use of language and images, we can sketch a theory that will enable us to identify practical methods for heuristic image use in contemporary society. Language and images need not compete; exaggerated claims for the capacity of either language or artistic images only prevent recognition of the proper bailiwick and particular effectiveness of each. Images are powerful, and the most powerful images accomplish with skill and economy what they do best: formation by attraction. Language is also powerful; language is therapeutic; its role is to anticipate and to analyze misunderstandings of self and world.

Training in Image Use

In Chapter 6 we discussed the images available daily to North Americans, and we looked at the specialized attention to language training in our culture. We were able to find no comparable training in image use, even for those who might search for such training. In this chapter we have outlined a theory, drawn from historical theory and practice, of the optimal relation of language and images in continuing human development.

We are almost ready now to explore a method by which we as individuals might take responsibility for our own visual training, thereby becoming skilled in the critical use of images. A cultural and personal imbalance is created by the provision of linguistic training, at least for those who are willing to seek it and sacrifice for it, without a corresponding training in image use. This imbalance is a cultural problem, but individuals can address it both for personal growth and in the faith that real change in individuals is the basis of all cultural change. Training onself in image use, understood in this light, becomes a matter of moral and social responsibility; it is not primarily narcissistic, even though benefit to oneself may initially be the most evident result.

But do we really need visual training? Before we are fully convinced of the need for a critical use of images, we must overcome a certain inertia caused by our skepticism over the idea that images affect us. Surely, we reason, the effect of any particular image is diluted or discharged by the multiple and diverse images to which we are exposed daily. We are willing to grant that images may inform or entertain us, but not that they can operate independently of our conscious minds to give shape to our desire, to channel our longing, to make us who we are.

In contrast to modern ideas of the ineffectualness of images, we have considered the medieval visual ray theory of physical vision, by which the object that engages one's visual ray becomes a permanent part of one's soul, even if it recedes from the mind and is "forgotten." At the end of the last century, Freud's theory of repression formulated something similar to this medieval theory. We are shaped, Freud said, more directly and more powerfully by what we have "forgotten" than by what we remember.[24] Understanding the intricate operation of one's psyche, Jung said, comes by recovering the images associated with strong experiences.

Nevertheless, the theories of Freud and Jung have not been specifically applied to physical vision, and contemporary ideas continue to minimize the importance of images in shaping character and personality. In contrast, medieval theory may seem to us superstitious, overscrupulous, or even paranoid. If we were to apply the medieval theory in the modern world, we would have a full-time job avoiding images that overtly or covertly foster the marginalization and oppression of human beings. On the other hand, if we accept the modern idea of vision, an idea that flatters our sense of independent and autonomous conscious choice, we consider ourselves unaffected by the images surrounding us. Neither of these ideas seems fully satisfactory.

As we have said, a person's self-image, values, and longing are shaped by the visual objects of her or his habitual attention. In our culture, whether we acknowledge it or not, images retain their role of formation by attraction. All of us to some degree, and some of us to a massive degree, are addicted to the publicly available images with which we live: press photographs, television news and programming, advertising images. Without a daily dose of the terrifying but titillating images of disaster, war, and accident supplied by news photography, we feel disoriented. Our need to feel in touch with events around the world often masks the extent to which our affective lives are shaped by media images. I am not advocating that we be uninformed of the significant events occurring in our world but simply that we become aware of how compulsively engaged we are with media images.

How can we distinguish between visual addictions and our efforts as responsible citizens to keep ourselves informed? One can give up, for a specified time, the object to which one suspects oneself addicted. Significant news, for example, is easy to learn from a friend. But to the extent that one is addicted, feelings of more or less severe discomfort and disorientation will accompany withdrawal from newspapers or television news. Addiction, we must remember, does not imply that the object of the addiction is bad but only that one's relation to it is compulsive. The overcoming of an addiction is therefore not a judgment on the object but is undertaken in the interest of more personal freedom.

But perhaps we are not so strongly addicted to media images as to require such a fast. And visual fasts, of course, do not train vision, even though they may be a useful preliminary. Ultimately we are interested not in fasts from media images but in selecting the types of images we want to entertain habitually and in using those images responsibly and productively.

There are three main steps in training oneself to choose and use images. The first step sounds simple, but it is perhaps the most difficult because it assumes in advance some measure of the awareness one is trying to acquire. The first step is to become aware of the messages one receives from the images with which one lives. One might, for example, change the pace at which one usually reads the newspaper in order to look more slowly and closely at the content, composition, and themes of news photographs. Or one might scan more rapidly than usual the photographs in a newspaper or magazine, attempting to analyze these images as a *group* of mutually reinforcing messages, as a complex unit of visual communication.[25]

Another exercise for becoming aware of the messages received from media is careful comparison of texts and images. We have discussed the denotation or linguistic anchorage of media images; the text, as Barthes said, "remote controls" the reader "towards a meaning chosen in advance." [26] We usually see in the image what its caption directs us to see. A comparison of the text and the image, in which we attempt to distinguish or separate the messages coming to us from each, may reveal some puzzling discrepancies between the messages we receive. The text, although we anticipate that it will corroborate the image, may contradict the message of the image, thereby establishing a perceptual tension of which we had been unaware. Or, as I have already suggested, the text may function as a distraction for the conscious mind, while the image plants its message on unconscious anxieties or longings. In any case, the exercise of determining the relationship of text to image will bring to our awareness aspects of media communication we had not been aware of but had nevertheless been affected by, at least to some degree.

The second step in visual training, to be undertaken when we have detected and dealt with our compulsiveness in relation to media images and when we have learned to notice and formulate the particular messages we receive from images and texts, is to begin to ask questions about media images. I have defined the primary tasks of culture as first, making available to people exemplary models for the conceiving and managing of physical existence, and second, coordinating individual desires so that the community is consolidated rather than disrupted by particular individual energies and longings. We must ask ourselves whether and how the images with which we live contribute to these cultural tasks. We live in a time when it is dangerous to ignore the visual images that inform us about who we are as bodies. The nuclear world desperately needs both responsible critique of media images and discovery of the visual images that train us to notice and find precious— too precious to blow up—the natural world of bodies and the body of the earth, our mother.

Is my sense of social and political responsibility informed and developed by the press photographs I contemplate daily? Or am I habituated to such massive doses of media violence and human pain that my sense of moral outrage and responsibility is dulled? [27] Can I locate, in my daily fare of images, a supply of images that affirm me and help me to explore what it is to be a woman of my age in my culture? Or do media images tell me that I am the wrong sex, the wrong age, or the wrong color? These and many other questions must be asked and answered personally and honestly.

A description of the third step will make it evident that these steps are not necessarily sequential but that they should be ultimately integrated in selecting and using images. The first two steps should give us a basis for choosing fruitful and life-enhancing images or types of images. It is impossible not to see some of the images of the daily newspaper while seeing others, but it is possible to reject publications or television programs that regularly feature images by which one does not want to be shaped. The first two steps may result in the sacrifice of images that titillate without informing or that attract one to dangerous or destructive values and goals. In the third step, however, one selects and develops a repertoire of images, chosen both because they attract and because from them one receives visual messages that help one to visualize — to envision — personal and social transformation and thus to focus the energy of attention and affection with more clarity.

The development of a repertoire of images initially consists of looking at a variety of images — both the images one is accustomed to seeing every day and those especially sought out — while observing oneself for spontaneous interested response. We must gather the images that immediately engage us, that strike us as important. And we must place these images where we see them daily, in a variety of moods and situations. The images we select will probably fall into two types: Either they *express* a valued aspect or quality of our experience or they *compensate,* offer alternatives to, our individual experience. The dark-skinned Madonna on my wall does not express, but it visually compensates, the pace of my day. We need images that express — that help us to "see" — what we are about, and we need images that re-present — that make present — aspects of human possibility we have known, perhaps only momentarily.

Moreover, we need a repertoire of images not only because we have many strongly felt but vaguely focused longings but also because the eye habituates itself to images seen daily. Although images do not themselves change, we do, and so the images we find expressive or compensatory at one time are likely to lose their effectiveness for us at another time, or even in another mood.

A critical image user is ruthless, humble, and not impressed by titles or "greatness." Like Socrates, who listened only to his daemon, we must listen only to the sense of importance and delight that identifies for us a visual image we can use. It may be the label of a can or it may be a painting that we go to see again and again in a museum. A line, a color, may be enough to touch us; we will contemplate that line, that color, until we recognize in it, perhaps, the perfect mother none of us has ever known, the stimulating or comforting touch for which we long when we feel "the mortal cold of the universe." [28]

An image conveys a specific and precise message to a particular viewer. Although a variety of messages may be received from the same image by different viewers, this does not mean that the message one viewer receives is vague. The viewer may at first be able only to speak vaguely about the particular attraction for him that the image has. He must even restrain himself from prematurely fixing in language the meaning for him of the image or kind of image. The urge to name must be disciplined by long, silent contemplation, until we understand the significance we first perceived only as a vague feeling about the importance of the image. Freud was speaking metaphorically when he wrote, in *The History of the Psychoanalytic Movement*, "I learned to restrain speculative tendencies and to look at the same things again and again until they themselves begin to speak." [29] We have only to return this metaphor to its original visual paradigm to have in it a description of the result of looking at the same image again and again; the image itself begins to speak.[30]

Images and Religion

The historical association of artistic images and religion was not accidental. Religion needs images to fulfill its formative role in human life. Until the sixteenth century, art and religion were interwoven, their interdependence assumed. Sixteenth-century reformers preached against exaggerated concentration on religious images and corresponding neglect of religious language. They recalled Christians to language use in liturgy, religious education, and private devotional practice. Even in the Roman Catholic reform, the religious value of images was questioned and, although it was affirmed by the Council of Trent, has come to be of minor importance for many North American Roman Catholics. In both Catholic and Protestant reformations, the therapeutic capacity of religious language was explored and extended as never before.

With the continued renunciation of images in Protestant worship and their diminished importance in Roman Catholic worship, the ancient function of images — that of cumulatively drawing the worshipper to imitate and participate in the qualities and way of life formulated by the image — has been neglected. Contemplation — concentrated meditation traditionally focused by an image — is largely ignored.[31] Neglect of images is neglect of contemplation. The religious affections, traditionally formulated and trained by images, are not effectively engaged in the worship of christian communities when images play no part in liturgy and devotional practice. In such a situation, there is a lack of balance between language, which plays so dominant a role in worship, and images, which either are entirely absent or are ignored. The intellect, engaged by language, is religiously trained, but the emotions are less effectively engaged. Through the use of images, historical Christians were moved first to imitate and then to assimilate the strength, the courage, and the love they contemplated in religious art. *Theoria* — contemplation in which one is lifted out of one's familiar world and into the living presences of the spiritual world — begins with physical vision, with a trained and concentrated seeing that overcomes conceptual barriers between the visible and the spiritual worlds.

Like langauge, contemplation can form community; it is not — or not necessarily — a solitary, individualistic activity. Those who gaze together at a religious image share participation in the spiritual world made present in its visual representation. To participate with others in the spiritual world is primarily to be *physically* present, that is, to have one's senses engaged:

It is only in a derived sense that presence at something means also a kind of subjective attitude, that of attention to something. Thus, to watch something is a genuine mode of sharing.[32]

If christian faith were simply a system of ideas, a conceptual scheme, or if it were a subjective state, physical presence at the corporate worship of a christian community would be unnecessary. It would even be a distraction from concentration on certain ideas or the cultivation of a certain attitude. But christian worship is not primarily a gathering of the like-minded. It is a gathering of human bodies to be with one another in the acknowledgment that human existence originates in and is drawn toward love. Worship is primarily response *in kind* to love, the origin, center, and goal of life; because of this, vision, the engagement of attention and affection, is a fundamental aspect of worship.

Community founded on the gathering of body/beings for communal participation in the spiritual world embodied in religious images is not the same as community based on a collection of individual subjective consciousnesses. The "transindividual reality of the subject," posited and addressed by language, is not community. Certainly, both intellect and affections need to be summoned and addressed in worship, but exclusive attention to intellect or subjective consciousness will, because of the universality of language, necessarily ignore particularity in the interest of achieving unified subjective attitudes. Community founded on bodily presence, engaging physical senses, does not negate but glories in the diverse particularities of human beings. Its model of community is the spiritual world presented in images in which values are embodied in historical figures immediately recognizable by their specific physical characteristics. These characteristics quickly became stylized in western medieval religious art because they were so prominently featured — the flowing red hair of Mary Magdalene, Saint Paul's bald head, the mascot lion of Saint Jerome. When images are used in worship, language, in which the individual's experience is formulated in predetermined categories, is balanced by implicit affirmation of the particularity of each worshipper.

Images belong to worship. Religion needs images to accomplish its task of formation by attraction; art also needs an essentially religious vision if it is to present human life in its most profound and comprehensive scope.[33] Religion without artistic images is qualitatively impoverished; art without religion is in danger of triviality, superficialty, or subservience to commercial or political interests.

If religious images are denied a central role in worship, churches will succeed in training only the language-using subjective consciousness so skillfully evoked in Martin Luther's call for exclusively verbal worship:

A right faith goes right on with its eyes closed; it clings to God's Word; it follows that Word; it believes the Word.[34]

Contemplation, *theoria,* the community of the diverse particular human beings who "see" God in participation in the love of God, whose lives are in the process of being formed to that normative vision, begins with visual perception. But it begins with vision not to move on as quickly as possible, leaving such "crutches" far behind; visual images are to be used, in the words of Thomas Aquinas, "not as a passing stimulus, but as an enduring foundation." [35]

Finally, since christian churches have relinquished the task of providing life-orienting images, secular culture has seized the opportunity of filling the void. In the absence of religious images, secular images function as life-orienting; they do provide messages from which people form self-images, values, and attitudes. These images, however, are not presented to place human life in its broadest and deepest context but to perpetuate a consumer culture. Images become idolatrous when they function as life-orienting but serve the private commercial gain of a few individuals. Images, in their ancient role of formation by attraction, are as effective as ever, but churches, in abdicating responsibility for the training of vision, have failed to provide both life-orienting images and training in their critical appreciation.

"To Understand Through the Eyes" [36]

This book has explored the assumptions and methods of contemporary hermeneutics to discover an alternative to the political and intellectual history that has until recently been regarded as universal "human" history. We have examined the dependence of political and intellectual history on the written texts of historical language users, usually the most privileged and atypical members of their communities. And I have proposed that media images, available to all and in daily use in historical communities, can be used as evidence of the ideas, attitudes, and values of those persons who were not primarily language users but image users, whose sense of self and relationship was informed by images rather than words.

In the traditional method of historical inquiry, dependent on verbal evidence from the past, we can identify the structure of noninclusive social and cultural institutions. Not only has a certain sex, class, and race been selected as uniquely interesting and significant, but also a certain function of human beings, developed to an unusual degree by intensive linguistic training, has been identified as the center and essence of human personhood. The antecedents of this center, which we have called individual subjective consciousness or ego, have been sought in the past. But the historical antecedents of people who understand themselves primarily as determined by the body and its location in the life cycle, or by relationship to a family or community, have not, until recently, been sought.

Historians have not originated this exclusive interest in one aspect of human being; probably they have not even been very influential in perpetuating it. We are not seeking a new *villain*, but rather we wish to detect, in historical work that has produced only the history of language users, the structure of oppression. Oppression, whether social, political, academic, or personal, always begins by identifying the physical characteristics, work, and values of a part of a community as right, true, and beautiful; persons who differ are disregarded, even if their work is crucial to the life of the community, their values are held by a majority of people, and their perspective provides the primary energy for the functioning of the community. The structure of oppression appears in historical study that has been directed toward the recovery of a *part* of human being, devaluing implicitly, if not explicitly, those persons who have not had opportunity or perhaps have not been interested in developing that part.

If my analysis is persuasive, its result should not be to make the reader despair because we have identified yet another area in which sexism, racism, agism, intellectualism, and elitism are subtly and ubiquitously woven through the fabric of contemporary society. If we have discovered the structure of oppression in hermeneutics, it was in order to propose a method that begins to elicit a more comprehensive understanding of people of the past.

Each of us has a responsibility to identify the small daily messages and methods — in media, in our work or academic disciplines, in our homes and institutions — that perpetuate the oppression of human beings. The first step is to recognize the structure of oppression by which one aspect of human being is exclusively valued. The persons who epitomize this aspect, often having developed it at the expense of development in other areas, become the models of the society. Once one is sensitized to this structure, one can readily detect it wherever it occurs. The important point is not that some forms of oppression are heinous while others are harmless. A society desensitized and habituated by small daily forms of oppression is vulnerable to large-scale oppression.

If we have assimilated Foucault's description of the operation of power from a "myriad of tiny points" that "go right down into the depths of society," [37] we have also abandoned the search for a "villain." Like Pogo, we have seen the enemy — and it is us. But if this is the case, change can begin with us.

It can begin with the reintegration of our alienated and manipulated capacity to "understand through the eyes," the neglected and oppressed aspect of ourselves. The exercise and strengthening of our visual understanding by disciplined critical image use is not, of course, an alternative to political and social action toward the alleviation of oppression. But it must accompany these efforts if an ideology of inclusiveness is not to remain abstract. Inclusiveness must begin with and be supported by a genuine and thoroughgoing appreciation for the mode of perception — once called the "queen of the senses" — that is most capable of receiving and delighting in the sensible world of bodies and things in all their multiplicity, particularity, and diversity.

Notes

Selected Bibliography

Index

Notes

Preface

1. Jacques Lacan, *The Language of the Self: The Function of Language in Psycho-analysis,* trans. Anthony Wilden (Baltimore: Johns Hopkins University Press, 1968), p. 39.
2. Michel Foucault, *Language, Counter-Memory, Practice: Selected Essays and Interviews,* trans. Donald F. Bouchard (Ithaca, N.Y.: Cornell University Press, 1977), p. 206: "Representation no longer exists."

Chapter 1   Introduction

1. Clifford Geertz, *The Interpretation of Cultures* (New York: Basic Books, 1973), p. 119.
2. Rudolf Arnheim, *Art and Visual Perception* (Berkeley: University of California Press, 1965), p. 31.
3. Jonathan Edwards, *Personal Narrative,* vol. 1 of *The Works of President Edwards,* ed. Samuel Austin (Worcester, 1808), pp. 61–62.
4. For example, Calvin's description of justification as "quickening" (*vivificatio*), overcoming the sluggishness, torpor, and inertia of "normal" perception, is a description of the agility of perception in which the natural world is seen in its authentic being — as created by God and demonstrating "without interruption and without silence" the glory of God. See Margaret R. Miles, "Anthropology, Theology, and the Human Body in Calvin's *Institutes,*" *Harvard Theological Review* (July 1981) pp. 303–323.
5. Augustine, *Confessions* 13.9.
6. Rudolf Arnheim, *The Dynamics of Architectural Form* (Berkeley: University of California Press, 1977), p. 208.
7. Plato, *Phaedrus* 250; see also Plotinus Ennead 1.6.4: "These experiences must occur whenever there is contact with any sort of beautiful thing, wonder and a shock of delight and longing and passion and a happy excitement."
8. Susanne Langer in *Philosophical Sketches* (New York: Mentor, 1962), p. 79.
9. Langer, *Philosophical Sketches,* pp. 80–81; see also p. 83: "Most people are so embued with the idea that feeling is a formless, total organic excitement in men as in animals that the idea of educating feeling, developing its scope and quality, seems odd to them, if not absurd. It is really . . . at the very heart of personal education."

10. "Sacred art functions to synthesize a people's ethos . . . the tone, character, and quality of their life, its authentic style and mood — and their world view — the picture they have of the way things, in sheer actuality, are, their most comprehensive ideas of order." Geertz, *Interpretation of Cultures*, pp. 89–90.

11. Arnheim, *Art and Visual Perception*, p. 31.

12. This description apparently originated with E. Renan, *Histoire des origines du christianisme*, vol. 3, *Marc Aurele et la fin du monde antique*, 6th ed. (Paris, 1891), pp. 539ff. See the following article for a description of the development of this hypothesis, its "repeated assertion" that has "raised to the level of established truth what was initially a matter of scholarly opinion," and a rebuttal of the hypothesis: Sister Charles Murray, "Art and the Early Church," *Journal of Theological Studies* (Oct. 1977), pp. 303–345.

13. Michael Gough, *The Early Christians* (London: Thames and Hudson, 1961), p. 101. The new subjects of church painting and mosaic in the fourth century do not appear one after the other as a slowly developing iconography, Gough writes: "the majority appear simultaneously and with a consistency of iconography that suggests an earlier period of development from a recognized prototype."

14. See Murray, "Art and the Early Church," and Aiden Nichols, O.P., *The Art of God Incarnate: Theology and Image in Christian Tradition* (London: Darton, Longman, and Todd, 1981).

15. Ernst Kitzinger describes the critical appropriation of images in his distinction between portrait images and the depictions of scriptural or historical scenes. Portrait images, with their "haunting, quietly hypnotic quality," were considered more likely to arrest the absorbed attention of the viewer to themselves. They resembled pagan cult images much more closely than did scenes in which the viewer's attention was directed to an action. The perception of an action included the viewer as participant in the dynamic momentum of a scene whose activity was only momentarily frozen so that the viewer could enter it. It may have been the great popularity of portrait images from the end of the sixth century on that led to the iconoclastic crisis in the East in the eighth century, rather than the inherent danger that all images would capture the viewer's attention without reference to the prototype of the image. "On Some Icons of the Seventh Century," in *Late Classical and Early Medieval Studies in Honor of Albert Matthias Friend, Jr.*, ed. Richard Krautheimer (Princeton: Princeton University Press, 1955), pp. 88–95.

16. Among recent scholarship on the iconoclast controversy, see especially Anthony Bryer and Judith Herrin, eds., *Iconoclasm*, Papers given at the Ninth Spring Symposium of Byzantine Studies (Birmingham, Ala.: Center for Byzantine Studies, University of Birmingham, 1977); Joseph Frary, "The Logic of Icons," *Sobornost*, ser. 6, no. 6 (Winter, 1972), pp. 394–404; Leonide Ouspensky, *Theology of the Icon* (Crestwood, New York: St. Vladimir's Seminary Press, 1978); John Stuart, *Ikons* (London: Faber and Faber, 1975).

17. Erwin Panofsky, *Gothic Architecture and Scholasticism* (Latrobe, Pa.: Archabbey Press, 1948); *Abbot Suger on the Abbey Church of St. Denis* (Princeton: Princeton University Press 1946), p. 20. See also the use of visual images in the work of cultural historians such as Jacques Le Goff, *The Birth of Purgatory* (Chicago: University of Chicago Press, 1984); L. K. Little, "Pride Goes Before Avarice: Social Change and the Vices in Latin Christendom," *American Historical Review* 76 (1971), pp. 16–49; André Vauchez, *La sainteté en Occident aux derniers siècles du Moyen Age* (Rome: Ecole française de Rome, 1981).

18. Panofsky, *Gothic Architecture,* p. 39.

19. Panofsky, *Gothic Architecture,* p. 24.

20. Roland Barthes's distinction: "The language of the image is not merely the total-ity of utterances emitted, it is also the totality of messages received." *Image-Music-Text* (New York: Hill and Wang, 1977), p. 47. See also Rudolf Berliner, "God Is Love," *Gazette des Beaux-Arts,* ser. 6, no. 42 (1953), p. 22: "Before 1800 the evident and the intended meaning of a religious image do not necessarily coincide."

21. The weakening of the original import of an image by its removal from its in-tended location is intimated in Carl C. Christensen's description of the policy of the iconoclasts of the French Revolution: "to preserve the proscribed monuments by re-moving them from the original settings with their strong emotional and intellectual associations and installing them in neutral museums where, torn from their cultural context, they might be regarded as mere 'art.'" *Art and the Reformation in Germany* (Athens, Ohio: Ohio University Press, 1979), p. 107; see also Stuart, *Ikons,* p. 24.

22. See Margaret R. Miles, "Vision: The Eye of the Body and the Eye of the Mind in Augustine's *De Trinitate* and Other Works," *Journal of Religion,* (April 1983), pp. 125–142. Cf. Plato *Tim.* 45c; Aristotle rejects this account of physical vision (*De anima* 2.8, 419a: "Vision occurs when the sensitive faculty is acted upon"; but the re-vival of popular Platonism in the first century A.D. ensured the dominant influence of Plato's theory throughout the medieval period.

23. No claim is made here that all medieval people knew this theory and would have described their visual experience in its terms; rather, there is much evidence that the theory accepted and often reiterated by classical and medieval philosophical thinkers was an articulation of common experience.

24. Contemporary studies treating visual experience in later-twentieth-century cul-ture include Wilson Brian Key, *Subliminal Seduction* (New York: New American Library, 1974), and *Media Sexploitation* (New York: New American Library, 1976); Jerry Mander, *Four Arguments for the Elimination of Television* (New York: Morrow Quill, 1978); Marie Winn, *The Plug-In Drug* (New York: Viking, 1977).

25. For a description of the prevalent cosmological interpretation of centralized church architecture in eastern Orthodox Christianity and in the west in the medieval period, see Gerhart B. Ladner, "St. Gregory of Nyssa and St. Augustine on the Sym-bolism of the Cross," in *Late Classical and Early Medieval Studies,* pp. 88–95 .

26. This strategic position was sometimes occupied by a depiction of the Virgin "enthroned, with the Child in her arms or on her lap, within a mandorla of light." André Grabar, "The Virgin in a Mandorla of Light," in *Late Classical and Early Medieval Studies,* p. 305.

27. Robert Ornstein, *The Psychology of Consciousness* (New York: Penguin, 1972), chap. 2, passim.

28. A. Sheridan, *Michel Foucault* (New York: Tavistock, 1980), p. 114. Through-out this book, I use Clifford Geertz's definition: "Sociology of knowledge deals with the social element in the pursuit and perception of truth, its inevitable confinement to one or another existential perspective." "Ideology as a Cultural System," in *Ideology and Its Discontents,* ed. David E. Apter (New York: Macmillan, 1964), p. 49. See also Judith Plaskow, *Sex, Sin and Grace: Women's Experience and the Theologies of Reinhold Niebuhr and Paul Tillich* (Washington, D.C.: University Press of America, 1980), p. 173: "The fact that neglect of women's experience always involves neglect of some aspect of human experience does not mean that theology can move directly from preoccupation with male experience to concern for 'universal human experience'

... Maleness and humanity have too long been identified for 'the feminine' and women's experience to be incorporated in the doctrine of God and theological anthropology other than deliberately."

29. William E. Connolly, "Theoretical Self-Consciousness," *Polity* 6 (Fall 1983), p. 25: "A perspective is a set of presumptions about social and political life derived from selective social experience; the conceptual system it sustains focuses on those aspects of the environment most congruent with those presumptions and tends to divert attention away from other possible dimensions. Since the investigator is seldom sharply aware of his own perspective and its role in inquiry, he is likely to ignore or underplay its tendency to push his interpretations in a particular direction."

30. The English word *text* is derived from the Latin *textus,* meaning texture or woven structure. Although all the meanings of *text* listed in *Webster's Unabridged Dictionary* refer to verbal texts, I will sometimes refer to visual "texts" and will argue their capacity for enriching the "texture" of historical understanding and interpretation.

31. For a description of the variety of evidence from texts and records on the experience of historical women, see Sheila Ryan Johansson, "Herstory as History: A New Field or Another Fad?" in *Liberating Women's History,* ed. Berenice A. Carroll (Chicago: University of Illinois Press, 1976).

32. Elisabeth Schüssler Fiorenza, *In Memory of Her* (New York: Crossroads, 1983); see also Frances and Joseph Gies, *Women in the Middle Ages* (New York: Crowell, 1978), esp. chap. 4, "Eve and Mary."

33. Relevant here is Wilhelm Dilthey's important reminder that "we must understand a period of history as being centered upon itself and not just as a preliminary stage to our own time." H. P. Rickman, ed., *Pattern and Meaning in History* (New York: Harper, 1961), pp. 81–82. See also Beverly Harrison's caution against "an internalized ideology about ourselves which contradicts our actual history." "The Power of Anger in the Work of Love," *Union Seminary Quarterly Review* 36 (1981), p. 45.

34. P. V. Charland, *Madame sainte Anne et son culte au moyen age 1–3* (Quebec, 1911–1929).

35. For a discussion of medieval iconoclasm, see William R. Jones, "Art and Christian Piety: Iconoclasm in Medieval Europe," in *The Image and the Word,* ed. Joseph Gutman (Missoula, Mont.: Scholars Press, 1977), pp. 75–105.

36. Victor Turner and Edith Turner, *Image and Pilgrimage in Christian Culture* (New York: Columbia University Press, 1978), p. 235.

37. See Luther's *Against the Heavenly Prophets in the Matter of Images and Sacraments,* LW 40, pp. 79ff. In 1537 Luther wrote: "In the papacy artists have pictured the Virgin Mary as showing the Lord Christ the breasts at which he had nursed, as gathering emperors, kings, princes, and lords under her cloak, as protecting them and pleading with her dear son to drop his wrath and penalties over them. Therefore everybody called upon her and honored her more than they did Christ. In this way the Virgin Mary turned into an abomination or into an idol and an offense, though without her fault." Quoted in Christensen, *Art and the Reformation,* p. 56.

38. How can a historian determine which texts and which images belong to the same discourse and thus have a relationship to one another? Before proceeding to interpretation, she must establish and be prepared to demonstrate which of the following range of possible relationships between a text and an image exists: At the strongest level of relationship, the visual image may be mentioned in the text; this is relatively rare, however. At the second level, the text may discuss a building, painting, or mosaic

of the style and subject known to have been in the same vicinity and contemporaneous with the author of the text. Third and more frequent, a work may be in the vicinity and contemporaneous with a written text although the text makes no mention of it. These levels of relationship are all strong enough to warrant the assumption of a discourse common to text and image. Fourth, the text may have been written in the same geographical area somewhat later than the visual work, so that the author of the text could certainly have had access to it. This level of relationship is conjectural and warrants only a tentative mutual interpretation of text and image. At the weakest usable level of relationship, the text and the image may belong to the same local tradition at different times. The relationship of a visual work to a verbal text within the christian west but at different times and places falls below any usable relationship for interpretation within a mutual discourse.

Chapter 2 *Hermeneutics and the History of Image Users*

1. Hans-Georg Gadamer, *Truth and Method* (New York: Seabury, 1975), p. 432. In this chapter I have used male pronouns wherever I considered them to designate more accurately than inclusive language the origin or adherents of particular ideas.

2. Jürgen Habermas, *Knowledge and Human Interests* (Boston: Beacon, 1968), p. 314.

3. Jacques Lacan, *The Language of the Self: The Function of Language in Psychoanalysis,* trans. Anthony Wilden (Baltimore: Johns Hopkins University Press, 1968), p. 67; I understand "ego" to be roughly synonymous with "subjective consciousness," as the human function that is structured by language. "Ego" emphasizes the motivational aspect of this activity, while "subjective consciousness" emphasizes the intellectual aspect. Cf. Habermas, *Knowledge and Human Interests,* p. 224: "unconscious" equals "delinguisticized." See also Lacan, *Language of the Self,* p. 20: "The unconscious is that part of the concrete discourse insofar as it is transindividual, which is not at the disposition of the subject to reestablish the continuity of his conscious discourse."

4. Lacan, *Language of the Self,* p. 19: "The Word confers a meaning on the functions of the individual; its domain is that of the concrete discourse, insofar as this is the field of the transindividual reality of the subject."

5. Quoted by Lacan, *Language of the Self,* p. 13.

6. Thomas Szasz, *The Myth of Psychotherapy* (New York: Anchor Doubleday, 1978), pp. 19, 130ff.

7. Habermas, *Knowledge and Human Interests,* p. 241.

8. The rectification of language as therapeutic is not a new idea; it was thoroughly described by Confucius. See also Robert Cushman's discussion of Plato's view of language in *Therapeia: Plato's Conception of Philosophy* (Westport, Conn.: Greenwood, 1958).

9. As, for example, in the rhetoric of Alcoholics Anonymous, "one day at a time," "easy does it," and "first things first" are simple, even cliché concepts that nevertheless have proved to have therapeutic value.

10. The first popular name for Freudian psychoanalysis was the "talking cure."

11. With the disdain of a language user for non–language users, Roland Barthes adds that "the mechanistic conception of language" forgets that language creates rather than represents universal values. *Image-Music-Text* (New York: Hill and Wang, 1977), p. 199.

12. Michel Foucault, *The Archeology of Knowledge* (San Francisco: Harper Torch-

books, 1972), pp. 226–227: "What is an educational system, after all, if not a ritualization of the word; if not a qualification of some fixing of roles for speakers; if not the constitution of a (diffuse) doctrinal group; if not a distribution and an appropriation of discourse, with all its learning and its powers?"

13. Lacan, *Language of the Self*, p. 19.

14. Lacan, *Language of the Self*, p. 64: "Language is not immaterial. It is a subtle body, but body it is."

15. Gadamer, *Truth and Method*, p. 493: "I want to argue for the pretention to universality of the act of understanding and of speaking. We can express everything in words, and can try to come to agreement about everything."

16. Gadamer, *Truth and Method*, p. 401.

17. See p. 20 in this book.

18. Michel Foucault, *Language, Counter-Memory, Practice: Selected Essays and Interviews*, trans. Donald F. Bouchard (Ithaca, N.Y.: Cornell University Press, 1977), p. 207.

19. Habermas, *Knowledge and Human Interests*, p. 264.

20. Michel Foucault, *Power/Knowledge*, ed. Colin Gordon (New York: Pantheon, 1972), p. 58.

21. Foucault, *Power/Knowledge*, p. 59.

22. Michel Foucault, *Discipline and Punish: The Birth of the Prison* (New York: Pantheon, 1977), p. 27.

23. Foucault, *Discipline and Punish*, pp. 26–27.

24. It may seem ironic that, although I wish to carry on without the traditional villains — the church, hierarchical social arrangements, or an individual whose ideas pervade Christian history — the "bad guy" role is still present, played by "individual subjective consciousness" and its adoption as an organizing assumption. It is, however, a different thing to identify within a well-defined discourse — late-twentieth-century academic discourse in the history of ideas in general and historical theology in particular — a constellation of ideas that prevent that discourse from moving toward a more inclusive historical inquiry. Within its original discourse — late-eighteenth-century philosophy — the identification of the "transcendental ego" or subjective consciousness was revelatory and liberating for those involved in the discourse. I am not interested in identifying the subjective consciousness as formulated and developed across discourses, but only in analyzing its adequacy and usefulness within our discourse. I assume that if the idea is still with us it must be exercising "strong power," an attraction that must be understood before it can be effectively questioned in the interest of more inclusive historical study.

25. Foucault, *Discipline and Punish*, pp. 26–27.

26. Foucault, *Power/Knowledge*, p. 119.

27. Foucault, *Power/Knowledge*, p. 57.

28. Foucault, *Language, Counter-Memory, Practice*, p. 213.

29. Foucault, *Power/Knowledge*, p. 59.

30. I am using the term "interest" here in the strong sense described by Habermas, *Knowledge and Human Interests*, p. 287: "The proposition that interest inheres in reason has an adequate meaning only within idealism, that is, only as long as we are convinced that reason can become transparent to itself by providing its own foundation . . . But if we comprehend the cognitive capacity and critical power of reason as deriving from the self-constitution of the human species under contingent natural conditions, then it is reason that inheres in interest."

31. Roland Barthes, *Elements of Semiology,* trans. A. Lavers and C. Smith (New York: Hill and Wang, 1976), p. 95.

32. See Foucault's detailed critique of the transtemporal continuity of ideas and statements, *Archeology of Knowledge,* pp. 21ff.

33. Foucault, *Archeology of Knowledge,* p. 100.

34. Foucault, *Archeology of Knowledge,* p. 176.

35. Foucault, *Archeology of Knowledge,* p. 149.

36. Foucault, *Archeology of Knowledge,* p. 149.

37. Clifford Geertz, *The Interpretation of Cultures* (New York: Basic Books, 1973), p. 106.

38. Geertz, *Interpretation of Cultures,* p. 20; see also p. 29.

39. Geertz, *Interpretation of Cultures,* p. 26.

40. I am indebted to the analytic ideas of cultural anthropologists; they should be taken much more into account in historical work, especially their recognition of the extent to which the study of an alien culture requires the suspension of cultural presuppositions, the acknowledgment of the perspective of the anthropologist, and the necessary incompleteness of description. Clifford Geertz writes, "Nor have I ever gotten anywhere near to the bottom of anything I have ever written about ... Cultural analysis is intrinsically incomplete." *Interpretation of Cultures,* p. 29.

41. Geertz, "Ideology as a Cultural System," in *Ideology and Its Discontents,* ed. David E. Apter (New York: Macmillan, 1964), p. 25.

42. Geertz, "Ideology as a Cultural System," p. 25.

43. Joseph Frary, "The Logic of Icons," *Sobornost,* ser. 6, no. 6 (Winter 1972), p. 398.

44. Marina Warner, *Alone of All Her Sex* (London: Quartet, 1978), p. 107.

45. Warner's interest in exposing the power politics of the early-medieval Roman church is also apparent in her interpretation of textual evidence. Compare, for example, the following quotations, both of which treat approximately the same information, but from the perspective of different interests: Santa Maria Antiqua "became the first church in Rome where the Church usurped the functions of the civil authorities, where an ecclesiastical diaconate took over such civil duties as the care of the sick and the old, hospitality to wayfarers, and the distribution of bread to the poor." Warner, *Alone of All Her Sex,* p. 106. "With the progressive weakening of the Byzantine administration in the last third of the sixth century, the Church had to take on by herself, through force of circumstance, nearly the entire task of feeding the people of Rome; only rarely could the government assist in combatting the endemic threat of famine." Richard Krautheimer, *Rome: Profile of a City, 312–1308* (Princeton: Princeton University Press, 1980), p. 71.

46. Warner, *Alone of All Her Sex,* p. 107.

47. See Augustine's description of social hierarchy as evidence of the Fall. The dislocation of true justice, that is, equality of all human persons, is only partially and temporarily compensated for Augustine by his insistence on the servanthood of rulers. *De civitate Dei* 19.15.

48. This line is also taken by André Grabar in *Christian Iconography: A Study of Its Origins,* Bollingen Series, no. 35, (Princeton: Princeton University Press, 1968), p. xlv: "The image is a means of conveying information ... a language." See also Rudolf Berliner, "The Freedom of Medieval Art," *Gazette des Beaux-Arts,* ser. 6, no. 28 (1945), pp. 267–268, for a discussion of prechristian and philosophical statements

concerning figurative art as "an autonomous method of acquiring knowledge otherwise unobtainable."

49. The capacity of images for resting the mind has been seen as undesirable for people whose minds are in need of stimulation and challenge rather than rest.

50. Quoted in L. W. Barnard, *The Graeco-Roman and Oriental Background of the Iconoclastic Controversy* (Leiden: Brill, 1974), p. 101.

51. I do not wish to argue, as does Hugh of St. Victor, for a depreciation of words, a "hierarchy of expressive media in which speech is secondary to knowledge acquired without words as intermediaries." (Berliner, "Freedom of Medieval Art," p. 277). Hugh's objection was to exclusive religious dependence on words and was based on changing definitions of the meanings of words as well as on the inevitable ambiguity of all words and their lack of competency to reveal "the invisible world" of religious meaning. As Rudof Berliner put it: "If words [are] not exempt from misunderstanding and [need] explanation they have no basic advantage over pictures" (p. 277).

52. "Intellectualizing" is not the exclusive prerogative of educationally privileged people, as Roland Barthes makes clear in his description of the stereotype as a popular "form of opportunism" in which one "sides with the power of language." *Image-Music-Text*, p. 199.

53. Frary, "Logic of Icons," p. 398.

54. Frary, "Logic of Icons," p. 397: "As soon as we know the rules, we can 'read' the icon." See also John Stuart, *Ikons* (London: Faber and Faber, 1975), who says that Russians use the same word to denote painting and writing, so that "it is said of an icon painter that he 'writes' (*pisat*) an icon. Thus the icon is nearer to hieroglyphics than to art" (p. 146). See also Davidson and Lytle, *After the Fact: The Art of Historical Detection* (New York: Knopf, 1982), p. 114, who discuss American Indians' notion that drawing is a kind of writing.

55. Barthes, *Image-Music-Text*, p. 39.

56. This description of the perspective of human being as primarily ordered by physical existence is dependent on Descartes's definition of "body" as animated, possessing feeling and psychological predicates, able to perform any functions — breathing, sleepwalking, voluntary and involuntary motions — that do not require the attention of consciousness. If I were to assume an earlier definition of body — Augustine's, for example — in which the body, without the presence of the animating soul, is literally a corpse, I would not be able to suggest a perspective from which consciousness is an epiphenomenon of body.

57. Ernst Jones wrote that "although there are thousands of symbols in the sense that the term is understood in analysis, all of them refer to the body itself, to kinship relations, to birth, to life, and to death." "The Theory of Symbolism" (1916), quoted by Lacan, *Language of the Self*, p. 58.

58. Consider Leo Frobenius' report of an Abyssinian woman's statement quoted by Joseph Campbell, *The Masks of God: Primitive Mythology* (New York: Viking, 1959), pp. 351–352: "A woman's life is quite different from a man's . . . A man is the same from the time of his circumcision to the time of his withering. He is the same before he has sought out a woman for the first time, and afterwards. But the day when a woman enjoys her first love cuts her in two. She becomes another woman on that day. The man is the same after his first love as he was before. The woman is from the day of her first love another. That continues so all through life. The man spends a night by a woman and goes away. His life and body are always the same. The woman conceives. As a mother she is another person than the woman without child."

59. Robert C. Neville, *Reconstruction of Thinking* (Albany, N. Y.: SUNY Press, 1981), p. 181.

60. Neville, *Reconstruction*, p. 181.

61. Neville, *Reconstruction*, p. 182: "One derives one's being from within the natural processes, and exhibits that being by responding to those processes. One's spontaneity arises by integrating the forces of natural processes into one's comportment as a natural event."

62. Hypatios, archbishop of Ephesus (531–538), quoted in Anthony Bryer and Judith Herrin, *Iconoclasm*, Papers given at the Ninth Spring Symposium of Byzantine Studies (Birmingham, Ala.: Center for Byzantine Studies, University of Birmingham, 1977), p. 181. Also see a similarly contemptuous modern statement: "For centuries, therefore, when the illiterate masses were unable to think in the abstractions of verbal imageries, architectural symbolism was a natural way of imaginative thinking because it was only by means of comprehensible forms that ideas, intuitions, and beliefs could have any convincing reality and popular validity." E. Baldwin Smith, *Architectural Symbolism of Imperial Rome and the Middle Ages* (Princeton: Princeton University Press, 1956), p. 5.

Chapter 3   *"The Evidence of Our Eyes": Fourth-Century Roman Churches*

1. Ernst Kitzinger, "The Cult of Images in the Age Before Iconoclasm," *Dumbarton Oaks Papers* 8 (1954), p. 146.

2. I have not been able to distinguish, among the fragmentary visual evidence extant from the fourth century, messages likely to have been received by various age, sex, and social class groups within the christian community. Part of the reason for this, I think, is that the discovery of a *via universalis,* heretofore only suggested or longed for by philosophers such as Porphyry, made appreciation of particularity secondary. The *via universalis* is a theme that was little developed in the fourth century. Our own situation is in this respect very different from that of fourth-century Christians; having been conditioned to universalization of the perspective of one particular human experience for many centuries, we are beginning, with a sense of exciting revelation, to understand the importance of attending to the experience of particular groups and persons. We will simply need to apply a hermeneutics of generosity to fourth-century people for whom the idea of universality was new, revolutionary, and exciting.

3. Consonant, however, with Jewish monotheism.

4. For example, Julian, the pagan emperor (361–363) describes Jesus as saying, "Whosoever is an adulterer, whosoever is a murderer, whosoever is accursed and wicked, let him be of good cheer and come; for I will wash him in this water and at once make him clean, and, if he falls into the same sins again, I will allow him to smite his breast and strike his head and become clean." *Convivium* 336; quoted in Arthur Darby Nock, *Essays on Religion and the Ancient World,* vol. 1 (Oxford: Clarendon, 1972), p. 132.

5. Sister Charles Murray, "Art and the Early Church," *Journal of Theological Studies* (Oct. 1977), p. 303.

6. Murray, "Art and the Early Church," p. 327.

7. Murray, "Art and the Early Church," p. 317.

8. Murray, "Art and the Early Church," p. 309; A. Perkins, *The Art of Dura Europus* (Oxford: Oxford University Press, 1973), p. 56.

9. Murray, "Art and the Early Church," p. 315.

10. Murray, "Art and the Early Church," p. 315.

11. Murray, "Art and the Early Church," pp. 323–324.

12. *Patrologia Latina*, 77, col. 1027–1028, 1128–1130.

13. There does seem to have been, however, one apparently unambiguous local rejection of the placement of images on church walls by a local synod, the Council of Elvira (c. 300). See Murray, "Art and the Early Church," pp. 317–318.

14. See Chapter 2, note 62 in this book.

15. *Patrologia Graeca* 46, col. 572.

16. Rudolf Berliner argues that "a purely hedonistic conception of art" was as alien to classical Greek and Roman writers as it was to fourth-century Christians. The true function of artistic representation was to present an invisible spiritual essence which, assiduously gazed on, was capable of making the viewer wise. "God Is Love," *Gazette des Beaux-Arts*, ser. 6, no. 42 (1953), pp. 267ff. Compare Plotinus: "The wisdom of the gods and the blessed is not expressed in propositions but by beautiful images." *Enneads* 5.8.5. Berliner's argument is important as a refutation of a common assumption among art historians that christian art, because of its didactic content, was a departure from classical art, which was solely concerned with visual form and beauty. One statement of this assumption appears in Charles Rufus Morey, *Early Christian Art* (Princeton: Princeton University Press, 1953), p. 59: "The world was to lose, for Christian eyes, its intrinsic beauty."

17. See on this point Augustine's scornful dismissal of religious art as a substitute for the study of scripture. Facts, he wrote, cannot be expected from paintings; "they have deserved to be mistaken who have researched Christ and his apostles not in the Holy Scriptures but on painted walls." *De concensu Evangel.* 1.9.

18. *Patrologia Latina*, 41, col. 850ff.

19. Richard Krautheimer estimates the population of Rome in 312 to have been approximately 800,000; of this, up to one-third were Christians or sympathized with Christians. *Rome: Profile of a City, 312–1308* (Princeton: Princeton University Press, 1980), p. 18.

20. Emile Mâle, *The Early Churches of Rome*, trans. David Buxton (London, Ernest Benn, Ltd., 1960), p. 53.

21. Krautheimer, *Rome*, p. 18.

22. Murray, "Art and the Early Church," pp. 344–345.

23. Paul Finney, "Antecedents of Byzantine Iconoclasm: Christian Evidence Before Constantine," in *The Image and the Word*, ed. Joseph Gutman (Missoula, Mont.: Scholars Press, 1977), p. 40.

24. Krautheimer, *Rome*, pp. 18–19.

25. House churches like this were also used by Jewish and Mithraic communities; examples are the Jewish house synagogue at Dura Europus and various sites in Rome. Mithraic meeting houses are indicated under the present San Clemente and the Basilica Porta Maggiore in Rome. See Lloyd M. White, *Domus Ecclesiae — Domus Dei*, Yale University dissertation, 1982 (Ann Arbor: University Microfilms International), and John F. Baldovin, *The Urban Character of Christian Worship in Jerusalem, Rome and Constantinople from the Fourth to the Tenth Centuries: The Origins, Development, and Meaning of Stational Liturgy*, Yale University dissertation, 1982 (Ann Arbor: University Microfilms International).

26. Ironically, Dura Europus "survived" to our time because it was destroyed in its own time. Its walls were reinforced shortly before the Persian invasion of 256, and the houses against the walls were buried until they were discovered in the twentieth century. Mâle, *Early Churches of Rome*, pp. 43–44; C. H. Kraeling, *The Excavations at Dura*

Europus: Final Report, vol. 8, part 2, *The Christian Building* (New Haven, Ct.: Dura Europus Publications, 1967).

27. Mâle, *Early Churches of Rome*, p. 43.

28. It is evident that the christian community had grown dramatically even before 313, numbering 50,000 (or about 5 percent of the population) by the mid-third century, before the decline in population during the perilous years 250–270. R. Krautheimer, *Studies in Early Christian, Medieval, and Renaissance Art* (New York: New York University Press, 1969), p. 2. Also see n. 19 above. During the third century, there were only two persecutions in Rome, lasting two years each. The Roman christian community by 313 was therefore a large and relatively affluent group, owning property, administering an impressively efficient organization for aid to the poor, taking charge of its own cemeteries, and determining church discipline and practice. Most third-century christian congregations were not in hiding, and their places of worship were known to their neighbors and even to state authorities.

29. The *Acts of Polycarp* mentions commemorative services at the tombs of martyrs and family members; see also Krautheimer, *Studies in Early Christian, Medieval, and Renaissance Art*, p. 19.

30. A catalog of subjects discovered thus far in Roman catacombs can be found in A. Nestori, *Repertorio, Topographia della Pitture della Catacombe Romane* (Città de Vaticano: Pontificio Istituto di Archeologia Cristiana, 1975), pp. 183ff.

31. For a description of the earliest portraits of Christ, see S. G. F. Brandon, "The Portrait of Christ: Its Origin and Evolution," *History Today* 23 (1971), pp. 473–481.

32. J. Stevenson, *The Catacombs: Rediscovered Monuments of Early Christianity* (London: Thames and Hudson, 1978), p. 61; see also Paul Corby Finney's suggestions that a more or less representational art may have differentiated proto-orthodox from gnostic art in the first centuries of the christian era: "If Gnostics made pictures, they were probably esoteric and fantastic, laconic signs and symbols devoid of narrative content." "Did Gnostics Make Pictures?" in *The Rediscovery of Gnosticism*, ed. Bentley Layton (Leiden: E. J. Brill, 1980), p. 450.

33. Stevenson, *Catacombs*, p. 34.

34. Stevenson, *Catacombs*, pp. 53–54.

35. Although some scenes of martyrdom exist from the time of persecution, these are rare in early christian art. One example is the fresco in the third-century remains of a christian house under the basilica of Ss. Giovanni e Paolo in Rome, depicting the beheading of three martyrs. See Stevenson, *Catacombs*, p. 38, for other examples.

36. Mâle, *Early Churches of Rome*, p. 24.

37. Clement of Alexandria 7.3.14; trans. and ed. Henry Chadwick, *Alexandrian Christianity* (Philadelphia: Westminster, 1954).

38. There is no question of destruction of any images by Christians in the third century: "No instances of such destruction are recorded, no attacks on religious properties, whether public, official monuments (for example those attached to the state religion), or private monuments, domestic chapels and cult places, painting, statues, and other religious arts in private ownership. Finney, "Did Gnostics Make Pictures?," p. 27.

39. Murray, "Art and the Early Church," p. 322.

40. Murray, "Art and the Early Church," pp. 321–323.

41. The *tituli* was originally a marble slab engraved with the owner's name, serving as proof of his ownership of the property. The term was extended to designate the house and property.

42. Krautheimer has shown that "what we might call the 'normal early Christian basilica' evolved only during the second half of the fourth and the fifth centuries." *Early Christian and Byzantine Architecture* (London: 1965), p. 42. Cf. Frederic van der Meer's discussion of Christian basilicas in *Early Christian Art* (Chicago: University of Chicago Press, 1967), pp. 53ff. Van der Meer's statement "The churches of the faith have remained as constant and unchanging as the faith itself" (p. 53) seems purposely ambiguous; the context, however, makes it clear that the statement intends not ambiguity but accuracy.

43. Eusebius was not a sycophant as he is often presented. See Sister Charles Murray on this point also. "Art and the Early Church," pp. 334–335; also see T. D. Barnes, *Constantine and Eusebius* (Cambridge, Mass.: Harvard University Press, 1981), pp. 104, 266.

44. Eusebius *Ecclesiastical History* 10.2.1, trans. G. A. Williamson (Baltimore: Penguin, 1966).

45. Eusebius *Ecclesiastical History* 10.4.58.

46. Eusebius *Ecclesiastical History* 10.44.2.

47. Eusebius *Ecclesiastical History* 10.4.67.

48. *Vita Constantini* 53; trans. in *A Select Library of the Nicene and Post Nicene Fathers*, 2nd ser., vol. 1 (Grand Rapids, Mich.: The Christian Literature Company, 1890).

49. Since Lactantius (*De moribus persecutorum*) describes the destruction of the church as taking only a few hours, it is unlikely that it was a very large or substantial building.

50. Whatever the dangers and difficulties of a mixture of political and religious powers, these are incomparably more glaring to twentieth-century people than they were to fourth-century people, for whom a strongly coordinated system of social, religious, and political power meant that some rather concrete and fundamental hopes for internal and external peace, food, and other necessities of everyday life that were dependent on such a government might be realized.

51. Krautheimer, *Studies in Early Christian, Medieval, and Renaissance Art*, p. 5.

52. Krautheimer, *Studies in Early Christian, Medieval, and Renaissance Art*, p. 8.

53. The spatial separation of clergy from laity has been described by Krautheimer as "a separation of more and less important parts," a "hierarchic separation." *Studies in Early Christian, Medieval, and Renaissance Art*, p. 7. Another interpretation of this phenmenon is possible, and perhaps both need to be made so that neither interpretation can claim finality; both must have been held by people at different times or by different people at the same time. In the new mammoth churches, distinguishing between clergy participating in the service in their various roles and laity participating in the service in other but no less important roles must have seemed mandatory to churches unaccustomed to the crowds of new converts. There must have been a need to give order to these potentially chaotic assemblies of standing or even, as in contemporary churches frequently visited by large numbers of tourists, sauntering people. Order inevitably produces hierarchy, but I think we should at least note a difference between a desire to establish a hierarchy of less and more important participants in worship and a desire for orderly worship. We must note also the variety of seating arrangements in local churches: In the Orleansville Cathedral in North Africa, clergy were enthroned in the high apse above the congregation, while at Aquileia, they were seated on the same level. Krautheimer, *Early Christian and Byzantine Architecture*, pp. 23–24.

54. It is important not to overinterpret liturgical requirements as determining the

architectural form of fourth-century churches. Church shapes ranged from round to rectangular, and liturgical actions could be assimilated to buildings of the most various internal design. Interior furniture likewise was variously placed according to local custom; sometimes the altar stood near the wall of the apse, sometimes in the middle of the nave, sometimes in front of the apse. There was no completely standard placement, just as there was no standard architectural design in fourth-century christian churches. See Jean Lassus, *The Early Christian and Byzantine World* (London: Paul Hamlyn, 1967), p. 41.

55. Tertullian tells us of this custom in *De Poententibus* 7; *Patrologia Latina* 1, col. 1352. Durandus of Mende mentions this custom as still practiced at the end of the thirteenth century: *Rationale divinorum officiorum* 6.56.11.

56. Krautheimer, *Early Christian and Byzantine Architecture*, p. 43.

57. The *agape,* or communal meal, died out only in the fourth century, apparently due to the unmanageable size of congregations. Originally, Christians brought gifts for this meal, but when the meal was discontinued as impractical, participation in the offertory procession was considered an obligation up to about the eleventh century. It was not considered sufficiently forceful for each member of the congregation to be merely represented in the offering; rather, each had to *present* a symbolic offering. Theodor Klauser, *A Short History of the Western Liturgy,* 2nd ed., trans. John Halliburton (Oxford: Oxford University Press, 1979), p. 110.

58. Mâle, *Early Churches of Rome,* p. 53.

59. Fourth-century churches in and about Rome that have survived to the present have often been altered to give the dim light that was valued later, at the time of reconstructions of the building. Frequently half of the windows have been covered over.

60. Krautheimer, *Early Christian and Byzantine Architecture,* p. 25; Constantine's oratory in Constantinople still had a representation of Constantine as sun god as late as 1105. See E. Baldwin Smith, *Architectural Symbolism of Imperial Rome and the Middle Ages* (Princeton: Princeton University Press, 1956), pp. 47–48, n. 138; p. 90, n. 54.

61. Krautheimer, *Early Christian and Byzantine Architecture,* p. 43.

62. Krautheimer, *Early Christian and Byzantine Architecture,* p. 44.

63. According to the *Liber Pontificalis,* the figure of Christ was five feet tall and weighed 120 pounds; each of the apostles was five feet tall and weighed 90 pounds. The figures facing the apse were as follows: a five-foot Christ, weighing 140 pounds; and four silver angels, each five feet tall and weighing 105 pounds, with precious stones set in their eyes and holding spears. The entire structure weighed 2,025 pounds. M. Teasedale-Smith, "The Latin Fastigium: A Gift of Constantine the Great," *Rivista di archeologia Cristiana* 44 (1970), pp. 149–715.

64. Krautheimer, *Early Christian and Byzantine Architecture,* p. 26.

65. Samuel Laeuchli has contrasted the inclusivity of christian art, as evidenced in extant floor mosaics from the cathedral of the important fourth-century seaport of Aquileia, with the exclusivity of the Creed of the Council of Nicea. *Religion and Art in Conflict* (Philadelphia: Fortress, 1980), chap. 6, passim. My own thesis differs from Laeuchli's in that I do not understand verbal and visual religious formulation as in conflict but rather as complementary, as I discuss later.

66. Stevenson, *Catacombs,* p. 39.

67. Stevenson, *Catacombs,* p. 21.

68. Michael Gough, *The Origins of Christian Art* (London: Thames and Hudson, 1973), p. 105.

69. Stevenson, *Catacombs,* pp. 82, 92.

70. An important study by Emerson H. Swift of the stylistic origins of late-classical christian art rejects the suggestion that this distinctive feature, frontality of presentation, came into Roman art from "oriental" influences. Swift demonstrates instead the stylistic continuity of imagery in fourth-century christian buildings with Roman popular art of the earlier centuries. In earlier catacomb art, for example, the figures are usually presented frontally, directly engaging the viewer. Moreover, the frontality of the art of Roman catacombs was "far more extreme than can be discovered in any of the Asiatic sarcophagi." *Roman Sources of Christian Art* (New York: Columbia University Press, 1951), p. 160.

71. Swift, *Roman Sources,* p. 158.

72. P. Styger, *Die altchristliche Grabeskunst* (Munich: J. Kösel and F. Pustet, 1927), p. 71. Styger found that of fifty-six Old Testament figures mentioned in contemporary prayers, thirty can be found in fourth-century paintings or carved sarcophagi.

73. See Francis Yates, *The Art of Memory* (Chicago: University of Chicago Press, 1966), for a fascinating discussion of the ancient art of memory, in which the architectural features of a well-known building were mentally connected to stanzas or lines of a long poem so that the reciter could mentally enter the building and, as he recited the poem, collect the various parts of the poem from their architectural setting. Something like this may have informed the subjects painted in churches and catacombs; they may have been mnemonic aids to prayer.

74. See the portrait busts of Constantine in which the whole animation and energy of the body is concentrated in his visual ray trained on the unseen world of spiritual realities. Also see *De vita Constantini* 4.15: "How deeply his soul was impressed by the power of divine faith may be understood from the fact that he ordered his portrait to be stamped on the gold coin of the empire with the eyes uplifted as in the posture of prayer to God: and this money became current throughout the Roman world. His full-length portrait was also placed over the entrance-gate at the palaces in some cities, eyes up-raised to heaven, and hands outspread as if in prayer."

75. Best described by H. P. L. Orange and P. J. Nordhagen, *Mosaics,* trans. Ann E. Keep (London: Methuen and Company, 1958).

76. Orange and Nordhagen, *Mosaics,* p. 42.

77. Orange and Nordhagen, *Mosaics,* p. 42.

78. See, for example, Origen's nostalgia when he wrongly assumed that the times of persecution were over: "Those were the days when Christians were really faithful, when the noble martyrdoms were taking place, when, after conducting the martyrs' bodies to the cemeteries, we returned thence to meet together, and the entire church was present without being afraid, and the catechumens were being catechized during the very time of the martyrdoms and while people were dying who had confessed the very truth unto death . . . Then we knew and saw wonderful and miraculous signs. Then there were true believers, few in number, but faithful, treading the straight and narrow way that leads to life. But now, when we have become many, out of the multitude which profess piety there are extremely few who are attaining to the election of God and to blessedness. *Homilies in Jeremiah* 4.3.

79. Although Constantinian churches were not centrally located in Rome and did not possess elaborate facades, they were very noticeable from the outside because of their enormous size; internally, of course, they were elaborately visible in the ways we have described.

80. See Erwin R. Goodenough's statement: "The great contribution of catacomb art

is to show us a faith much simpler and more direct than the faith of the involved theologians of the time." "Early Christian Catacomb Art," *Journal of Biblical Literature* 81 (1962), p. 141. Stevenson remarks that the literary sources of early Christianity give an impression that "Rome was swarming with heretics and schismatics in the early centuries." *Catacombs,* p. 109.

81. See André Grabar's discussion in chap. 6, "Dogmas Represented by Juxtaposed Images," in his *Christian Iconography: A Study of Its Origins,* Bollingen Series, no. 25 (Princeton: Princeton University Press, 1968).

82. It is not clear to me why naturalistic treatment of scenes from the natural world must be interpreted simply as holdovers from classical art; Christians may have adopted the naturalistic style of Hellenistic art not because they did not know how to give their religious ideas any other visible form but because they found this style congruent with the high value of the created world. When the former interpretation is given to explain early christian use of a naturalistic style, it is usually based on the claims that Christians had no appreciation of the natural world for reasons endemic to christian "otherworldliness." See Grabar, *Christian Iconography,* pp. 49–50: "indifferent to the beauties of the visible world and its vain appearances, the early Christians contented themselves with the most summary depictions of things seen and discountenanced any sort of naturalism"; also see Morey, *Early Christian Art,* p. 59: "The world was to lose, for Christian eyes, its intrinsic beauty."

83. Stevenson finds three possible meanings indistinguishably interwoven in catacomb banquet scenes: a Eucharistic or *agape* meal, a pagan funereal banquet, and the banquet of the blessed in heaven. *Catacombs,* p. 94.

84. See. L. W. Barnard's argument that pagan symbols were used by "conscious choice" by Christian artists as apologetics. "Early Christian Art as Apologetic," *Journal of Religious History,* vol. 10, no. 1 (June, 1978), pp. 20–31.

85. See especially Smith's researches, *Architectural Symbolism* and also *The Dome: A Study in the History of Ideas* (Princeton: Princeton University Press, 1950). The former book gives a detailed account of the "extent to which the patrons of architecture, the state and the church, succeeded in embodying ideas of heavenly powers, universal authority, and awe-inspiring grandeur" in architecture (p. 3).

86. See Orange and Nordhagen, who follow Dygge's interpretation: "In the basilica designed for worship the whole building is directed axially to the center of worship, the altar, which is placed in front of the vaulted apse under a celestial canopy, *ciborium,* in just the same way as the imperial *palatium sacrum* was related axially to its center of worship at the rear, the emperor enthroned beneath the *ciborium.*" *Mosaics,* pp. 17–18.

87. Smith, *Architectural Symbolism,* p. 3.

88. See Klauser, *Short History,* for a discussion of the imperial connotations of clergy dress in the fourth century (p. vi). As early as 318, Constantine made bishops state officials by giving them "power of jurisdiction in civil proceedings between Christians and other Christians . . . between Christians and non-Christians, and no one was allowed to appeal against their judgments" (p. 33).

89. The earliest extant publicly accessible crucifixion depictions are on a panel from the wooden doors of Santa Sabina on Rome, between A.D. 422 and 440; an ivory box from southern Gaul, made for a private owner and hence not associated with public worship, may be a bit earlier. Gough, *Origins of Christian Art,* pp. 120–121, 130.

90. Robert A. Markus, *Christianity in the Roman World* (London: Thames and Hudson, 1947), p. 87.

91. *De vita Constantini* 2.56.

92. *Code Theod.* 26.1.2, quoted in C. N. Cochrane, *Christianity and Classical Culture* (Oxford: Oxford University Press, 1940), p. 327. Significantly, legislation against paganism began in 382 with "the nationalization of the temples and of their treasures (including the statues of the gods) which were thrown open to the public as monuments of art." Cochrane, *Christianity,* p. 329. Also see chap. 1, n. 21, in this book.

93. Augustine *De civitate Dei* 10.32; cf. John J. O'Meara, *Porphyry's Philosophy from Oracles in Augustine* (Paris: Etudes Augustiniennes 1959), p. 144.

94. Augustine *De civitate Dei* 10.32.

95. Confusion of late-fourth-century art with the art of fifty years later, led Klauser, for example, to write: "For it was in this century [fourth] that Christ began to be looked upon as a ruler who as the 'Pantocrator' governed the whole of creation. As a result of this conception whenever Jesus was portrayed in the art of that period he assumed the outward marks of imperial rank; he was the ruler who sat on a throne adorned with jewels and purple cushions, who wore the royal halo, whose foot and hand were kissed, who was surrounded by a heavenly cortege of palace and much else besides." *Short History,* p. 36.

96. Compare the triumphant Christ of the Santa Pudenziana apse mosaic whose unassuming humble demeanor and dress emphasize simultaneously his triumph and his accessibility with Cochrane's description of the increasing inaccessibility of the emperor: "Successive enactments restricted to a privileged few the right of 'touching the purple' and of 'adoring his serenity.' As for the masses, for whom the imperial person was inaccessible, they had to be content with prostrating themselves before the 'sacred portraits.' " *Christianity,* p. 321.

Chapter 4 *Images of Women in Fourteenth-Century Tuscan Painting*

1. Edwin Ardener, "Belief and the Problem of Women," in *The Interpretation of Ritual,* ed. J. S. La Fontaine (London: Tavistock, 1972), p. 137.

2. Ardener, "Belief," p. 136.

3. Ardener, "Belief," p. 152.

4. Elisabeth Schüssler Fiorenza has outlined a feminist critical hermeneutics for the reconstruction of "a common historical experience of women as unconsciously collaborating or struggling participants in patriarchal culture and history." *In Memory of Her* (New York: Crossroads, 1983), p. 31. The goal of this hermeneutics is the recovery of a detailed picture of both the form and style of patriarchal oppression and the power of women in historical christian communities. One of the "methodological rules for dealing with the information of androcentric texts" is analysis of these texts "in their specific socio-political context in order to establish their function" (p. 60). It is at this point that the analysis and interpretation of the visual images commonly and constantly available to particular historical communities become a necessity. Images constitute an essential part of the cultural context, a vivid primary communication without which any analysis of context is seriously incomplete and often distorted. The context of an androcentric text can be supplied only partially from other androcentric verbal texts. Stepping outside the evidence of verbal texts altogether by attention to visual images can often reveal a crucially important cultural communication that will alter our reconstruction of the context.

5. Recognition of this ambiguity was difficult for me and delayed the writing of this chapter for several weeks while I first tried to find ways to dissolve the ambiguity in a more comprehensive and unified argument — in spite of having written in chapter 2 of the value of allowing contradictions to show! Failing to find the more comprehensive

argument, I then undertook to understand its structure and meaning. I had wanted to claim that it was in images that women found a range of models on which to pattern their self-images and behavior. This thesis is not untrue, but neither is it the whole picture. It is an important and neglected part of the picture, and thus it is valuable to point it out and to demonstrate it as fully as possible. But the usefulness of images for women must not be permitted to obscure the different usefulness they held for men.

6. Jane Gallop, *The Daughter's Seduction: Feminism and Psychoanalysis* (New York: Cornell University Press, 1982), p. 35.

7. Ardener, "Belief," p. 35.

8. R. Fawtier, *Sainte Catherine de Siena* (Paris: Librarie Gallimard, 1921), p. 222.

9. For accounts of visions in which the figures of the vision appear "in the forms which they have in painting," see O. Lehmann Brockhaus, *Schriftquellen zur Kunstgeschichte des 11. und 12. Jahrunderts für Deutschland, Lothringen, und Italien* (Berlin, 1938).

10. Interesting in this connection and testifying to the importance of vision in worship is the late, medieval practice, unknown in Rome until the end of the thirteenth century, of the elevation of the communion bread during mass for an extended period so that people might gaze on it. *The New Catholic Encyclopedia*, vol. 9 (New York: McGraw-Hill, 1967), p. 422, reports that this aspect of the mass became so vital a part of the Eucharist that people would shout to the priest to raise it higher if they were unable to see it and would consider gazing on the elevated host as a substitute for receiving it, frequently leaving the church after the elevation.

11. For expenditure in Tuscany on art, see Millard Meiss, *Painting in Florence and Siena After the Black Death* (New York: Harper Torchbooks, 1964), pp. 78ff.

12. Bruce Cole, *Giotto and Florentine Painting 1280–1375* (New York: Harper and Row, 1976), p. 18.

13. The trend toward stronger light in churches than in Romanesque and Gothic buildings began in the fourteenth century. A century later, by the beginning of Renaissance, "a brightness had been achieved that displeased conservative souls." Paul Frankl, *The Gothic: Literary Sources and Interpretations Through Eight Centuries* (Princeton: Princeton University Press, 1960), p. 219.

14. The new use of images attracted considerable attention and discussion, apparently even when they were in chapels designed for the private use of wealthy families. A letter written on January 9, 1305, by monks of a hermitage church close to the Scrovegni Chapel in Padua, which was newly erected and painted by Giotto, complains that the wealthy Enrico Scrovegni had been given a permit "to erect a small church, almost in the manner of an oratory, for himself, his mother and his family, and that people ought not to be allowed to frequent this church." Quoted in Cole, *Giotto*, p. 65. Apparently both the prescribed modest scale of decoration and its private use were being flagrantly ignored, thereby attracting worshippers away from the nearby hermitage church, an enormous, dark building without decoration.

15. M. Baxandall, *Painting and Experience in Fifteenth Century Italy* (Oxford: Oxford University Press, 1972), p. 41.

16. Quoted in Baxandall, *Painting and Experience*, p. 41.

17. *Rationale divinorum officiorum* 3.4. Gregory the Great's classical statement on the practical value of images was quoted frequently by medieval authors as authoritative — in the medieval sense of "authoritative," that is, a formulation that both validates and is validated by contemporary experience. Gregory had written his statement to Bishop Serenus of Marseilles in 787: "One thing is the adoration of an image; an-

other thing is to learn what to adore from the story rendered by the image. For what the Scripture teaches those who read, the same the image shows to those who cannot read, but see; because in it even the ignorant see whom they ought to follow; in the image those who do not know better are able to read." *Episutla* 11.13, *Patrologia Latina* 77, cols. 1128–1129.

18. Rudolf Berliner, "The Freedom of Medieval Art," p. 273.

19. *Meditations on the Life of Christ: An Illustrated Manuscript of the Fourteenth Century,* trans. Isa Ragusa and Rosalie B. Green (Paris: Bibliothèque Nationale, Ms. Ital. 115; Princeton: Princeton University Press, 1977), p. 3.

20. *De administratione,* quoted in Erwin Panofsky, *Abbot Suger on the Abbey Church of St.-Denis* (Princeton: Princeton University Press, 1946), p. 21.

21. *Adnotationes mysticae in Psalmos CXIII,* P.L. 196, col. 337. Barbara Nolan contrasts Richard's teaching that the full beatific vision can occur in this life with Augustine's cautious "We walk more by faith than by sight" and his frequent quoting of 1 Cor. 13:12: "We see now through a mirror and in an enigma, then, however, face to face." *The Gothic Visionary Perspective* (Princton: Princeton University Press, 1977), p. 31. See also Margaret R. Miles, "Vision: The Eye of the Body and the Eye of the Mind," *Journal of Religion* (April, 1983), pp. 125–142.

22. Thomas Waley, *De modo comonendi sermones,* quoted in Baxandall, *Painting and Experience,* p. 64.

23. Meiss, *Painting in Florence and Siena,* p. 130. For medieval religious drama, see David M. Bevington, ed. and trans., *Medieval Drama* (Boston: Houghton Mifflin, 1975); O. B. Hardison, Jr., *Christian Rite and Christian Drama in the Middle Ages* (Baltimore: Johns Hopkins University Press, 1969); William Tydeman, *The Theatre in the Middle Ages* (New York: Cambridge University Press, 1978); Karl Young, *The Drama of the Medieval Church,* vol. 2 (Oxford: Oxford University Press, 1933).

24. *Meditations on the Life of Christ,* p. 139.

25. *Meditations on the Life of Christ,* p. 309.

26. *Meditations on the Life of Christ,* p. 167.

27. *Meditations on the Life of Christ,* p. 150.

28. For example, the popular legend that Mary Magdalene and John the Evangelist were married at Cana where Christ performed his first miracle is rejected as "false and frivolous" by Jacobus de Voragine in *The Golden Legend.* The tale claimed that Christ called John to follow him directly after the wedding feast and Mary Magdalene, in anger at being thus preemptorily jilted, became a prostitute.

29. *Meditations on the Life of Christ,* pp. 138–9.

30. *Meditations on the Life of Christ,* pp. 32–3.

31. The description in the *Meditations on the Life of Christ* of Joseph's despondency can account for Filippo Lippi's panel painting of a nativity scene in which Joseph sits, resting his chin on his hand, a conventional gesture of discouragement (Florence, Uffizi, about 1455). San Bernardino of Siena objected to such depictions of Joseph in a sermon: "Joseph was a cheerful old man, and should be shown so." Quoted in Baxandall, *Painting and Experience,* p. 61.

32. *Meditations on the Life of Christ,* p. 387.

33. Despite occasional complaints by theologians about particularly misleading images, no one to my knowledge argues against all use of religious images. See Berliner, "Freedom of Medieval Art," pp. 281ff., for a discussion of some "reservations" and complaints by theologians against antidogmatic images. Unlike sixteenth-century

iconophiles, fourteenth-century theologians were apparently able to distinguish between "use" and "abuse."

34. Baxandall, *Painting and Experience*, p. 48.

35. Baxandall, *Painting and Experience*, p. 45.

36. Jacobus de Voragine, *The Golden Legend*, trans. Granger Ryan and Helmut Ripperger (New York: Arno, 1969).

37. Another liturgical use of illuminated manuscripts that demonstrated the centrality of images in liturgy is the following. From high pulpits, lit by candlesticks, the *Exultet* was read from a long illuminated scroll. "On these scrolls, the subjects mentioned in the *Exultet* were illustrated by lively miniatures, usually painted upside-down in relation to the text, so that as the deacon intoned the verses, the congregation could watch this medieval form of 'moving pictures' slowly descending from the pulpit." Georgina Masson, *The Companion Guide to Rome* (London: Collins, 1972), pp. 339–40.

38. But see Sixten Ringbom's interesting thesis that pictorial formulations served as inspiration for literary analogy, not vice versa. *Icon to Narrative* (Åbo, Finland: Åbo Akademi, 1965), p. 19. See also Meiss, *Painting in Florence and Siena*, chap. 5. George La Piana has demonstrated the origin of a Latin liturgical office from a *representatio*, or extraliturgical drama which itself derived from Byzantine iconography of the early life of the Virgin. "The Byzantine Iconography of the Presentation of the Virgin Mary to the Temple and a Latin Religious Pageant," in *Late Classical and Medieval Studies in Honor of Albert Matthias Friend, Jr.*, ed. Richard Krautheimer (Princeton: Princeton University Press, 1955), pp. 261ff.

39. G. Boccaccio, *Decameron* 6.5, trans. F. Winwar (New York: Modern Library, 1955), p. 365.

40. M. R. James, *The Apocryphal New Testament* (Oxford: Oxford University Press, 1926).

41. *Meditations on the Life of Christ*, pp. 337–8.

42. Meiss, *Painting in Florence and Siena*, p. 131.

43. Private devotional images also appeared for the first time in the late thirteenth and early fourteenth century. Erwin Panofsky, *Festschrift für Max J. Friedlander* (Leipzig, 1927), pp. 264ff. See also Meiss, *Painting in Florence and Siena*, p. 145: "These images ... embody in the most distinctive and novel way those tendencies apparent in all the art of this period to establish a direct, sympathetic, and intimate emotional relationship between the spectator and the sacred figures."

44. "Secularized" here means simply that most of the large commissions for painting came from the guilds or from wealthy private individuals rather than from churches and monasteries. The term seems to me ill-advised in that it connotes to us a departure from religious interests. In fact, religious subjects were being painted — and seen — outside churches in a variety of public and private buildings. This trend thus involved the appropriation and extension of religious themes by the laypeople who commissioned them rather than any rejection of religious art.

However, the "secular and communal" commissioning of art for public places should not be understood to imply that a large share in the selection of sites, artists, subjects, and styles belonged to the increasingly important middle class. Towns were controlled by guilds of the great merchants, bankers, industrialists, and professional men, but large segments of the population, such as workers in the major industry of Florence, the manufacture and refinement of cloth, were excluded by law from forming or joining a guild. For example, only in 1378 were painters allowed to form an independent *mem-*

brum of the guild of physicians and apothecaries, to which they had belonged as dependents of the apothecaries since 1314. Meiss, *Painting in Florence and Siena,* p. 59. The argument for the popular significance of painting in this chapter does not assume a democratic base for the commissioning of art but rests on a lively popular exposure to and interest in the viewing of paintings.

45. M. Baxandall, *Giotto and the Orators* (Oxford: Clarendon, 1971), p. 62.

46. Baxandall, *Giotto and the Orators,* p. 14.

47. Baxandall, *Painting and Experience,* pp. 118ff.

48. Millard Meiss documents a change in style and taste around 1350, under the massive shock of the Black Death, to the distinction of Christ and other figures by "elevation, immobility, isolation, and frontality." The style of the ducento, with its greater ability to reassure the viewer of divine protection in the face of overwhelming loss and misery, was to a large extent reinstated in the second half of the fourteenth century. Yet it was the influence of Giotto's naturalistic style that was to reemerge in Masaccio's frescoes for the Brancacci Chapel, which ushered in Renaissance painting. Frankl, *The Gothic,* p. 241.

49. Quoted in Marina Warner, *Alone of All Her Sex* (London: Quartet, 1978), p. 213.

50. "Come, my chosen one, I shall place you on my throne."

51. "His left hand should be under my head, and his right hand will embrace me."

52. A collection of diptychs in the Louvre in Paris offers a clue as to the intended theological meaning of the associated themes of Mary as Queen of Heaven and Bride of Christ. One side of these diptychs displays the coronation of the Virgin, while the other side shows the crucifixion. In the first, Mary, a human being, is elevated to the height of the spiritual cosmos, partaker in divinity; on the opposite side, Christ is shown at the nadir — from a human perspective — of his earthly career, dying and thus participating fully in the human condition. Humanity is divinized in Mary, and divinity is humanized in Christ, a graphic portrayal of the access of every human being to salvation. Jacobus de Voragine wrote that Mary is the neck that joins Christ, the head of the church, to the faithful, the body of Christ.

53. Paul Hetherington, *Pietro Cavallini: A Study in the Art of Late Medieval Rome* (London: Sagittarius, 1979), p. 94: "The selection of subjects treated in the mosaics does not correspond to any one textual source . . . nor does it have a recognizable theological basis, such as the group of Marian feasts drawn up at the Council of Toulouse in 1229. The subjects must therefore be regarded as a personal selection."

54. Meiss, *Painting in Florence and Siena,* p. 132.

55. Meiss, *Painting in Florence and Siena,* pp. 151–152.

56. Warner, *Alone of All Her Sex,* p. 200.

57. See James H. Stubblebine, *Giotto: The Arena Chapel Frescoes* (London: Thames and Hudson, 1969), for a discussion of the "unusually elaborate participation" of the Virgin in the Last Judgment, a participation for which there exists "no prototype" (pp. 90, 175).

58. *Meditations on the Life of Christ,* p. 335.

59. Although not defined as Roman Catholic dogma until Pope Pius XII's bull *Munifcentissimus Deus* in 1950, a long tradition of apocryphal stories, popular devotional works, and iconography preceded the official acceptance of the Virgin's bodily assumption.

60. The dogma of the Immaculate Conception was proclaimed by Pope Pius IX

only in 1854, but, as in the case of the dogma of the bodily assumption, this formal dogma was long anticipated in popular literature and painting.

61. Jacobus, *Golden Legend*, p. 150.

62. V. Saxer, *La Culte de Mary Magdalene en Occident, des Origines a la fin du moyen age* (Paris, 1959), p. 2: (1) the sinful woman of Luke 7:36–50; (2) sister of Martha, Luke 10:38–42; (3) sister of Lazarus, weeping for the death of Lazarus, John 11:1–45; (4) anointing Christ's feet with perfume, John 12:1–8; (5) being delivered from seven devils, Luke 8:2, Mark 16:9; (6) following Jesus to Judea, Matt. 27:55–56, Mark 15:40–41, Luke 23.49; John 19:25; (7) at the resurrection of Christ, Matt. 28:1–10, Mark 16:1–8, Luke 24:1–10, John 20:1–10; (8) as the first to see Christ after the resurrection, John 20:11–18, Mark 16:9–11. See also Warner, *Alone of All Her Sex*, Appendix B, "A Muddle of Marys," pp. 344–345.

63. Gregory the Great conflates several gospel accounts: *Hom.* 33.1, *Patrologiae Latina*, 76, col. 1238.

64. Extreme reluctance to relinquish a tradition of such devotional vigor, even when demonstrated as inaccurate, is shown in the declaration of the theology faculty of the University of Paris in 1521 that Lefevre's teaching was "dangerous." Only the personal intervention of Francis I saved Lefevre from condemnation as a heretic. Saxer, *La Culte de Mary Magdalene*, p. 12.

65. John 20:17.

66. The image of the Magdalene at the foot of the cross appears first in the late twelfth century but achieved its greatest popularity in the trecento in Italy.

67. *Meditations on the Life of Christ*, p. 170. Cf. the anonymous fourteenth-century English vernacular treatise *The Cloud of Unknowing*, 16: "her sorrow was more heart-felt, her longing more grievous, her sighing more profound, her languishing nearly fatal, because she wanted to love God more."

68. *Meditations on the Life of Christ*, p. 171.

69. *Meditations on the Life of Christ*, p. 172.

70. *Meditations on the Life of Christ*, p. 308.

71. *Meditations on the Life of Christ*, p. 362.

72. For example, images of infantile dependency and weakness, such as presented in the popular subjects of the nursing Virgin, the Madonna of the Cradle, and the like, may have been compensatory and healing in the medieval situation of minimal parenting, but the same image, in a society that protects and cushions its young against economic necessity, could certainly be counterproductive. In the latter type of society, images that challenge people to maturity, autonomy, and independence would be productive.

73. See Eileen Power, "The Position of Women,'" in *The Legacy of the Middle Ages*, ed. G. C. Crump and E. F. Jacobs (Oxford: Clarendon 1926), pp. 401–434.

74. Stanley Chojnacki, "Patrician Women in Early Renaissance Venice," *Studies in the Renaissance* 21 (1974), pp. 176–203.

75. Chojnacki, "Patrician Women," pp. 186–187.

76. Angela of Foligno, *The Book of Divine Consolation*, trans. Mary G. Steegmann (London: Chatto and Windus, 1909), p. 5.

77. Dante Alighieri, *La Vita Nuova* 2, trans. Barbara Reynolds (Hammondsworth, Middlesex: Penguin, 1969).

78. Dante, *La Vita Nuova* 19: "To look at her, her virtue then he knows, / For, greeting him, salvation she bestows."

79. Chojnacki, "Patrician Women," pp. 186–187.

80. Hannah Arendt has richly demonstrated this in her study of revolutions, *The Origins of Totalitarianism* (New York: Meridian, 1958).

81. Gallop, *The Daughter's Seduction*, p. 35. Even the Virgin is, however, sometimes depicted as jealous and demanding; see Warner, *Alone of All Her Sex*, pp. 156–159 and pl. XIX.

82. See R. Bridenthal and C. Koonz, eds., *Becoming Visible: Women in European History* (Boston: Houghton Mifflin, 1977), especially "Sanctity and Power: The Dual Pursuit of Medieval Women," pp. 90–118. Also see Eileen Power, "The Position of Women."

83. Chojnacki, "Patrician Women." See also C. Bynum, *Jesus as Mother: Studies in the Spirituality of the High Middle Ages* (Berkeley: University of California Press, 1982), p. 143. Writing of literary imagery, Bynum concludes, "There is little evidence that the popularity of feminine and maternal imagery in the high Middle Ages reflects an increased respect for actual women by men."

84. Aristotle *Historia animalium* 608B; *Politics* 1252B.

85. Vern L. Bullough, "Medieval Medical and Scientific Views of Women," *Viator: Medieval and Renaissance Studies* 4 (1973), pp. 487–493.

86. One example of combined ignorance, prejudice, and theological rationalization in a medieval theologian and popular writer is Jacobus de Voragine's teaching that the soul is infused in a male fetus forty days after conception. A female fetus takes twice as long — eighty days — to "complete." This difference, Jacobus writes, can be "explained by three spiritual reasons, disregarding the physical ones": (1) Christ's birth as a male honored men and "endowed them with more grace"; (2) woman has sinned more than man and therefore "should be unhappier"; and (3) "woman has troubled God more than has man because she has sinned more." *Golden Legend*, p. 150.

87. For example, Marina Warner writes: "every facet of the Virgin had been systematically developed to diminish, not increase, her likeness to the female condition. Her freedom from sex, painful delivery, age, death, and all sin exalted her *ipso facto* above ordinary women and showed them up as inferior." *Alone of All Her Sex*, p. 153.

88. Catherine apparently learned to read by the time she was twenty-three, but by then her spiritual life and career were already established. She learned to write later than that and always preferred to dictate her voluminous correspondence. Since she lived only to the age of thirty-three (a suspect age, possibly hagiographical embellishment — Christ and also Mary Magdalene, who was "dear to the Dominican order," died, according to legend, at thirty-three) — her literacy occurred relatively late in her life. Robert Fawtier and Louis Canet, *La Double Experience de Catherine de Benincasa* (Paris, 1948), p. 48.

89. For a discussion of the literary and visual images on which the spiritual life of Saint Catherine of Siena was patterned, see Meiss, *Painting in Florence and Siena*, pp. 112ff.: (the gift of her heart to God); pp. 108ff. (the marriage of Christ); and p. 107 (her vision of the Madonna and Child).

90. Jacobus, *Golden Legend*, pp. 708ff.

91. Raymond of Capua, *The Life of Catherine of Siena*, trans. Conleth Kearns, O.P., pt. 3, ch. 15 (Wilmington, Delaware: Michael Gazier, 1980).

92. There is evidence that at least one group of women, namely monastic women, did not use religious feminine imagery to any significant extent. Discussing the use of feminine imagery by thirteenth- and fourteenth-century monastic women, Bynum writes: "For women do not use the image of mother-Jesus as one of their primary ways of speaking of union ... To them, Christ is the bridegroom, and all kinds of passionate

sexual language serves as a metaphor for union with a male God." *Jesus as Mother*, p. 162.

93. See, for example, Warner as quoted in n. 87 above.

94. In other words, its linguistic aspect. The "symbolic" is the order of language; the semiotic is "a more archaic dimension of language, pre-discursive, pre-verbal, which has to do with rhythm, tone, colour, with all that does not immediately serve for representation . . . The semiotic is always traversing language, always a bodily presence disruptive to the sublimated symbolic order." Gallop, *The Daughter's Seduction*, p. 124.

95. This definition of "semiotic" agrees with Saussure's description of semiology as dealing with "the science of signs, of which linguistics is only a part." *Course in General Linguistics* (1916), quoted in Roland Barthes, *Elements of Semiology*, trans. A. Lavers and C. Smith (New York: Hill and Wang), p. 11.

96. As, for example, John Berger does in *Ways of Seeing* (London: Penguin, 1977).

Chapter 5 *Vision and Sixteenth-Century Protestant and Roman Catholic Reforms*

1. *Luther's Works*, general ed. Helmut Lehmann (vols. 1–30, St. Louis: Concordia; vols. 31–55, Philadelphia: Fortress Press, 1955–   ) vol. 29, p. 244. I am grateful to Jared Wicks, S.J. of the Gregorian Pontifical University, Rome, for drawing my attention to this quotation.

2. I will consistently refer to the sixteenth-century reforming movement within the Roman Catholic church as the "Catholic reformation" rather than the "counter reformation." The former term more accurately and realistically acknowleges the continuity of the sixteenth-century Catholic reform with medieval movements of reform such as the Devotio Moderna. The term "counter reformation," which began to be used only in the nineteenth century, implies that reform within the Roman church occurred as a reaction to Protestant reform, a highly misleading way to designate this dynamic and largely effective historical movement.

3. For a description of the visual theory of the thirteenth-century philosopher Robert Grosseteste, see A. C. Crombie, *Medieval and Early Modern Science* (New York: Doubleday, 1959).

4. E. Demoutet, *Le désir de voir l'hostie et les origines de la dévotion au Saint-Sacrament* (Paris, 1926).

5. Quoted in J. A. Jungmann, S.J., *The Mass of the Roman Rite: Its Origins and Development*, trans. F. A. Brunner (New York: Benzinger Brothers, 1951), vol. 1, p. 121.

6. C. Garside, *Zwingli and the Arts* (New Haven: Yale University Press, 1966), p. 93.

7. Theodor Klauser, *A Short History of the Western Liturgy*, 2nd ed., trans. John Halliburton (Oxford: Oxford University Press, 1979), p. 121.

8. "Elevation in the Mass," *New Catholic Encyclopedia* (New York: McGraw Hill, 1967), vol. 5, pp. 265–266.

9. David C. Lindberg, *Science in the Middle Ages* (Chicago: University of Chicago Press, 1978), p. 340. See also Crombie, *Medieval and Early Modern Science*, p. 104: "Material light, traveling with enormous though finite velocity, passed from the object seen to the eye"; but in the act of looking, "something psychological 'went forth' from the eye."

10. Lindberg, *Science*, p. 352.

11. Bernd Moeller, "Piety in Germany Around 1500," in *The Reformation in Medieval Perspective*, ed. Steven E. Ozment (Chicago: Quadrangle, 1971), pp. 50–75. We should also remind ourselves that this understanding of visual participation as the most important aspect of the worshipper's participation in the liturgy of the Eucharist can be traced to the origins of christian liturgy. The exclusion of catechumens, from early christian worship after the service of the Word consisted of their withdrawal into curtained alcoves adjacent to the nave. Here the catechumens could hear the words but not see the actions of the celebrant. Only on the completion of an exacting course of instruction and after baptism were the catechumens permitted visual participation — that is, *active* participation — in the liturgy. Thus, the educational significance of the words of the liturgy was recognized and implemented, while visual participation became the goal of completed instruction and full membership.

12. J. A. Jungmann, S.J., *The Mass: An Historical, Theological, and Pastoral Survey* (Collegeville, Minn.: Liturgical Press, 1976), pp. 198–199; Klauser, *Short History*, pp. 98–99. Several modern historians of the sixteenth century describe late-medieval religion and popular piety as characterized by "feminine religiosity": Lionel Rothkrug, *Religious Practices and Collective Perceptions: Hidden Homologies in the Renaissance and Reformation* (Waterloo, Ont.: Historical Reflections, 1980), p. 184; Francis Oakley, "Religion and Ecclesiastical Life on the Eve of the Reformation," in Steven Ozment, *Reformation Europe: A Guide to Research* (St. Louis: Center for Reformation Research, 1982), p. 17. Oakley describes spirituality in England, Italy, Germany, and the Netherlands in the early sixteenth century as "a particular confluence of Dominican theology and care of souls, vernacular preaching, feminine piety." These authors do not define what they mean by "feminine" religiosity or piety, but it is clear that they use the term as a pejorative contrast to the piety of the reformation era. It would be of the greatest interest for my thesis if a close relationship could be established between women and image use, implying that if images are the primary religious communication, women will have an advantage. Rudolf Arnheim informs me, however, that "from all the evidence we have from children's drawings, there is no indication that girls have more of a natural affinity to imagery than boys." Personal communication, August 1984. Rather, image use is, I think, automatic for persons of both sexes who have not received specific training in the substitution of language use for image use.

13. In many areas the situation was much worse. The *Libellus ad Leonem Decem* (1513), a plan for general reform in Italy drawn up by Fathers Giustiani and Quirini, "chiefly deplored the ignorance of the regular clergy," thousands of whom could not "adequately read or write." "In the whole multitude of the religious, scarcely two in a hundred or perhaps two in a thousand can be found who can read the daily services." Quoted in Denis Hay, *The Church in Italy in the Fifteenth Century* (New York: Cambridge University Press, 1977), p. 63.

14. See, for example, the list of stylized gestures enjoined on English preachers by the 1520 edition of the *Mirror of the World*, quoted in W. S. Howell, *Logic and Rhetoric in England, 1500–1700* (Princeton: Princeton University Press, 1956), pp. 89–90.

15. Francis Haskell, *Patrons and Painters* (London: Chatto and Windus, 1963), p. 64.

16. Haskell, *Patrons and Painters*, p. 69.

17. Oakley, "Religious and Ecclesiastical Life," pp. 7–8.

18. Garside, *Zwingli and the Arts*, p. 89.

19. Quoted in Carl C. Christensen, *Art and the Reformation in Germany* (Athens,

Ohio: Ohio University Press), p. 22. See also *Huldrich Zwinglis Sämtliche Werke* (Leipzig, 1927), vol. 4, pp. 101, 102, 104, 107, 108, 109, 110, 125, 139, 146–147.

20. Garside, *Zwingli and the Arts,* pp. 92–93.

21. Howard Hibbard, "Ut picturae sermones: The First Painted Decorations of the Gesù," in *Baroque Art: The Jesuit Contribution,* ed. R. Wittkower and I. B. Jaffe (New York: Fordham University Press, 1972), p. 30.

22. Theological arguments concerning images by leading Protestant reformers have been thoroughly and perceptively discussed in the following works related to the given reformers: Zwingli, in Garside, *Zwingli and the Arts;* Luther and Karlstadt, in Christensen, *Art and the Reformation.* Original documents on the subject of iconoclasm in southern Germany and German-speaking Switzerland are collected in H. Rott, *Quellen und Forschungen zur südwest-deutschen und schweizerischen Kunstgeschichte in XV. und XVI. Jahrhundert* (Stuttgart, 1933–1936).

23. Meister Eckhart, "This Is Another Sermon," in *Meister Eckhart,* trans. Raymond Blakeney (New York: Harper and Row, 1941), p. 108.

24. *Luther's Works,* vol. 12, pp. 325–326.

25. Quoted by Elizabeth L. Eisenstein, "The Advent of Printing and the Protestant Revolt," in Robert M. Kingdon, *Transition and Revolution* (Minneapolis: Burgess, 1975), p. 238.

26. Konrad Escher, "Das Grossmünster am Vorabend der Reformation," *Zwingliana* 4 (1921–1928), pp. 447–485; *Die beiden Zürcher Münster* (Fravenfeld und Leipzig, 1928); P. Meyer, *Schweizerische Münster und Kathedralen des Mittelalters* (Zurich, 1945).

27. G. Germann, *Der protestantische Kirchenbau in der Schweiz* (Zurich, 1963); Richard Zurcher, *Die Kunstlerische Kultur in Kanton Zurich: Ein geschichtlicher Uberblick* (Zurich, 1943).

28. Garside, *Zwingli and the Arts,* pp. 86–87.

29. Christensen, *Art and the Reformation,* p. 81.

30. Garside, *Zwingli and the Arts,* pp. 159–160.

31. Quoted by Garside, *Zwingli and the Arts,* p. 160.

32. Carl C. Christensen, "Patterns of Iconoclasm in the Early Reformation: Strasbourg and Basel," in *The Image and the Word,* ed. Joseph Gutman (Missoula, Mont.: Scholars Press, 1977), p. 119.

33. Christensen, *Art and the Reformation,* p. 107.

34. Christensen, *Art and the Reformation,* p. 107.

35. See Craig Harbison, *The Last Judgment in Sixteenth-Century Northern Europe: A Study in the Relationship Between Art and the Reformation* (New York: Garland, 1976), for a treatment of the iconography of this subject before and during the reformation era.

36. Quoted by Miriam Crisman, *Strasbourg and the Reform* (New Haven: Yale University Press, 1967), p. 148.

37. Fritz Schmidt-Clausing, *Zwingli als Liturgiker: Eine liturgiegeschichtliche Untersuchung* (Göttingen, 1952).

38. Quoted in Jaroslov Pelikan, *Luther the Expositor* (St. Louis: Concordia, 1959), pp. 63–64.

39. Pelikan, *Luther the Expositor,* pp. 63–64.

40. Henry-Russell Hitchock, *German Renaissance Architecture* (Princeton: Princeton University Press, 1981), p. 201; Eugenio Battisti, "Reformation and Counter-Reformation," *Encyclopedia of World Art* (1966), vol. 11, cols. 894–916.

41. Battisti, *"Reformation and Counter-Reformation,"* col. 898.

42. Klauser, *Short History,* pp. 102, 106.

43. *Luther's Works,* vol. 21, p. 54, "The Magnificat," prologue.

44. *Luther's Works,* vol. 40, pp. 99–100, "Against the Heavenly Prophets."

45. Rudolf Berliner, "The Freedom of Medieval Art," *Gazette des Beaux-Arts,* ser. 6, no. 28 (1945), p. 285.

46. Christensen, *Art and the Reformation,* p. 25; Karlstadt, *Von Abtuhung der Bilder und das keyn Betdler unther den Christen seyn sollen* (1522), ed. Hans Leitzmann (Bonn, 1911), n. 74.

47. Quoted in Garside, *Zwingli and the Arts,* p. 76; *Huldreich Zwinglis Sämtliche Werke,* in *Corpus Reformation,* ed. Emil Egli, Georg Finsler, Walter Köhler (Leipzig, 1927), vol. 91, 3, 906, 1–2.

48. See also Zwingli's admission: "Images are able to delight me less since I cannot see them well." Garside, *Zwingli and the Arts,* pp. 4, 84, 24–25. Zwingli was nearsighted.

49. Harold J. Grimm, *The Reformation Era, 1500–1650* (London: Macmillan, 1954), p. 187.

50. Some limited iconoclasm occurred in Rome in 1527, and in 1558 the Bishop of Aquileia removed some images from churches. Battisti, "Reformation and Counter-Reformation," col. 901.

51. In Italy, the only churches in which images were absent were two Waldensian churches in the small towns of Angrogna and Ciabas, both built in 1555. Battisti, "Reformation and Counter-Reformation," col. 902.

52. Battisti notes that in Italy the famous architect Vasari "devoted himself to this type of remodeling" "Reformation and Counter-Reformation," col. 898.

53. G. Dorfles, quoted in Battisti, "Reformation and Counter-Reformation," col. 898.

54. *De. Histor. sanct. imag. et pict.,* lib. 2, cap. 54.

55. Emile Mâle, *L'Art Religieux après le Councile de Trente* (Paris: Librairie Armand Colin, 1932), p. 22.

56. Hibbard, "Ut picturae sermones," p. 40.

57. On Roman Catholic reform architecture, see Pietro Pirri, S.J., *Giovanni Tristano e i Primordi della Architettura Gesuitica* (Rome, 1955).

58. "Discourse on Rome," quoted by Haskell, *Patrons and Painters,* p. 63.

59. My thesis does not require that I take up the question, much discussed by historians of art and architecture, as to whether the wishes of the Jesuits were faithfully carried out in the decoration of the Gesù, begun but not completed by Cardinal Farnese. On the one side, the poverty of the Jesuits is cited to support the argument that patrons were able to do whatever they liked in the decoration. Haskell, *Patrons and Painters,* p. 65. On the other side, Hibbard's discussion of the iconographic scheme of the nave chapels demonstrates the coherence of the chapel iconography and concludes that records indicating an early ("1580s, if not before") Jesuit-controlled program for these decorations are correct: "The patrons may have had some limited say in the character of the program — as they surely had their choice of artists for the altarpieces — but the coherence of the chapel iconography did not allow room for much independent choice of subject." Hibbard, "Ut picturae sermones," p. 34. Against Haskell's argument of Jesuit poverty, see also Leif H. Monssen, "Rex Gloriose Martyrum: A Contribution to Jesuit Iconography," *Art Bulletin* 8 (March 1981), p. 131.

60. Monssen, "Rex Gloriose Martyrum," p. 130.

61. St. Giovanni dei Fiorentini in Rome is an intact example of a sixteenth-century

Jesuit church that is decorated relatively simply and whitewashed throughout the nave and apse. Only the side chapels are decorated with paintings, sculpture, and stucco. From this church one can recover a sense of what worship in the Gesù was like in the sixteenth century, before its apse, the two large transept chapels, and the vault of the nave were decorated. Also, a painting by Andrea Sacchi, *Urban VIII Visiting the Gesù on October 2, 1639 During the Centenary Celebrations of the Jesuit Order,* shows the unpainted nave vault and dome. Ann S. Harris, *Andrea Sacchi* (Oxford: Phaidon, 1977), pl. 130.

62. Battisti, "Reformation and Counter-Reformation," col. 898.

63. Battisti, "Reformation and Counter-Reformation," col. 898.

64. See, for example, Augustine's description of the resurrection body of saints as characterized primarily by a mobile weightlessness: "The bodies of the saints, then, shall rise again free from every defect, from every blemish, as from all corruption, weight, and impediment. For their ease of movement shall be as complete as their happiness. Whence their bodies have been called spiritual, though undoubtedly they shall be bodies and not spirits." *Enchiridion* 91.

65. The word "experience" has become trite and vague through honorific overuse. Yet I do not know what other word to use to suggest that entering a building and looking around, although perhaps primarily a visual activity, is not entirely a visual experience. If it were, one could get as much from a careful documentary film in which the camera took the perspective of a person entering a building and looking, from different positions and angles, at each architectural and decorative feature. The primary relation, only partly mediated visually, is that of one's body to the spatial dimensions of the building.

66. Hibbard, "Ut picturae sermonae," p. 35.

67. *Luther's Works* vol. 40, p. 84.

68. For example, in the question of infant baptism, Zwingli's attempt to establish the practice as biblical by quoting Christ's "Let the little children come to me" and by citing the Acts account of the baptism of the jailer and his household — presumably containing small children — was rejected by Conrad Grebel and his Anabaptist circle.

69. Many quotations on Luther's position on social anarchy could be cited. One interesting exposition of the necessity and value of strong government occurs in the 1528 treatise *Instructions for the Visitors of Parish Pastors in Electoral Saxony,* which was penned by Melanchthon but commonly attributed to Luther and included among his writings because he approved it, wrote its preface, and revised subsequent editions. Among the most important duties of pastors was to instruct people that they must "learn to see God in government" and thus not merely to respect government but to have "sincere love towards it." *Luther's Works,* vol. 40, pp. 281ff.

70. See Thomas Tentler's neutral use of the term "social control" to describe one of the agenda of confessors' manuals at the end of the medieval period. "The *Summa* for Confessors as an Instrument of Social Control," in C. Trinkhaus and H. Oberman, *The Pursuit of Holiness in Late Medieval and Renaissance Religion* (Leiden: E. J. Brill, 1974), p. 135.

71. *Luther's Works,* "On Keeping Children in School" (1530): "This seems to be a real masterpiece of the devil's art. He sees that in our time he cannot do what he would like to do; therefore he intends to have his own way with our offspring. Before our very eyes he is preparing them so that they will learn nothing and know nothing. Then, when we are dead, he will have before him a naked, bare, defenseless people with whom he can do as he pleases" (vol. 46, p. 217).

72. Strauss, *Luther's House of Learning* (Baltimore: Johns Hopkins University Press, 1978), p. 131.

73. Quoted by Thomas Trexler, "Ritual in Florence: Adolescence and Salvation in the Renaissance," in Trinkhaus and Oberman, *Pursuit of Holiness,* p. 233.

74. It is evident in Luther's sermon "On Keeping Children in School" (1530) that his first educational concern was the training of good pastors. His eulogy of the good pastor makes such pastors the goal of education: "There is no dearer treasure, no nobler thing on earth or in this life than a good and faithful pastor and teacher." *Luther's Works,* vol. 46, p. 233. He argues, however, against parents who are already skeptical of the usefulness of a Lutheran education, that knowledge of a little Latin will not damage a son's ability to earn a living if he does not become a pastor (p. 231). Lutheran success in achieving an educated ministry and its relative failure to achieve an educated public are reflected in Lionel Rothkrug's analysis of vernacular literature in book fair catalogs in Germany in the seventeenth century. Until about 1770, the authors of vernacular literature were "almost all Protestant clergymen, their sons, or men who had studied for the ministry . . . German Protestant clergy virtually monopolized the production of vernacular literature for more than two centuries after the Reformation." *Religious Practices,* p. 196.

75. Quoted in Gerald Strauss, *Luther's House of Learning,* p. 131; A letter from a Dutch Protestant woman, in prison and about to be executed for religious reasons, to her infant daughter, born in prison, illustrates the high value placed on language-centered education: "run not in the street as other bad children do. Take up a book, take up a book and learn to see that which concerns your salvation." Quoted in Hans J. Hillerbrand, *Christendom Divided* (New York: Corpus, 1971), p. 67.

76. *Luther's Works,* vol. 46, p. 218. Elizabeth L. Eisenstein estimates the sales of Luther's thirty publications between 1517 and 1520 to have been well over 300,000 copies. "The Advent of Printing," p. 235.

77. Eisenstein, "The Advent of Printing," p. 237.

78. Eisenstein, "The Advent of Printing," p. 236. But see an argument that "the printed illustration, not the printed word, is the reason why the press in the West proved to be a dramatic change" in Margaret Hagen, ed., *The Perception of Pictures* (Boston: Academic Press, 1980), p. 190.

79. Ozment, *Reformation Europe,* pp. 86–87. See also R. W. Scribner, *For the Sake of Simple Folk: Popular Propaganda for the German Reformation* (New York: Cambridge University Press, 1981).

80. Strauss, *Luther's House,* p. 127.

81. Ozment, *Reformation Europe,* p. 87.

82. Ozment, *Reformation Europe,* p. 89.

83. Luther's translation of the Bible was not the first edition of a German Bible; an edition was published in Zurich and Worms in 1529 that used some of Luther's translations. The first edition of Luther's New Testament, published in 1522, was sparsely illustrated, but subsequent editions were more fully illustrated. The 1534 edition of the whole Bible in German had 177 woodcuts, not counting title pages and decorative initials. More than 500 illustrations were prepared for the Wittenberg edition, published during Luther's lifetime. Christensen, *Art and the Reformation,* p. 169.

84. *Luther's Works,* vol. 40, p. 99.

85. See Hans Freiherr von Campenhausen, "Zwingli und Luther zur Bilderfrage," in *Das Gottesbild in Abendland,* ed. Günther Howe (Wittenberg und Berlin, 1959), pp. 139–172.

86. Quoted by Erwin Panofsky, *Symbols in Transformation* (Princeton: Princeton University Press, 1969), p. 16; interesting also in this connection is P. A. Florensky's article "The Icon Related to Oil Painting and Engraving: Metaphysical, Sensual, and Rational Art Forms," an appendix in John Stuart, *Ikons* (London: Faber and Faber, 1975), in which the claim is made that oil painting is best suited to conveying the sensual aspect of life because it has "something in common with the object portrayed," while engraving, with its asensual quality, is better suited to conveying rational concepts (p. 150).

87. Quoted by Wolfgang Stechow, *Northern Renaissance Art, 1400–1600: Sources and Documents* (Englewood Cliffs, N.J.: Prentice-Hall, 1966), p. 111. On Dürer's use of words in paintings, see Christensen, *Art and the Reformation*, pp. 181–206.

88. Panofsky, *Symbols in Transformation*, p. 9.

89. See, for example, Hans Baldung's depiction of Luther as a Protestant saint, complete with halo, in Oskar Thulin, *Bilder der Reformation: aus den Sammlungen der Lutherhalle in Wittenberg* (Berlin, 1956), p. 30.

90. Panofsky, *Symbols in Transformation*, p. 30.

91. See, for example, Lucas Cranach's subjects, which include various saints, among them Mary Magdalene; a Madonna and Child; portraits of Luther and Katherina von Bora, his wife; classical subjects; Adam and Eve; Luther's mother and father; and so on. Max J. Friedlander and Jakob Rosenberg, *Die Gemälde von Lucas Cranach* (Berlin, 1932). A comparable range of traditional religious and classical subjects, along with subjects characteristic of reformation interests, is evident in the graphic work of Hans Baldung. Bearbeitet von Matthias Mende, *Hans Baldung Grien: Das Graphische Werke* (Verlag Dr. Alfuos Uhl, 1978).

92. See Oskar Thulin, *Cranach-Altare der Reformation* (Berlin, 1955), pp. 9ff., on the Stadtkirchenaltar in Wittenberg.

93. Louis La Favia, *The Man of Sorrows: Origin and Development in Florentine Trecento Painting* (The Hague: Sanguis 1980).

94. Cf. the strange woodcut of Lucas Cranach the Younger "Last Supper of the Lutherans, Luther Preaching, and the Fall of the Catholics into Hell" (c. 1540). Harbison, *Last Judgment*, pl. 89. In this woodcut Luther appears as judge, with his left hand consigning cowled monks to the flames of hell and his right pointing to a Lutheran communion table on which the Lord's Supper is being celebrated while a Lutheran congregation participates.

95. Thulin, *Bilder der Reformation*, p. 9.

96. See Battisti's statement: "A Protestant type of sacred art developed only in the north and east of Germany, which were the only areas to remain Lutheran." "Reformation and Counter-Reformation," col. 902. See also Carl Christensen, "The Reformation and the Decline of German Art," in his *Art and the Reformation*, ch. 5, pp. 164ff., which treats in some detail the "diminished employment and financial hardship" of painters and sculptors in Germany directly attributable to the Protestant reform. It is important to remember that the suddenly dramatically reduced demand for ecclesiastical art came after a half-century of unusual efflorescence and productivity in the arts.

97. Strauss, *Luther's House*, p. 303.

98. Introduction, *Luther's Works*, vol. 40, pp. 263ff.

99. Quoted in Strauss, *Luther's House*, p. 250. Also: "The pedagogical experiment was not a success" (p. 249). It was undermined, Strauss writes, by the reformer's "lack of compassion for the religious needs of ordinary people" (p. 302).

100. In fact, educated men who dabbled charmingly in the occult arts were not

persecuted and executed for their pursuits. See Eisenstein, "The Advent of Printing," pp. 358–362, for a discussion of the connection between the verbal media and witch-hunting in the sixteenth century. The witch craze, Eisenstein writes, "would not have preceded Gutenberg's invention." Also see H. C. Erik Midelfort's translation of a typical broadsheet — the first "newspapers" — reporting the trials, confessions, and executions of 114 witches in various small towns, in his "Were There Really Witches?" in Kingdon, *Transition and Revolution,* pp. 211–213, 195.

101. See Berliner, "Freedom of Medieval Art"; also his "God Is Love," *Gazette des Beaux-Arts,* ser. 6, no. 42 (1953).

102. The Jesuit Maselli wrote in 1610: "I do not know how those responsible for the enforcement of the decrees of the Council of Trent can excuse themselves for their grave negligence." *Vita della beata Vergine* (Venice, 1610), quoted in Berliner, "God Is Love," pp. 17–18.

103. Berliner, "Freedom of Medieval Art," p. 284.

104. Quoted in Hibbard, "Ut picturae sermones," p. 30.

105. Hubert Jedin, *A History of the Council of Trent,* 2 vols., trans. Ernest Graf (London: Nelson, 1957–1961), vol. 2, p. 123.

106. This does not deny the increasing importance of lay education in the work of the Jesuits and the Ursulines, "the earliest and greatest teaching order for women." A. G. Dickens, *The Counter Reformation* (London: Thames and Hudson, 1968), p. 74. But the Jesuit colleges were primarily for the training of Jesuit novices, and the Ursulines' first school was founded at Parma in 1595; public education was not a major movement in sixteenth-century Roman Catholic territories.

107. The first printing press in Italy was set up in the convent of Santa Scholastica at Subiaco in 1464. The first two books printed were Cicero's *De Oratore* and a work of Lactantius. An Italian translation of the Bible by Niccolò di Malermi was published in Venice in 1471, and a revision of this edition in 1477, but although the Council of Trent did not prohibit lay reading of the Bible, neither was it encouraged in Catholic territories.

108. Herwarth von Rottgen, "Zeitgeschichtliche Bildprogramme der Katholischen Restauration under Gregor XIII (1572–1585)," *Münchner Jahrbuch der Bildenden Kunst* (München, 1975), pp. 89–122; Paolo Prodi, *Ricerche sulla Teorica delle Arti Figurative nella Riforma Cattolica* (Rome, 1962); John B. Knipping, *Iconography of the Counter Reformation in the Netherlands,* 2 vols. (Leiden: A. W. Sijthoff, 1974).

109. See the statement of the novelist Patrick White in *Riders in the Chariot* (New York: Viking, 1961), p. 27: "in the last light, illumination is synonymous with blinding."

110. Historian of Catholic reform art Emile Mâle says that he knows of no examples of depictions of saints in ecstasy before the seventeenth century; *L'Art Religieux,* p. 172.

111. Léon Dewez and Albert van Iterson, "Le lactation de saint Bernard: Legende et iconographie," *Cîteaux in de Nederlanden* 7 (1956), pp. 165–189.

112. See the multitude of sixteenth-century symbols and images of death and motifs for reminding a person of the brevity of life: *Europe in Torment, 1450–1550: An Exhibition by the Department of Art, Brown University* (Providence, R.I.: Brown University Press, 1974). See also Kathleen Cohen's discussion of tomb art in *Metamorphosis of a Death Symbol: The Transi Tomb in the Late Middle Ages and the Renaissance* (Berkeley: University of California Press, 1973).

113. Mâle, *L'Art Religieux,* p. 207; Monssen, "Rex Gloriose Martyrum," p. 133.

114. Quoted by Thomas Buser, "Jerome Nadal and Early Jesuit Art in Rome," *Art Bulletin* 57 (1976), p. 425. Ignatius's successor, Diego Laynez, wrote of him: "He thought to himself that even if no Scriptures had been given to us to teach us the truths of faith, he would nevertheless have determined to give up life itself for them, purely on account of what he had seen with the soul." Quoted in Dickens, *Counter Reformation*, p. 75.

115. Quoted by Mâle, *L'Art Religieux*, p. 30.

116. Mâle writes that, while the medieval saints performed miracles, the Catholic reform saints "were themselves miracles." *L'Art Religieux*, p. 152.

117. Giovanni Battista Cavelieri, *Ecclesiae militantis triumphi sive amabilium martyrium gloriosa* (Rome, 1585).

118. The Catacomb of Priscilla, the most painted of the pre-Constantinian catacombs, was opened in 1578 (Baronius, *Annales eclesiastici*, Anno 130, cap. 30); other catacombs, opened for generations but ignored until the later sixteenth century, were now seen by Catholics as "proof of their claims for the existence of thousands of early Christian martyrs as mentioned in the legends." Buser, "Jerome Nadal," p. 432. In fact, no martyrdom painting exists in the pre-Constantinian catacombs.

119. Mâle points out that the first Jesuit martyrs were not killed by the half-savage natives of these continents, but by Calvinists in 1570; a ship carrying forty Jesuits on their way to missions in Brazil was attacked by Huguenots. The Jesuits, who would not defend themselves, were massacred.

120. Paintings by Pomarancio, among the first paintings of the Gesù, are in the chapels on the right and on the left as one enters the church. They are a Crucifixion of Peter and a Beheading of Paul.

121. Francis Haskell has argued that sixteenth-century Jesuits were indifferent to style, and even to quality, in painting but were concerned exclusively with compelling subject mater. *Patrons and Painters*, pp. 68, 83, 93. The practical rather than artistic aims of early Jesuit art are also emphasized by Hibbard, "Ut picturae sermonae," pp. 3, 12–13.

122. For example, in Haskell, *Patrons and Painters*, p. 53.

123. Buser argues that the scenes in Santo Stefano Rotondo were influenced by the illustrated English Protestant book by John Foxe, *Acts and Monuments of These Later and Perilous Days*, published in 1563 to publicize the Protestant martyrdoms of the sixteenth century under English Catholic monarchs. It is a highly interesting and provocative suggestion, implying the significance of printed, illustrated martyrdom accounts not only for English Protestants but also for English Catholics, such as George Gilbert, the wealthy Englishman who financed the first martyrdom illustrations in the Jesuit English College in Rome. For treatment of images in the English reformation, see J. Phillips, *The Reformation of Images: Destruction of Art in England, 1535–1660* (Berkeley: University of California Press, 1973).

124. I do not differentiate between education and propaganda; "education," used honorifically, and "propaganda," used pejoratively, often apply the same techniques and shade off imperceptibly into one another.

125. *Luther's Works*, vol. 40, p. 280.

126. Dickens, *The Counter Reformation*, p. 68.

127. See geographical charts of territories adhering to Protestantism and those remaining Roman Catholic in 1550, compared with the same in 1650. Battisti, "Reformation and Counter-Reformation," col. 895.

Chapter 6   Image and Language in Contemporary Culture

1. Beaumont Newhall, *Photography: A Short Critical Essay* (New York: Museum of Modern Art, 1937), p. 77.

2. James C. Kinkaid, *Press Photography* (Boston: American, 1936), p. 65.

3. John Berger, *About Looking* (New York: Pantheon, 1980), p. 49.

4. John Berger, *Ways of Seeing* (London: Penguin, 1977), p. 48.

5. Newhall, *Photography*, p. 80.

6. Roland Barthes, *Image-Music-Text* (New York: Hill and Wang, 1977), p. 40.

7. See John Berger's essay "Photographs of Agony," in his *Ways of Seeing*, for a discussion of war photographs as art: "The possible contradictions of the war photograph now become apparent. It is generally assumed that its purpose is to awaken concern. The most extreme examples . . . show moments of agony in order to extort the maximum concern. Such moments, whether photographed or not, are discontinuous with all other moments. They exist by themselves. But the reader who has been arrested by the photograph may tend to feel this discontinuity as his own moral inadequacy. And *as soon as this happens his sense of shock is dispersed* . . . his own moral inadequacy may now shock him as much as the crimes being committed in the war. In both cases, the issue of the war which has caused the moment is effectively depoliticized. The picture becomes evidence of the general human condition. It accuses nobody and everybody" (emphasis mine), (p. 39).

8. Jerry Mander, *Four Arguments for the Elimination of Television* (New York: Morrow Quill, 1978), p. 171. See also Marie Winn, *The Plug-In Drug* (New York: Viking, 1977); Michael Schudson, *Advertising: The Uneasy Persuasion* (New York: Basic, 1984); William Meyers, *The Image Makers* (New York: Times Books, 1984).

9. Berger, *Ways of Seeing*, p. 58.

10. Gregor Goethals, *The TV Ritual* (Boston: Beacon, 1982).

11. Goethals, *TV Ritual*, p. 54.

12. Michel Foucault, *Power/Knowledge*, ed. Colin Gordon (New York: Pantheon, 1972), p. 58.

13. Barthes, *Image-Music-Text*, p. 39.

14. The possibility of a "base rhetoric" of images should never be excluded — a rhetoric that is "always trying to keep individuals from the support provided by personal courage, noble associations, and divine philosophy." A base rhetoric can operate either through words or through images. Thomas Szaz, *The Myth of Psychotherapy* (New York: Anchor Doubleday, 1978), p. 130.

15. Foucault, *Power/Knowledge*, p. 57.

16. Jürgen Habermas, *Knowledge and Human Interests* (Boston: Beacon, 1968), p. 292.

17. Although the early psychoanalytic movement identified psychoanalysis as a science, recent scholarship is more interested in exploring the relation of psychoanalysis to the ancient self-reflective disciplines. See, for example, L. L. Whyte, *The Unconscious Before Freud* (New York: F. Pinter, 1960); Habermas, *Knowledge and Human Interests*; and Jacques Lacan, *The Language of the Self: The Function of Language in Psychoanalysis*, trans. Anthony Wilden (Baltimore: Johns Hopkins University Press, 1968).

18. Habermas, *Knowledge and Human Interests*, p. 241; Lacan, *Language of the Self*, p. 32: "the symptom resolves itself entirely in a Language analysis, because the

symptom itself is structured like a Language, because the symptom is a Language from which the Word must be liberated."

19. Habermas, *Knowledge and Human Interests*, p. 224: " 'Unconscious' means specifically delinguisticized."

20. Lacan, *Language of the Self*, p. 98, n. 23.

21. Habermas, *Knowledge and Human Interests*, p. 310.

22. Habermas, *Knowledge and Human Interests*, pp. 261–262: "Analytic insights possess validity . . . only after they have been accepted as knowledge by the analysand himself . . . Interpretations hold . . . only to the degree that those who are made the subject of individual interpretations know and recognize themselves in these interpretations."

23. Susanne Langer, *Philosophical Sketches*, chap. 1, n. 8.

24. Cf. Schleiermacher's comment on removing a work of art from the location for which it was created, quoted in Hans-Georg Gadamer, *Truth and Method* (New York: Seabury, 1975), p. 148: "A work of art too is really rooted from its own soil. It loses its meaning when it is wrenched from this environment and enters into general commerce; it is like something that has been saved from the fire but still bears the marks of the burning upon it."

25. See Gadamer, *Truth and Method*, p. 63: The experience of art "suddenly takes the person experiencing it out of the context of his life, by the power of the work of art, and yet relates him back to the whole of his existence." This statement fails to acknowledge the *sine qua non* of an "experience of art," the preparation brought to it by preliminary visual training. Gadamer compares the "experience of art" to a religious conversion in structure and describes it as the overcoming of the settled visual habits of a lifetime. Like religious conversion, however, it is more likely that this experience occurs to a person already prepared for it than as an unsought and unanticipated miracle.

26. Gadamer, *Truth and Method*, p. 125, n. 53.

Chapter 7   Language and Images: A Theory

1. John Wild, *Plato's Theory of Man* (Cambridge, Mass.: Harvard University Press, 1949), p. 36: the "inversion of reality" is the inevitable and involuntary condition of "natural man."

2. Robert Cushman, *Therapeia: Plato's Conception of Philosophy* (Westport, Ct.: Greenwood, 1958), p. 295.

3. *Epistula 7*.

4. Cushman, *Therapeia*, p. 66.

5. *Phaedrus* 276e.

6. *Phaedrus* 276a. Plato's uneasiness about the value of "thrice-removed images" should be noted.

7. *Phaedrus*, 275d. An interesting parallel can be found in Luther's distinction between written and spoken language. Although it is certainly not impossible that the word will be "heard" through written language, it is much more likely to confront the hearer in speech; see chap. 5, p. 104, above.

8. See the discussion of the universality of language in chap. 2, pp. 21ff.

9. Robert C. Neville, *Reconstruction of Thinking* (Albany, N.Y.: SUNY Press, 1981), pp. 23–24. See also Jean Bethke Elshtain, "Methodological Sophistication and Conceptual Confusion," in *The Prism of Sex: Essays in the Sociology of Knowledge*,

ed. Julia A. Sherman and Evelyn Torton Beck (Madison, Wis.: University of Wisconsin Press, 1979), pp. 229–252.

10. *Phaedrus* 251a. See also Plotinus *Ennead* 1.6.4: "These expressions must occur whenever there is contact with any sort of beautiful thing, wonder and a shock of delight and passion and happy excitement." The Athenian Platonic philosopher Damascius (c. 480) reports that he "broke into a perspiration from wonder and emotion" when he contemplated a statue of Aphrodite. R. Asmus, *Das Leben des Philosophen Isidorus* (Leipzig, 1911), p. 53.

11. "Your lovers of sights and sounds delight in beautiful tones and colors and shapes and in all the works of art into which these enter; but they have not the power of thought to behold and take delight in the nature of beauty itself. That power to approach beauty and behold it as it is in itself is rare indeed." See also *Symp.* 210a ff.

12. *Ennead* 4.3.11. See also *Ennead* 5.8.5: "The wisdom of the gods and the blessed is not expressed by propositions but by beautiful images."

13. *Phaedrus* 250d.

14. *De anima* 432a.17: "The soul never thinks without a mental picture." See also *De anima* 432a.9: "No one could learn or understand anything if he had not the faculty of perception; even when he thinks speculatively, he must have some mental picture with which to think."

15. Although for Plato himself the "divided line" is only conceptually divided, not divided in reality, popular Platonism tended, especially under the influence of middle Platonists like Numenius, to understand as separate in reality what Plato described as conceptually distinguishable.

16. Aquinas' *Opusc.* 16, *de Trinitate* 6.2, ad.5; emphasis mine.

17. P.G. 94, col. 1260. Also see Rudolf Berliner, "God Is Love," *Gazette des Beaux-Arts,* ser. 6, no. 42 (1953), p. 272.

18. See Aiden Nichols, O.P., *The Art of God Incarnate: Theology and Image in Christian Tradition* (London: Darton, Longman, and Todd, 1981), for a historical exploration of the implication of the incarnation for artistic representation.

19. *Republic* 598: "The art of representation . . . is a long way from reality . . . it grasps only a small part of any object, and that only an image." Porphyry relates that Plotinus refused to have his portrait painted, saying that "an image of an image" has little value. Porphyry, *Life of Plotinus,* in Stephen Mackenna, *Plotinus, The Enneads* (New York: Oxford University Press, 1934), p. 1.

20. Angels are never the primary subjects of medieval painting; they are used as contrast with the human figures depicted. Medieval people did not aspire to the qualities or characteristics of angels, with one notable exception — virginity, the "state of the angels." This state was considered, however, to be attainable only by a miracle, not the result of effort and repression. See the discussion of Gregory of Nyssa's treatise *De virginitate* in Margaret R. Miles, *Fullness of Life: Historical Foundations for a New Asceticism* (Philadelphia: Westminster Press, 1981), pp. 102–105.

21. The *via negativa* of eastern Christianity shows that it is possible for language users to understand and define the limitations of language, to be concerned that language not be granted more proficiency and a greater area of operation than is legitimate. In the eleventh century, Simeon, called in the Orthodox church the "New Theologian," expressed it as follows: "Do not try to describe ineffable matters by words alone, for this is an impossibility . . . but let us contemplate such matters by activity, labor and fatigue . . . In this way we shall be taught the meaning of such things as the sacred mysteries." *Orations* 26. See also John of Damascus, *The Orthodox Faith* 4.16. trans.

S.D.F. Salmond in *Select Library of Nicene and Post-Nicene Fathers,* Second series, vol. 9 (New York: Charles Scribner's Sons, 1899), p. 88.

22. Saul Bellow, *Mr. Sammler's Planet* (New York: Viking, 1969), pp. 228–229.

23. Gadamer, *Truth and Method,* p. 47.

24. Awareness of the phenomenon of unconscious motivation was certainly not new with Freud, but a description of the phenomenon with claims to scientific accuracy rather than poetic meaning was new. See Whyte, *The Unconscious Before Freud.*

25. For example, the *New York Times Magazine* often features articles on crime, war, and other forms of legal and illegal violence; the pictures accompanying these articles are frequently of dead, severely hurt, diseased, or undernourished persons. Advertising images alongside these feature articles are of luxury items — fur coats, liqueurs, expensive cars, and cigarettes. How do these juxtaposed images of conspicuous consumption and starving, damaged bodies combine to convey a complex message?

26. Roland Barthes, *Image-Music-Text* (New York: Hill and Wang, 1977), p. 40.

27. See Jonathan Schell, *The Fate of the Earth* (New York: Knopf, 1982), for discussion of the puzzling public lethargy in the face of nuclear threat.

28. The phrase is Albert Camus's.

29. Sigmund Freud, *History of the Psychoanalytic Movement,* vol. 14 of *The Complete Psychological Works of Sigmund Freud* (London: Hogarth Press, 1957), p. 22.

30. See John Dillenberger, "The Diversity of Disciplines as a Theological Question: The Visual Arts as Paradigm," *Journal of the American Academy of Religion* 48:2 (June 1980), p. 241: The discipline of seeing "comes by seeing over and over again."

31. Contemplation requires silence; historically, contemplation has been more central to worship when visual images were understood as coordinating and unifying worship. If everyone's eyes are shut, meditation *is* an individual activity, each person's thoughts going in idiosyncratic directions. The cohesiveness of worship, however, can be as readily achieved by each person *looking* at the same image as by each person *listening* to the same words. In contemporary churches, it is usually assumed that the cohesiveness of worship is guaranteed by maintaining an unbroken fabric of sound. Periods reserved for private devotions are limited to a few minutes directly before and after the service. Even then, an organ prelude and postlude, even if tasteful and beautiful, distracts from private prayer.

32. Hans-Georg Gadamer, *Truth and Method* (New York: Seabury, 1975), p. 111.

33. See T. R. Martland, *Religion as Art: An Interpretation* (New York: SUNY, 1981), p. 12: Art and religion "tell us what is; they do not respond to what is."

34. *Luther's Works,* general ed. Helmut Lehmann (vols. 1–30, St. Louis: Concordia; vols. 31–55, Philadelphia: Fortress Press, 1955–   ). "Lectures on Jonah" (Latin text), vol. 19, 1.1.

35. See p. 71, above.

36. "The inborn capacity to understand through the eyes has been put to sleep and must be reawakened." Rudolf Arnheim, *Art and Visual Perception* (Berkeley: University of California Press, 1954), p. 1.

37. See chap. 2, n. 23, above.

Selected Bibliography

General, Contemporary

Ardener, Edwin. "Belief and the Problem of Women." In *The Interpretation of Ritual,* ed. J. S. La Fontaine. London: Tavistock, 1972.

Arnheim, Rudolf. *Art and Visual Perception.* Berkeley: University of California Press, 1965.

——. *The Dynamics of Architectural Form.* Berkeley: University of California Press, 1977.

Barthes, Roland. *Elements of Semiology.* Trans. A. Lavers and C. Smith. New York: Hill and Wang, 1976.

——. *Image-Music-Text.* New York: Hill and Wang, 1977.

Berger, John. *About Looking.* New York: Pantheon, 1980.

——. *Ways of Seeing.* London: Penguin, 1977.

Carroll, Berenice A., ed. *Liberating Women's History.* Chicago: University of Illinois Press, 1976.

Foucault, Michel. *The Archeology of Knowledge.* San Francisco: Harper Torchbooks, 1972.

——. *Discipline and Punish: The Birth of the Prison.* New York: Pantheon, 1977.

——. *Language, Counter-Memory, Practice: Selected Essays and Interviews.* Trans. Donald F. Bouchard. Ithaca, N.Y.: Cornell University Press, 1977.

Gadamer, Hans-Georg. *Truth and Method.* New York: Seabury, 1975.

Gallop, Jane. *The Daughter's Seduction: Feminism and Psychoanalysis.* New York: Cornell University Press, 1982.

Geertz, Clifford. "Ideology as a Cultural System." In *Ideology and Its Discontents,* ed. David E. Apter. New York: Macmillan, 1964.

——. *The Interpretation of Cultures.* New York: Basic, 1973.

Habermas, Jürgen. *Knowledge and Human Interests.* Boston: Beacon, 1968.

Key, Wilson Brian. *Subliminal Seduction.* New York: New American Library, 1974.

Kincaid, James C. *Press Photography.* Boston: American, 1936.

Lacan, Jacques. *The Language of the Self: The Function of Language in Psychoanalysis.* Trans. Anthony Wilden. Baltimore: Johns Hopkins University Press, 1968.

Langer, Susanne. "The Cultural Importance of Art." In *Philosophical Sketches.* New York: Mentor, 1962.

Neville, Robert C. *Reconstruction of Thinking.* Albany, New York: SUNY Press, 1981.

Newhall, Beaumont. *Photography: A Short Critical Essay*. New York: Museum of Modern Art, 1937.

Ornstein, Robert. *The Psychology of Consciousness*. New York: Penguin, 1972.

Plaskow, Judith. *Sex, Sin, and Grace: Women's Experience and the Theologies of Reinhold Niebuhr and Paul Tillich*. Washington, D.C.: University Press of America, 1980.

Turner, Victor, and Edith Turner. *Image and Pilgrimage in Christian Culture*. New York: Columbia University Press, 1978.

Whyte, L. L. *The Unconscious Before Freud*. New York: F. Pinter, 1960.

Early Christian

Barnard, L. W. *The Graeco-Roman and Oriental Background of the Iconoclastic Controversy*. Leiden: Brill, 1974.

Bryer, Anthony, and Judith Herrin, eds. *Iconoclasm*. Papers given at the Ninth Spring Symposium of Byzantine Studies. Birmingham, Ala.: Center for Byzantine Studies, University of Birmingham, 1977.

Cushman, Robert. *Therapeia: Plato's Conception of Philosophy*. Westport, Ct.: Greenwood, 1958.

Fiorenza, Elisabeth Schüssler. *In Memory of Her*. New York: Crossroads, 1983.

Frary, Joseph. "The Logic of Icons." *Sobornost*, ser. 6, no. 6 (Winter 1972), pp. 394–404.

Gough, Michael. *The Early Christians*. London: Thames and Hudson, 1961.

Grabar, André. *Christian Iconography: A Study of Its Origins*. Bollingen Series, no. 35. Princeton: Princeton University Press, 1968.

Kitzinger, Ernst. "The Cult of Images in the Age Before Iconoclasm." *Dumbarton Oaks Papers* 8 (1954).

Perkins, A. *The Art of Dura Europus*. Oxford: Oxford University Press, 1973.

Kraeling, C. H. *The Excavations at Dura Europus: Final Report, vol. 8, part 2, The Christian Building*. New Haven: Dura Europus Publications, 1967.

Krautheimer, Richard. *Early Christian and Byzantine Architecture*. London: Pelikan, 1965.

———. *Rome: Profile of a City, 312–1308*. Princeton: Princeton University Press, 1980.

———. *Studies in Early Christian, Medieval, and Renaissance Art*. New York: New York University Press, 1969.

Laeuchli, Samuel. *Religion and Art in Conflict*. Philadelphia: Fortress Press, 1980.

Mâle, Emile. *The Early Churches of Rome*. Trans. David Buxton. London: Ernest Benn Ltd., 1960.

Markus, Robert A. *Christianity in the Roman World*. London: Thames and Hudson, 1974.

Murray, Sister Charles. "Art and the Early Church." *Journal of Theological Studies* (Oct. 1977).

Nichols, Aiden, O.P. *The Art of God Incarnate: Theology and Image in Christian Tradition*. London: Darton, Longman, and Todd, 1981.

Orange, H. P. L., and P. J. Nordhagen. *Mosaics.* Trans. Ann E. Keep. London: Methuen and Co., Ltd., 1958.

Panofsky, Erwin. *Abbot Suger on the Abbey Church of St.-Denis.* Princeton: Princeton University Press, 1946.

———. *Gothic Architecture and Scholasticism.* Latrobe, Pa.: Archabbey Press, 1948.

Smith, E. Baldwin. *Architectural Symbolism of Imperial Rome and the Middle Ages.* Princeton: Princeton University Press, 1956.

Stevenson, J. *The Catacombs: Rediscovered Monuments of Early Christianity.* London: Thames and Hudson, 1978.

Weitzmann, Kurt, ed. *Late Classical and Early Medieval Studies in Honor of Albert Matthias Friend, Jr.* Princeton: Princeton University Press, 1955.

Medieval

Baxandall, M. *Painting and Experience in Fifteenth Century Italy.* Oxford: Oxford University Press, 1972.

Berliner, Rudolf. "The Freedom of Medieval Art." *Gazette des Beaux-Arts,* ser. 6, no. 28 (1953).

———. "God Is Love." *Gazette des Beaux-Arts,* ser. 6, no. 42 (1945).

Bridenthal, R., and C. Koonz, eds. *Becoming Visible: Women in European History.* Boston: Houghton Mifflin Company, 1977.

Bullough, Vern L. "Medieval Medical and Scientific Views of Women." *Viator: Medieval and Renaissance Studies* 4 (1973), pp. 487–493.

Bynum, C. *Jesus as Mother: Studies in the Spirituality of the High Middle Ages.* Berkeley: University of California Press, 1982.

Chojnacki, Stanley. "Patrician Women in Early Renaissance Venice." *Studies in the Renaissance* 21 (1974), pp. 176–203.

Cole, Bruce. *Giotto and Florentine Painting, 1280–1375.* New York: Harper and Row, 1976.

———. *Sienese Painting from Its Origins to the Fifteenth Century.* New York: Harper and Row, 1980.

Crombie, A. C. *Medieval and Early Modern Science.* New York: Doubleday, 1959.

Gutman, Joseph, ed. *The Image and the Word.* Missoula, Mont.: Scholars Press, 1977.

Hetherington, Paul. *Pietro Cavallini: A Study in the Art of Late Medieval Rome.* London: Sagittarius, 1979.

Jungmann, J. A. *The Mass of the Roman Rite: Its Origins and Development.* Trans. F. A. Brunner. New York: Benzinger Brothers, Inc., 1951.

Lindberg, David C. *Science in the Middle Ages.* Chicago: University of Chicago Press, 1978.

Meiss, Millard. *Painting in Florence and Siena After the Black Death.* New York: Harper Torchbooks, 1964.

Stubblebine, James H. *Giotto: The Arena Chapel Frescoes.* London: Thames and Hudson, 1969.

Warner, Marina. *Alone of All Her Sex.* London: Quartet, 1978.

Sixteenth-Century Reformations

Battisti, Eugenio. "Reformation and Counter-Reformation." *Encyclopedia of World Art* (1966), vol. 11, cols. 894–916.

Christensen, Carl C. *Art and the Reformation in Germany*. Athens, Ohio: Ohio University Press, 1979.

Cohen, Kathleen. *Metamorphosis of a Death Symbol: The Transi Tomb in the Late Middle Ages and the Renaissance*. Berkeley: University of California Press, 1973.

Dickens, A. G. *The Counter Reformation*. London: Thames and Hudson, 1968.

Garside, C. *Zwingli and the Arts*. New Haven: Yale University Press, 1966.

Grimm, Harold J. *The Reformation Era, 1500–1650*. London: Macmillan, 1954.

Harbison, Craig. *The Last Judgment in Sixteenth-Century Northern Europe: A Study in the Relationship Between Art and the Reformation*. New York: Garland, 1976.

Haskell, Francis. *Patrons and Painters*. London: Chatto and Windus, 1963.

Hay, Denis. The Church in Italy in the Fifteenth Century. New York: Cambridge University Press, 1977.

Hitchcock, Henry-Russell. *German Renaissance Architecture*. Princeton: Princeton University Press, 1981.

Jedin, Hubert. *A History of the Council of Trent*. 2 vols. Trans. Ernest Graf. London: Nelson, 1957–1961.

Kingdon, Robert M. *Transition and Revolution*. Minneapolis: Burgess Publishing Company, 1975.

Mâle, Emile. *L'Art Religieux après le Councile de Trente*. Paris: Librairie Armand Colin, 1932.

Ozment, Steven E. *The Reformation in Medieval Perspective*. Chicago: Quadrangle Books, 1971.

———, ed. *Reformation Europe: A Guide to Research*. St. Louis: Center for Reformation Research, 1982.

Panofsky, Erwin. *Symbols in Transformation*. Princeton: Princeton University Press, 1969.

Phillips, J. *The Reformation of Images: Destruction of Art in England, 1535–1660*. Berkeley: University of California Press, 1973.

Rothkrug, Lionel. *Religious Practices and Collective Perceptions: Hidden Homologies in the Renaissance and Reformation*. Waterloo, Ont.: Historical Reflections, 1980.

Scribner, R. W. *For the Sake of Simple Folk: Popular Propaganda for the German Reformation*. New York: Cambridge University Press, 1981.

Strauss, Gerald. *Luther's House of Learning: Indoctrination of the Young in the German Reformation*. Baltimore: 1978.

Stechow, Wolfgang. *Northern Renaissance Art, 1400–1600: Sources and Documents*. Englewood Cliffs, N.J.: Prentice-Hall, 1969.

Trinkhaus, C., and H. Oberman. *The Pursuit of Holiness in Late Medieval and Renaissance Religion*. Leiden: E. J. Brill, 1974.

Wittkower, R., and I. B. Jaffe, eds. *Baroque Art: The Jesuit Contribution*. New York: Fordham University Press, 1972.

Index

Advertising, 130–133
Amiens, cathedral at, 76
Anabaptist movement, 112–113, 123
Andrew, Saint, 111
Angela of Foligno, 65, 84
Anne, Saint, 11, 77, 79
Anthony, Saint, 64
Aquila, Caspar, *Des Kleinen Catechismi Erklerung*, 118
Aquileia, cathedral at, 51, 52, 55
Aquinas, Thomas, 142–143, 152
Architecture, 58; images, liturgy, and, 48–55, 99–100; and images before Peace of the Church, 46–48
Ardener, Edwin, 63
Aristotle, 86, 142
Arius, 56
Arnheim, Rudolf, 4, 152, 191
Athanasius, *De Incarnatione*, 59
Augustine, Saint, 2, 7, 25, 42, 64–65; *The City of God*, 60; his theory of physical vision, 45; on *via universalis*, 60

Bacon, Roger, 97
Baglioni, Giovanni, 121
Barthes, Roland, 19, 129, 148
Battisti, Eugenio, 110
Baxandall, Michael, 74
Bellow, Saul, 1, 145; *Henderson the Rain King*, 131
Bernard of Clairvaux, Saint, 70–71, 120
Bernardino da Siena, Saint, 119
Bernini, Giovanni, *Ecstasy of St. Teresa*, 120
Berthold of Regensburg, 96
Black Death, 65
Boccaccio, Giovanni, 74; *Decameron*, 72
Body: images and life of the, 35–39; needed by present society, 132–133
Bogomils, 23

Bridget of Sweden, 85, 87
Bucer, Martin, 113

Calvin, John, 25, 101–102
Canisius, Peter, 110
Cantastorie, 68
Catacombs: fourth-century art of, 43, 46–47, 53–54, 58; orantes of, 48, 51
Cathars, 23
Catherine of Alexandria, Saint, 87
Catherine of Siena, Saint, 65, 85, 87, 88
Catholic reform (sixteenth century), 95–96, 108–113, 150; and architecture, images, and reform of liturgy, 99–100; and images, education, and propaganda, 118–122; success of, 124–125
Cavallini, Pietro, 76–77, 79
Chiesa del Gesù (Rome), 96, 100, 109–112, 120, 121, 124; Ignatius Loyola Chapel at, 121
Christ in Majesty, 8, 56
Churches, house (*tituli*), 48, 51
Church Order, Pseudo-Clementine, 48
Circignani, Niccolo (Pomarancio), 121, 122, 131
Clement of Alexandria, 48
Coherence, 26
Conflict, 26-27
Consciousness, *see* Subjective consciousness
Constantine, Emperor, 46, 49, 50–51, 52, 53, 58; Edict of Toleration of, 59; outlawing of crucifixion by, 59
Constantine V, Emperor, 121
Contemplation, 150–152
Continuity, 24–26, 36
Contradiction, 26–27
Council of Chalcedon (451), 26
Council of Hiereia (754), 44
Council of Nicaea, Second (787), 44